W9-AKY-235

THE BIG GUN

The forward twin 15in turrets of the battleship *Warspite*, probably taken shortly after the First World War. *Conway Picture Library*

THE BIG GUN

BATTLESHIP MAIN ARMAMENT 1860–1945

by Peter Hodges
Drawings by the author

NAVAL INSTITUTE PRESS

Library of Congress Catalog Card No 80-84051

ISBN 0-87021-917-0

Published and distributed in the United States of America by the Naval Institute Press, Annapolis, Maryland 21402

Printed and bound in the United Kingdom

Contents

Foreword

A large number of excellent books have been published on the design of battleships and some dealing with their guns have appeared in print, but little, if anything, has been written that explains how their weapons *functioned.* This, it seemed to me, has been a serious omission, for the mountings that carried some of the heaviest ordnance the world has seen were the very *raison d'être* for the battleship: although these great feats of engineering revolved within the ships that carried them, in the final analysis the design of the ship really revolved about them.

If the fundamental Naval Staff Requirement was for a vessel to carry a given number of heavy guns around the oceans of the world at an optimum surface speed, then the hull had to be designed to carry them and their ammunition, be armoured to protect them and the ship from enemy attack, and be engined and bunkered to provide the speed and endurance demanded. Thus, accommodation spaces and the domestic requirements of the gun crews and the engineers who 'steamed' the ships had to be taken care of, bringing in their wake supporters to deal with food, stores administration and so on.

In addition, there were subsidiary weapons: a secondary armament to deal with destroyers and their kin and, later, a tertiary armament to tackle aircraft at long and close range. All these weapons needed manning and their own crews needed space to live; the crews, moreover, had to be fed, paid and administered.

Ultimately however, the *offensive* power of the battleship centred on her main armament and those who served it. One can see the way that such a vessel grew around, perhaps, four twin turrets by considering that something like 350 men from a ship's company of 1200 were concerned solely with them and their control systems, and that their total combined weight was about 3000 tons on a displacement of 30,000 tons.

Perhaps the very proportions and the overall *presence* of a battleship has caused so much to be written about the vessel itself and so little about its weapons. I hope that this book will, at least in part, redress this imbalance. Its contents are the accumulation of data gathered during more than thirty years of naval service devoted exclusively to weapons and weapon-system engineering. During those years I found myself in appointments which gave me occasional access to archival records (with which, I am bound to day, few seemed to be in the least interested) but, in particular, I have to thank the captain of HMS *Excellent* (of many years ago) for permission to spend happy lunch-hours in the Wardroom Attic store, and Mr Susans, of Priddy's Hard Weapons Museum, for unfailingly showing me such courteous assistance. My thanks are also due to John Campbell and John Roberts for their help in providing me with information about the gun mountings of the major foreign naval powers.

1 The Development of Heavy Gun Mountings

If a mariner of the first Elizabethan era could have seen the ships of the young Queen Victoria when she ascended the throne in 1837, he might have been surprised by their size but he would rapidly have grasped the function of their sails and tackles, at first sight quite novel to him. When he came to look at the armament, he would have seen little difference in the style of the guns or of their carriages, and would probably have been more impressed by the presence of a flintlock (followed in due course by the percussion lock) as the primary means of firing than by anything else. Certainly he could have served the guns as ably as he had his Tudor queen. He, too, would have experience of swivelling pieces – albeit very small – so that even the most advanced contemporary gun carriage design of the revolving carronade style would simply be the natural extension of an existing idea, and he would probably have accepted that the cannon were muzzle-loaders knowing, perhaps, that early Tudor attempts at breech-loaders had proved unsuccessful.

Indeed, the state of affairs in 1837, when warships were still conventionally armed with broadside batteries of muzzle-loaders firing through gunports cut in the ship's side, was to obtain for some time. HMS *Warrior*, the first British ironclad, mounted 26 – 68pdrs and 8 – 7in breech-loading rifles (BLR) on the gundeck and six more BLRs on the upper. She was completed in 1861 and was followed into service in 1862 by her sister-ship *Black Prince*. *Warrior*'s ship rig, clipper bow and overall proportions gave her a most attractive profile. She is still afloat, and it is to be hoped that current efforts to restore her to her former glory will meet with the success that they surely deserve.

Her sister-ship's completion occurred in the same year as the famous American Civil War engagement between *Monitor* and *Merrimac*. The former (of the Northern or Federal forces) carried her guns in a revolving gun turret on the centreline and there can be no doubt that the emergence of this ship considerably influenced contemporary naval thinking. In Britain, it provided a powerful argument for Captain Cowper-Coles, who had been developing a turret mounting for some time and in 1860 had published plans for a ship with no fewer than nine twin turrets on the centreline. There was, however, substantial opposition to such ideas, not least due to the very real difficulties of providing clear arcs of fire in a rigged ship, and, despite Coles' lobbying, ships with broadside batteries continued to be built throughout the 1860s, although there was a move away from full-length gundecks towards a concentration of the main battery amidships – by now

The Armstrong 7in 110pdr breech-loader (BL) introduced into Royal Navy service in 1861. Due principally to the problems of providing an efficient, gas-tight breech block, these weapons did not prove successful and were soon superseded by the rifled muzzle-loader (MLR). *National Maritime Museum*

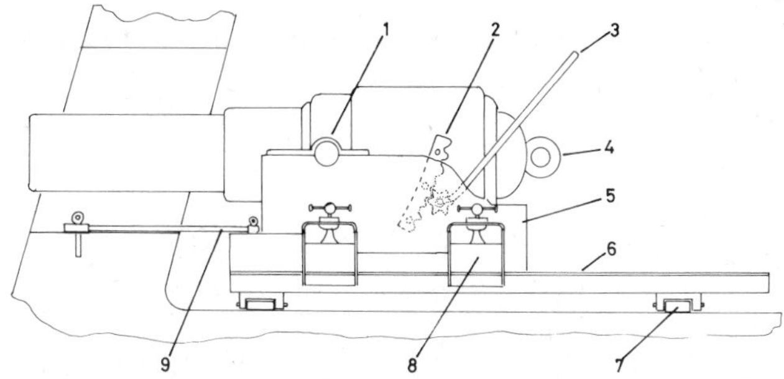

100pdr SMOOTH-BORE, 1862

1 Trunnion
2 Elevating arc
3 Elevating lever
4 Breeching ring
5 Carriage
6 Slide
7 Slide roller
8 Frictional compressor
9 Tie-link

consisting of muzzle-loading rifles (MLR) – supplemented by swivelling, or pivoted, bow- and stern-chasers. The ships themselves were often ugly in the extreme, with graceless hulls, ram bows and, still, a combination of sail and steam propulsion. The guns of the period showed few advances in design and although Mr Armstrong's breech-loader was officially adopted in 1859, as no means had yet been devised of positively locking the breech block into position, his gun was regarded with reservations.

The accompanying drawing shows a typical 100pdr smoothbore muzzle-loader of the mid-1860s. The carriage slid in recoil on twin beams, the latter running on rollers like the earlier carronade, and the barrel was elevated by a simple toothed arc and pinion operated by a large lever instead of by wedge-shaped quoins. Rope breechings were still in use, but the carriage was fitted with frictional 'compressors' which were then commonly employed in an attempt to absorb some of the recoil shock. They were very unsatisfactory in service because there was no method of setting them to a precise adjustment.

The irascible Cowper-Coles at last got his way when his ideas came to fruition with HMS *Captain*, a twin-turret ship of nearly 7000 tons. He was undoubtedly a man with very clear – and indeed sensible – views on the merits of turreted guns, but he was no ship designer. *Captain* sank in a heavy gale off Cape Finisterre in 1871 taking Cowper-Coles and all save eighteen of her crew to the bottom. Not unnaturally, the loss of Coles and his ship created something approaching panic; nevertheless, the seed had been sown, and thereafter the areas of controversy were between the 'turret' and 'barbette' advocates – and between those who favoured muzzle-loaders and those who recognised that the way ahead lay with the breech-loader.

Guns now tended to be judged neither by their calibre nor by the weight of their projectile but, oddly, by their *own* weight. Sometimes the calibre was included in the description, but an armament given as 'four 35-ton MLR' was met with quite frequently. Gunpowder was still used as a propellant and its violent and virtually uncontrollable expansion on exploding led to massively thick and disproportionate barrels.

The muddle over the definition of 'barbette' and 'turret' was to continue for many years but the installation mounted in HMS *Hotspur* of 1871 (see drawing) was indeed the nearest thing to the turret seen in a castle or similar military fortification. The fixed structure was pierced with four gunports and within it was set a turntable, revolved by

Above An Armstrong 7in 110pdr BL mounted on a wooden slide-carriage. Metal construction was substituted for wood in later mountings of this type and the means of controlling the recoil, run-out, elevation and training became more sophisticated as heavier guns and the need for greater accuracy necessitated the introduction of mechanical aids for the gun's crews. *National Maritime Museum*

Below Aboard the broadside ironclad *Minotaur* in the late 1860s. In the left foreground is a 7in MLR on a wrought iron slide-carriage. *Conway Picture Library*

Captain Scott's naval gun carriage and slide, introduced in 1871, provided improved recoil arrangements and mechanical training gear. The latter can be seen under the carriage, at the rear of the gun, and consisted of a mechanism on the carriage driving a pinion (visible below the carriage) which could run round a curved toothed rack, fixed to the deck. *National Maritime Museum*

Above A 9in MLR aboard the central battery ironclad *Iron Duke* in the 1870s. Note the ramming and sponging-out staffs hung from the deckhead above the gun. *National Maritime Museum*
Below A 10in 18-ton gun aboard the central battery ironclad *Sultan* in the 1890s. *National Maritime Museum*

a steam engine. The gun was carried on the normal mounting of the day, but had the refinement of geared training over a limited arc. By running the gun in, with the running-in winch, and revolving the turntable, it could be run out again (by tackles) through any of the four gunports, although its limited traverse did not enable it to cover every bearing. The turret was protected by 10in thick iron sandwiched with teak but was devoid of any form of gunport lids and its crew must have had a breezy time on occasions. Perhaps, however, they were less subject to being half choked by powder-smoke than might otherwise have been the case. Following are some examples of the heavy gun mountings employed in the Royal Navy between the introduction of the turret and the crystallization of ship and gun designs at the beginning of the 1890s.

BARBETTE MOUNTING, 1877

The arguments put forward by those in favour of the fixed 'barbette' style of mounting centred on the fact that, in general, they were sited higher than were the turrets of the day and were, therefore, more easily worked in bad weather when turrets often became untenable.

The guns were loaded at the 'run-in' position so that apart from the sighting numbers' position (usually behind an armoured hood or shield) all other members of the crew were within the protection of the barbette itself. The latter was sometimes known as the redoubt and was usually pear-shaped.

The contemporary hydraulic machinery was common to both barbette and turret arrangements and both had a turntable revolved by a hydraulic engine. The accompanying drawing shows the barbette mounting adapted for HMS *Temeraire* from its Moncrieff 'disappearing' land-based counterpart. The trunnions of the 11in muzzle-loading rifled gun were supported by two heavy, cranked trunnion-arms whose lower limbs were connected to a cross-head on the piston rod of the recoil and run-out arrangements. These were set centrally below the gun, within the revolving turntable, and internally were similar to the gear fitted in the *Royal Sovereign* class battleships (1889).

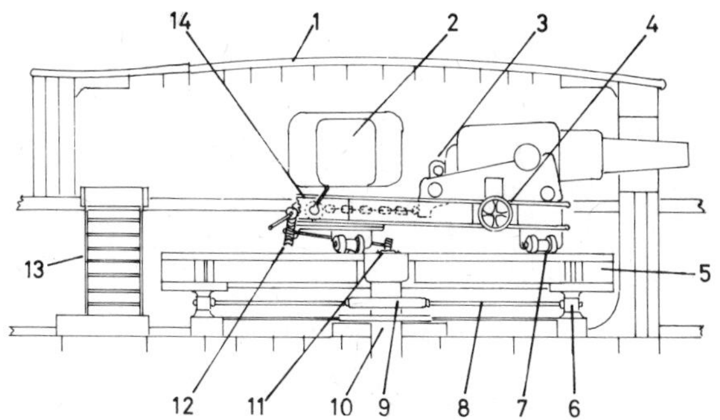

FIXED TURRET, 1871

1 Turret roof
2 Gunport
3 Breeching ring
4 Compressor wheel
5 Turntable
6 Training roller
7 Carriage traverse roller
8 Roller shaft
9 'Necklace' ring
10 Central tube
11 Traverse pinion
12 Traverse worm and wormwheel drive
13 Access ladder
14 Running-in crank

The 12in 25-ton MLR of the *Hotspur*. The gun is on a standard broadside mounting but the deck on which it stands is actually a turntable which enabled the weapon to be rotated to one of several ports within a 'fixed' circular armoured turret. *National Maritime Museum*

Inset A rear view of *Hotspur*'s 12in MLR. *National Maritime Museum*

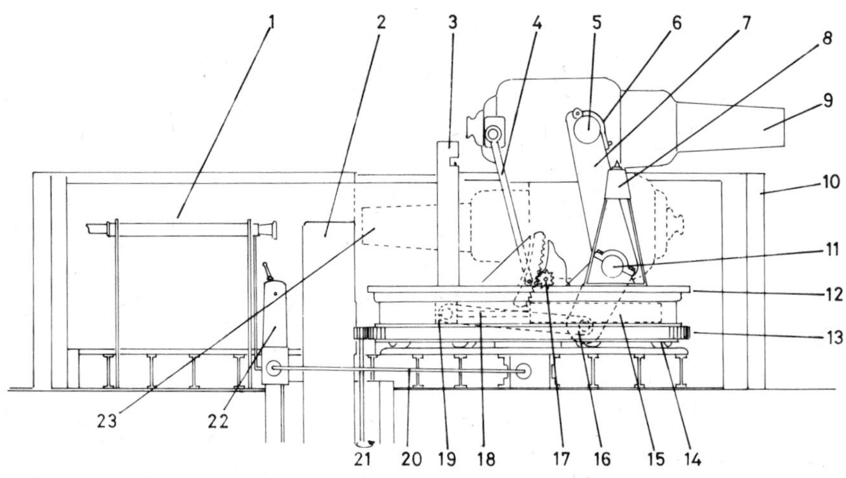

BARBETTE MOUNTING, 1877

1 Rammer
2 Ammunition trunk
3 Control and sighting position
4 Elevation link-rod
5 Trunnion
6 Trunnion cap
7 Cranked trunnion arm
8 Fore-sight
9 Barrel in firing position
10 Barbette
11 Trunnion arm axis
12 Turntable
13 Training rack
14 Turntable support wheel
15 Recoil and run-out cylinder
16 Link-arm
17 Elevating pinion
18 Recoil piston rod
19 Cross-head
20 Hydraulic lead to rotating structure
21 Training drive to training pinion
22 Control console for rammer and hoist
23 Gun in recoiled and loading position

A second connecting bar ran between the rear end of the barrel and a hand-worked elevation gearbox, and the complete assembly functioned like a pantograph. On gunfire, the recoil caused the gun to move backwards and downwards so it disappeared from sight behind the protection of the barbette armour. The moving elevation toothed quadrant was part of an arc struck from a centre such that, no matter at what elevation the gun was fired, the geometry of the pantograph caused it always to descend to the same lower position. The turntable was then revolved until the muzzles were in alignment with the fixed loading position under the protection of the ship's superstructure. This loading position for the gun is shown by broken lines in the drawing.

When loading was complete, the gun was trained back on to the firing bearing, whereupon, by admitting hydraulic pressure to the run-out cylinder, the gun was returned to its firing position. Aiming was from an armoured position projecting above the upper lines of the barbette armour; and because the geometry of the pantograph allowed the elevation to be pre-set, the gun could be run out and fired whenever it was tactically advantageous. *Temeraire* was unique in carrying this mounting, but is worthy of inclusion for its novelty.

One of the *Temeraire*'s 11in 25-ton MLRs in the raised (firing) position. *National Maritime Museum*

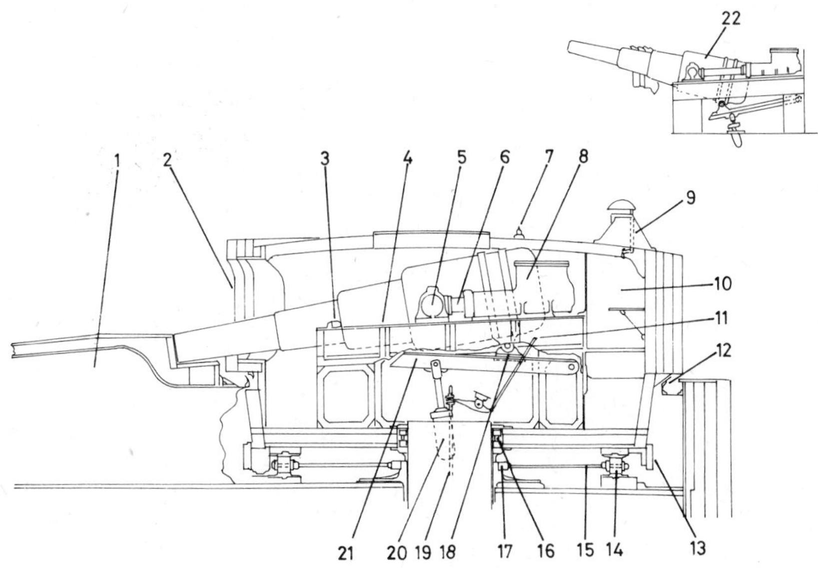

TWIN TURRET, 1881

HMS *Inflexible,* built at Portsmouth Dockyard and completed in 1881, was armed with two twin 81-ton gun turrets, with 17in frontal protection, disposed *en échelon* amidships (as were those of *Colossus*). The guns (of 16in calibre) were muzzle-loaders and fired a 1684lb projectile. They were longer barrelled than the guns described thus far and because of this – and to keep the turret to acceptable dimensions – they were loaded from an armoured glacis in the superstructure to which the gun returned when it had fired. The turret diameter was still large when compared to the projection of the barrels even when they were run out, and its circular drum shape, with slightly domed roof, was typical of the era. The guns of the period were constructed from a series of tubes shrunk over each other and the increased length in proportion to their maximum diameter gave them a more pleasing appearance.

The turntable arrangements, together with the glacis-mounted rammer and loading cage, remained much as before but the elevating gear was complex in the extreme. The gun trunnions were set into trunnion blocks which were free to move in recoil on a slide-way inclined upwards towards the rear. A piston was attached to the trunnion block and combined the duties of recoil damping and run-out by working in a cylinder fixed to the non-recoiling slide. A lug on the underside of the barrel was attached to a slipper-block which was also free to slide in recoil along the upper face of a beam, pivoted at one end and supported by a hydraulic ram at the other.

When the gun had been loaded, and trained away from the glacis, it was run out by the usual hydraulic process and thereafter it was elevated by allowing the elevating beam to depress. This created a most peculiar lever movement and the inset on the relevant drawing has been included to show the geometry of the gear at maximum elevation.

TWIN TURRET, 1881

1 Loading position in superstructure
2 Frontal armour
3 Run-out buffer stop
4 Slide
5 Trunnion
6 Recoil piston rod
7 Fore-sight
8 Recoil cylinder
9 Sight-hood cowl drive
10 Sighting compartment
11 Link-rod to power control lever
12 Weathering strips
13 Training rack
14 Training roller
15 Roller axis shaft
16 Thrust roller
17 'Necklace'
18 Sliding slipper-block
19 Control shaft on centre of rotation
20 Elevating ram
21 Elevating beam
22 Gun in run-out position

The interior of one of the turrets of HMS *Devastation* showing the breech ends of the two 12in 35-ton MLRs. *National Maritime Museum*

HMS *Inflexible*, which carried the largest muzzle-loading guns employed in British naval service – four 16in MLRs mounted in two twin turrets. *National Maritime Museum*

The shock of gunfire created thrusts in several directions but none was in line with the actual plane of the gun centre line and mechanically the design was a nightmare. In addition the gunport was very large – and unprotected – which must have made life very uncomfortable for the turret crew.

TWIN TURRET, 1887

Major changes came with the introduction of breech-loading guns in HMS *Colossus*. The 'sleeving' construction of the barrels had not been entirely satisfactory because each component had been machined from a solid billet and thus the 'grain' of the steel was not circumferential in direction. This was resolved by forging the strengthening members of the construction which ensured a much stronger 'wrap-around' granular structure.

The integral trunnion pins, which had been a fundamental feature of cannon for some 400 years, were abandoned in favour of straps which secured the gun to a saddle working on the slide. (The immediate benefit was that the guns could now be set more closely together whereas, before, their individual, adjacent trunnion pins had, of course, to clear each other in recoil.) Recoil was absorbed by the usual combined piston and cylinder slung under the slide, the latter being moved by hydraulic pressure, to depress, and the controlled release of liquid to exhaust, to elevate (the gun being 'tail-heavy'). The slide was pivoted close to the turret's gunport to allow for a smaller port opening and so relieve some of the problems experienced in *Inflexible*. As has been mentioned in the section on that ship, the turrets of *Colossus* were similarly disposed, and an inset to the drawing shows them in part-plan and part-side elevation. In passing it is worth remarking that this particular period coincided with the emergence of the very potent torpedo-boat and, in consequence, a secondary armament of lighter guns began to appear in warships.

BREECH MECHANISMS

The typical breech mechanism of this period was, by modern standards, a cumbersome device but in its day it marked an enormous advance in basic gun design. The drawing is based on the breech of the 12in 45-ton guns in *Colossus* but is applicable to the period generally.

The benefits of breech-loading were recognised almost from the inception of cannon and both the Chinese and the Tudors had attempted to perfect the scheme. Further attempts had been made by the early Victorians but none met with success, principally because no safe means could be devised of both locking and sealing the breech of the gun.

The breakthrough came with the invention by the French of the interrupted screw thread which functioned in much the same way as the familiar bayonet joint used on domestic lamp fittings. The required strength was achieved by the size of the threads and the length of the block, and most had five or six interruptions. Five meant that there were five segments threaded on the blocks, alternating with five segments machined away, with the female thread in the gun chamber similarly treated. The block could thus be entered into the breech to its full depth and locked by being revolved 36°. With six interruptions, only 30° of rotation was necessary. Because only half the surface of block and breech were threaded, this system gave only half locking power, so the blocks themselves had to be deep along the axis of the gun bore to give sufficient strength to withstand the force of the explosion in the chamber.

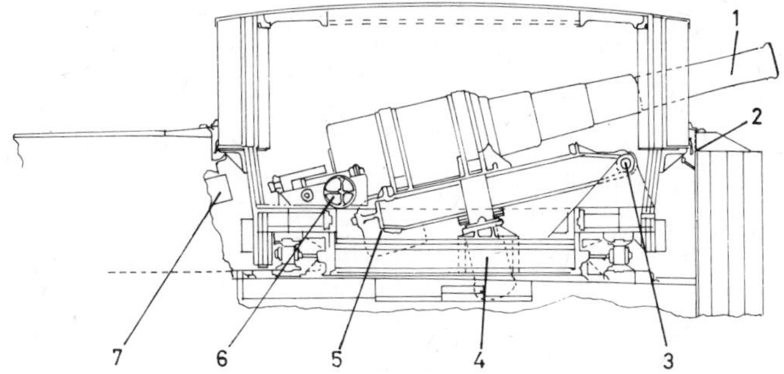

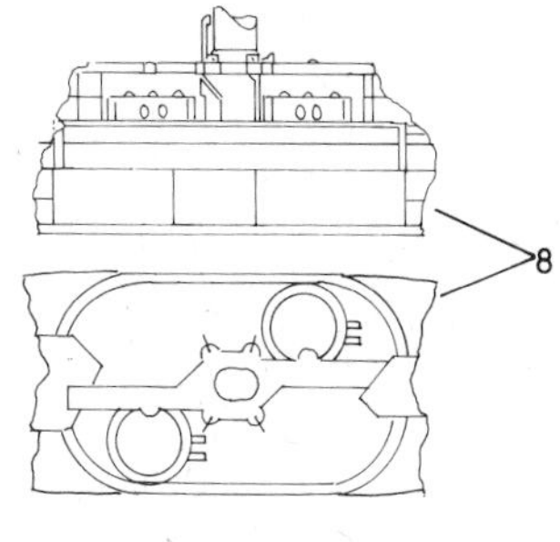

TWIN TURRET, 1887

1 Gun at run-in position
2 Weathering
3 Slide pivot
4 Elevating ram
5 Recoil cylinder
6 Breech-screw withdrawal gear
7 Rammer tube
8 Midship plan and elevation

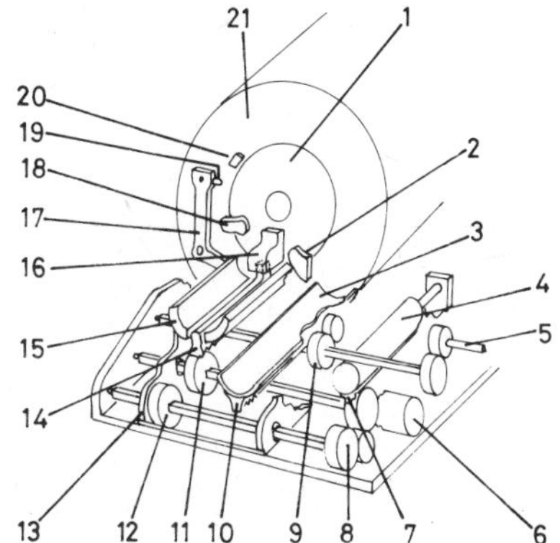

TYPICAL EARLY BREECH MECHANISM (*COLOSSUS* CLASS)

1 Breech-screw
2 Breech-screw projection
3 Loading tray
4 Withdrawing cylinder, moving over fixed piston
5 Hand-drive to loading tray
6 Saddle traversing cylinder
7 Toothed rack on underside of cylinder
8 Twin gear drive to withdrawing pinions
9 Loading tray reduction gears
10 Toothed rack on underside of loading tray
11 Primary extractor pinion
12 Secondary extractor pinion
13 Traversing saddle
14 Toothed rack on underside of extractor
15 Breech-screw support tray
16 Slotted lug on breech-screw engaged by extractor
17 Catch lever
18 Breech locking lug
19 Spring catch-bolt
20 Locking lug limit stop-plate
21 Breech-ring

Operation

Initially, with the breech block closed, 18 butts up against 19 and is locked in position by a spring catch (19) on 17. Slotted lug (16) lies at 8 o'clock, projection (2) is at 6 o'clock and the saddle (13) is traversed to the left, so that the loading tray (3) is in line with the chamber. On gunfire, the gun recoils and remains run-in. On traversing the saddle to the right, the saddle strikes the projection (2) and at the same time actuates lever (17) freeing 19 from 18.

Lateral movement of the saddle unscrews the breech-screw, disengaging its interrupted threads. At the fully unscrewed position, slotted lug (16) engages with the vertical 'toe' on the extractor; support tray (15) now being in line with the breech-screw. The drawing depicts the mechanism in this condition.

Operating the hydraulic cylinder (4) drives through gears 8 to the twin extractor pinions, which are mounted on square-section shafts along which they can slide during traversing. The primary pinion (11) draws the extractor to the rear, pulling the breech-screw bodily out of its breech-ring, the drive being maintained by secondary pinion (12) when the rack leaves 11.

The angled surface of the top faces of the support tray (15) 'dovetail' into the unthreaded 'interruption' of the breech-screw, preventing it from lifting. The saddle is then traversed, carrying the breech-screw clear to the left, at the same time aligning the loading tray with the chamber. Operating a handwheel drive (5), through gears 9 and rack 10, runs the loading tray forward into the breech-ring forming a bridge over the breech threads. Although not shown in the drawing, a second part of the loading tray was 'towed' behind the first.

On completion of loading, the loading tray is withdrawn, and the saddle is traversed right to bring the breech back into line with the breech-screw. The extractor movement is reversed and pushes the breech-screw home; traversing the saddle clear turns the screw, by 2, to re-lock it. Locking lug (18) passes behind 19, is trapped between the latter and 20. Finally, the gun is run-out to the firing position.

From the drawing it will be observed that the breech was unscrewed by bringing a power-operated saddle laterally sideways; it was withdrawn bodily backwards by an extractor, and then carried bodily sideways on the saddle to the left. This movement placed a loading tray in line with the open breech and in direct line with the ammunition cage and rammer. Saddle traverse and extraction was by power, while the loading tray was extendable into the chamber by hand-gearing so as to cover, and protect, the internal threads of the breech. When the gun had been loaded, the loading tray was withdrawn; the saddle traversed to the right to bring the breech block back to the gun; the 'extractor' pushed the block back into the breech; and, finally, by traversing the saddle back to the right the extractor was disengaged, at the same time screwing the breech home. Remembering that the gun was loaded in the 'run-in' condition and at maximum elevation, it will be noted that only under these conditions could the breech be opened or closed. The whole procedure was somewhat long-winded, loading and returning to an optimum firing bearing taking three minutes.

LATER GUN MOUNTINGS UP TO 1894

The next major group of British warships were the 'Admirals' of which there were six, nominally of the same class but differing considerably in performance and armament. The smallest, *Collingwood*, had two twin 12in guns; the middle group (*Rodney*, *Howe*, *Anson* and *Camperdown*) had twin 13.5in; and the largest, *Benbow*, had two single 16.25in, proudly described as 'the 110-ton gun'. All these weapons were mounted *en barbette* and those of *Benbow* caught the imagination of the public. Her guns were 30 calibre pieces employing a 960lb powder charge (in eight one-eighth charges) as the propellant for the 1800lb shell.

HMS *Benbow*, which carried two of the largest calibre guns ever fitted in a British battleship – 16.25in, 110-ton breech-loaders. In this case they were mounted in single open-topped barbettes but in the later *Victoria* and *Sans Pariel* they were fitted in twin turrets. *Conway Picture Library*

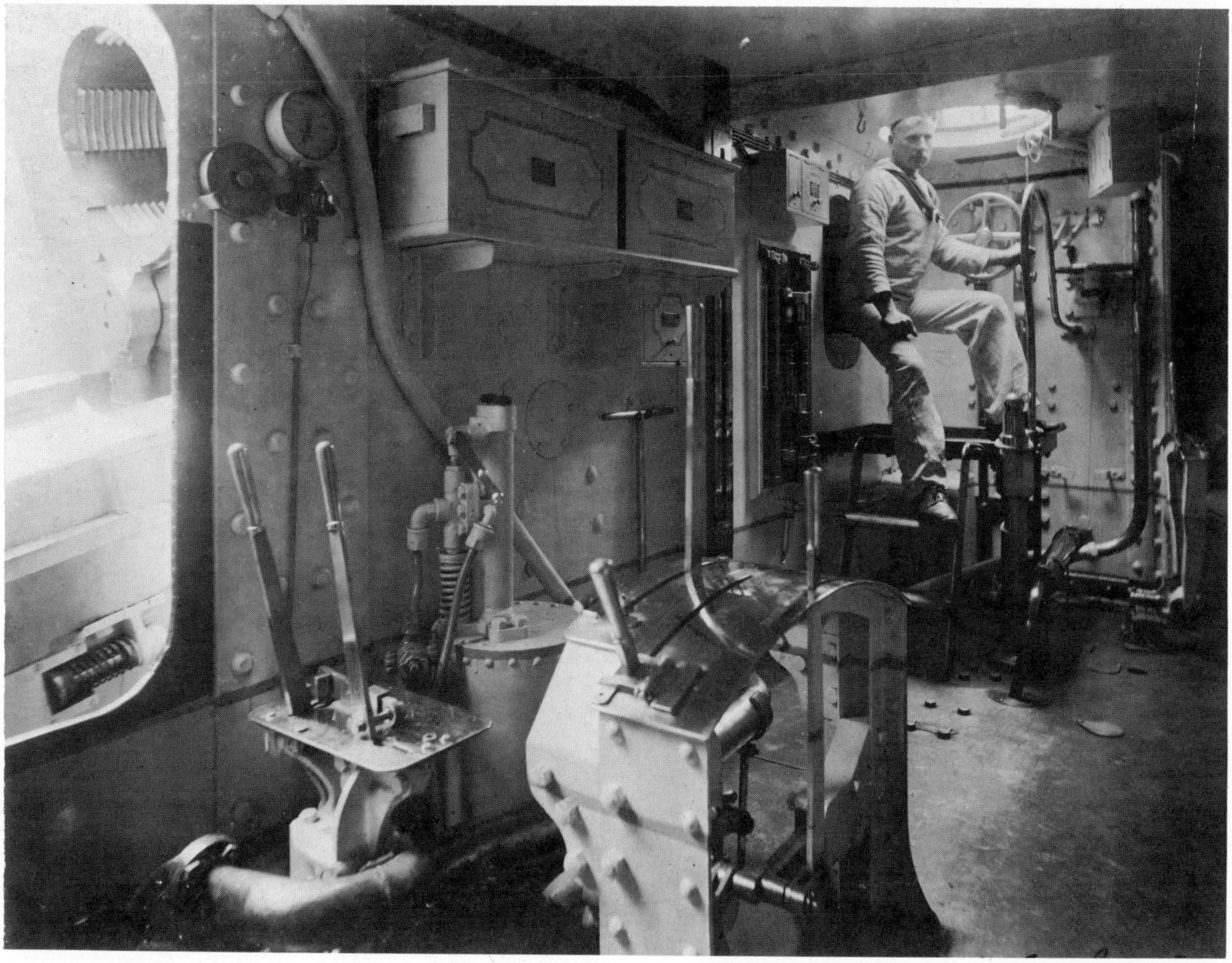

The interior, right side, of one of the barbette mountings of HMS *Repulse* (1892). In the foreground are a number of the control levers for the hydraulic system, and visible through the opening on the extreme left is the breech of the right 13.5in gun, its breech block removed. The seaman has his head partially through one of two sighting ports (the other being on the left side) provided in the thin splinter plating fitted across the top of the barbette. *Conway Picture Library*

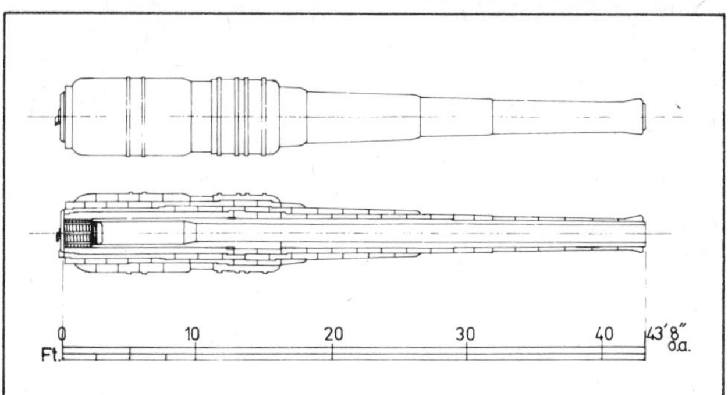

BRITISH 16.25in BL Mk I
Drawing by John Roberts

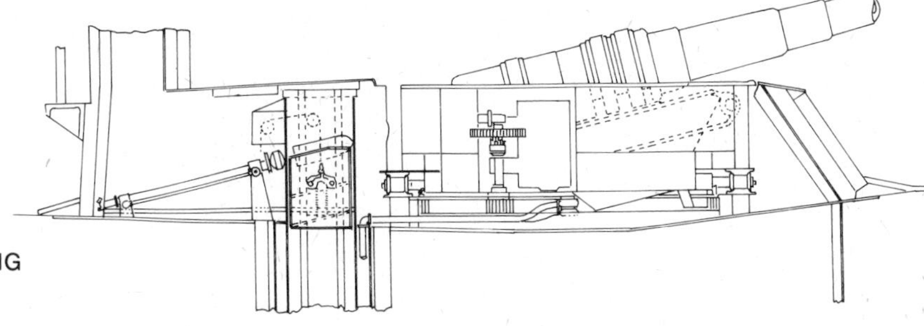

BRITISH 16.25in BL BARBETTE MOUNTING (*BENBOW*) – GENERAL ARRANGEMENT

VAVASSEUR BROADSIDE MOUNTING

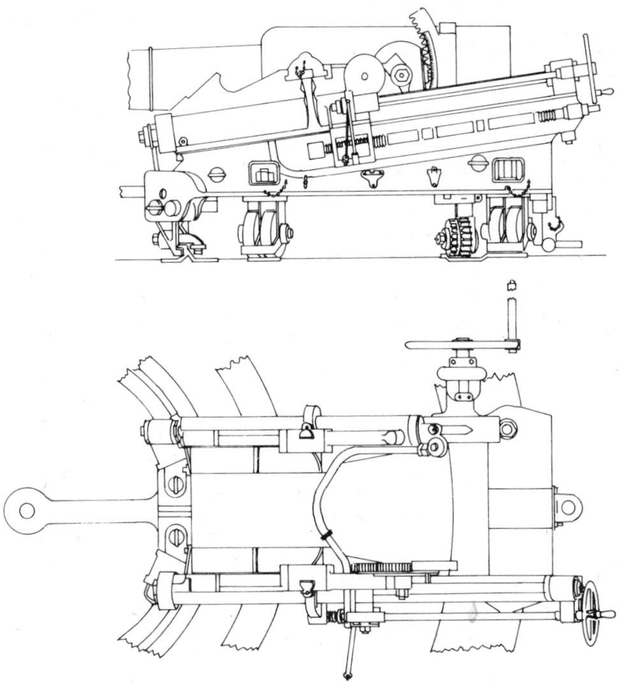

Apart from a succession of minor improvements to detail, none of the mountings of this period showed any fundamental changes in their hydraulic machinery. The guns were still loaded at the 'run-in' position, they were all tail-heavy, the breech mechanism was still of the *Colossus* style and the mounting invariably had to return to a loading position in alignment with the superstructure. However, although no major developments in the heavy gun mounting had occurred since the introduction of the breech-loading 12in, the design of lighter and handier weapons had been progressing apace, and at the same time cordite, as a propellant, was waiting in the wings.

The 'quick-firer' was by now very much in vogue and had risen in calibre to a 6in piece carried on an upper-deck shielded mounting. It fired a 100lb shell, could be hand-worked throughout and immediately presented a considerable hazard to the gun crews of those heavy guns mounted *en barbette* because they were largely unprotected, from above, against the effects of shell splinters. Thus it was that the death-knell sounded upon even the largest of the open-topped barbette-mounted guns and, with the introduction of the *Majestic* class of 1894, the steady march towards the sophisticated mountings of the twentieth century began.

There then followed several turret ships, one of which, the ill-fated *Victoria*, had a twin 16.25in turret forward, a single upper-deck mounted 10in aft, 12 broadside-mounted 6in generally disposed towards the quarters, and 21 light anti-torpedo-boat guns.

Although somewhat out of context, it might be remarked at this point that the secondary guns of the period were customarily carried on Vavasseur mountings. These were the invention of a Mr Vavasseur who, despite his probably continental heritage, was in the employ of the Elswick-based company of Sir W Armstrong. Early examples of this type had the old-fasioned 'carronade' style carriage but later models were fitted on central pivot mountings. Drawings of both styles appear in this book.

Two more ships of this period were *Nile* and *Trafalgar*, armed with 13.5in guns in twin fore and aft turrets, but the next major group were the *Royal Sovereign*s. Seven of the class had twin 13.5in *en barbette* (which typified the divergence of opinion of the day) but the eighth, *Hood*, had turret-mounted guns.

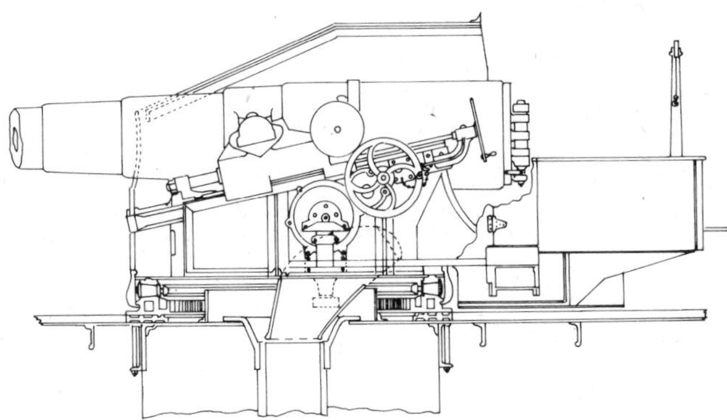

VAVASSEUR CP MOUNTING

TYPICAL HYDRAULIC RING MAIN (*QUEEN ELIZABETH*)

1 Lead to shell room
2 Isolating stop valve
3 Auxiliary maintenance pump
4 Turbo-pump unit
5 Lead to 'normal' training 'walking-pipe'
6 Lead to 'alternative' training 'walking-pipe'
7 Alternative lead to shell room

(Note: Turbo-pump units were normally connected to their 'own' turret.)

2 Gun Mounting Machinery

Although the steam-driven turntable already existed, it was hardly the medium to employ *within* a gun mounting, and so it was that, in 1874, the forward turret of HMS *Thunderer* was experimentally adapted for hydraulic power operation in order that it might be evaluated against her after turret which remained (as designed) entirely hand-worked.

The trial showed the powered turret in a very favourable light, particularly since it could be worked by 28 men whilst its partner aft needed a crew of 48. Thereafter, hydraulic machinery became more and more widely used and remained the principal power medium for gun mountings throughout the era of the battleship. It is still used extensively today, not only in gun mountings and missile launchers but also in the internal guidance systems of missles themselves. The only major rival to hydraulic power was electric drive which was employed by several naval powers, principally the USA, for heavy gun mountings. However, in several cases it was used in conjunction with hydraulic machinery while in others the system was tried experimentally only (eg the 12in mountings in the British battlecruiser *Invincible*).

Hydraulic machinery, generally, has a number of attributes which make it particularly suitable for gun mounting operation – and in the 1870s there was in any case little practical alternative. Engineers already had a great store of experience of reciprocating steam engines but the dangers of such machinery – to say nothing of its discomforts – in the confines of a turret need no elaboration. Hydraulic machinery, on the other hand, while using pistons, valves, pumps and engines very similar in design to their steam counterparts, was cool, quiet, safe and easy to control, and it used a *liquid* as distinct from a condensible gas.

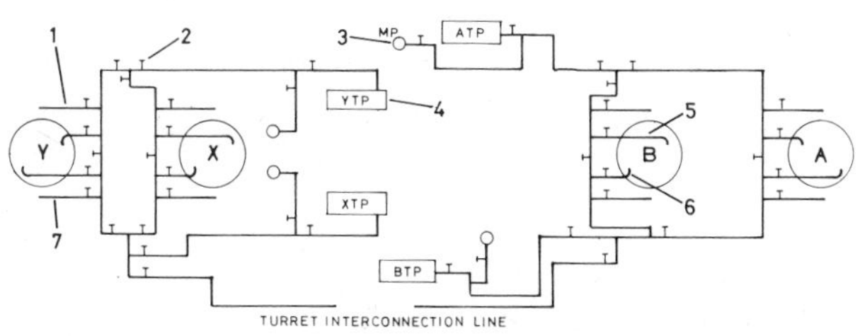

The significance of the last statement lies in the fact that a liquid (for practical purposes in hydraulic systems, at least) can be regarded as incompressible. Hence the liquid between two pistons can be regarded as a solid, but flexible, link and, disregarding leakage, no matter how tortuous the path the linking pipe make take, moving one piston will result in an immediate movement of the second. The descriptions of the various styles of machines which follow are dealt with collectively at this point to show hydraulic principles, and not all were necessarily applicable throughout. Nevertheless, once these principles are appreciated the later detailed descriptions of mounting machinery will be more readily understood.

From the earliest days, the British used water as a hydraulic medium in their heavy gun mountings and only with their triple 16in of the 1920s did they change to oil – reverting to water with the 14in twin and quad of the 1930s. However, in medium-calibre powered mountings, mineral oil was introduced after the First World War and is now exclusively used. In consequence of the use of water (which was fresh, not salt) almost all components of the hydraulic system as a whole were manufactured from copper or copper-based alloys with the obvious exceptions of pump pistons, valve stems and so on. Copper was used for the pipework which in the case of exhaust lines was often of considerable diameter so as to reduce back pressure by ensuring free exhaust flow.

Pipework was flanged with brass, and valve cases, manifolds and the like were generally manufactured from the bronze group. For this reason, with world material prices as they are (especially for copper alloy materials), the salvage of sunken vessels of the period can, in the long term, become a profitable enterprise. In the event of a major loss of water from the hydraulic mains tanks, salt water could be introduced by emergency stop valves but this was only resorted to *in extremis* because the eventual corrosive effect on the system was very severe.

From the outset, ships were fitted with some kind of ring-main of pressure pipes into which one or more steam-driven pumping engines discharged, drawing their intake from hydraulic tanks into which parallel exhaust lines discharged. They were fitted with automatic governors and idled until system pressure fell, when they automatically went 'on load' to restore the *status quo*.

A typical in-ship installation for a 15in battleship is shown in the accompanying drawing. As will be seen, it had a comprehensive arrangement of isolating valves, and alternative routes between pump units and individual mountings were available, although they were normally opened up to their 'own' pump. It will be noted, too, that each mounting had a duplicate on-mounting and off-mounting delivery (and exhaust) system, so that in the event of severe action damage to one side of the hull, the alternative hydraulic route could be opened up on the other. Earlier installations were obviously less complex but they nevertheless followed very similar lines.

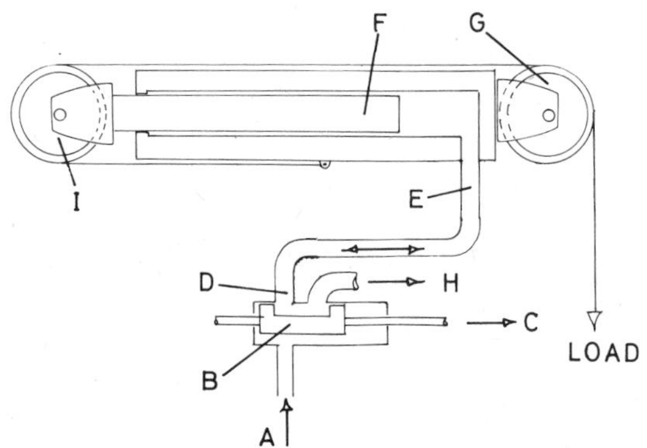

'D' SLIDE VALVE AND PLAIN RAM

'D' SLIDE VALVE AND PLAIN RAM

The plain ram was the simplest type of hydraulic machine and the drawing shows it controlled by a 'D' slide valve. This was commonly used in all fluid power systems (including, therefore, steam locomotives) and consisted of a box-shaped device designed to bridge the various ports cut in the valve casing. Pressure was always led to the top of these valves so as to press them downwards on to the internal valve body. To allow for this they were not a rigid fit on their control rods, but were allowed an element of 'float'. The mating surfaces of valve and valve body needed skilled preparation and the pressure effect upon the upper surface of the 'D' made them difficult to move if they were very large; some, therefore, had their own 'servo valve' included in the design of the main valve itself and it was the former that was moved by the external control rod. Moving the small servo valve caused the complete main valve to shift its position (at the same time shutting off pressure to the servo), so that the main valve then stopped in a new position. The 'D' slide type of valve was superseded by the piston type which was much easier to engineer and had wider applications in hydraulic systems.

At this point it must be made clear that *pressure* is only a means to an end and that it can only exist when the *flow* of liquid is restricted. Hydraulic machines require a flow of liquid to make them function and the pump supplying them must have a volumetric output which will cope with their demands. In general terms this maximum pump output should exceed the maximum possible demands that may be imposed upon it by the devices it serves. Thus a hydraulic system should include a pump unit which will initially discharge liquid into a totally closed-off series of pipes, leading to inactive machinery, so that the pressure set up in these pipes will always be sufficient to create the flow rate required in order that they may function at their designed speed.

Obviously the pipework and all the components, valves and gland-packings must be capable of withstanding the effects of this 'static' system pressure. Because, as has been said, liquids are to all intents and purposes incompressible, and because liquid pressure acts simultaneously in all directions, in a total hydraulic system pressure very quickly rises to its maximum when there are no flow demands. If such demands are suddenly made, flow commences and pressure drops, but if this pressure drop is instantly felt by the pump governor, or its equivalent, the pump will commence discharging to make up the pressure and so provide the flow rate.

An important point to realise, however, is the significance of pressure in terms of, say, pounds per square inch (of area) and the *force* which a pressure may exert when it is applied to a particular surface area. As an example, if a piston head has a surface area of 3 sq in and is subjected to a pressure of 100psi, its piston rod will exert a force of 300 pounds. There is clearly a very useful multiplication factor here, and much use has been made of it in the design of hydraulic machinery.

Returning to the drawing of the 'D' slide valve and plain ram it will be seen that it can only act in one direction under the influences of the system pressure supply at A. The slide valve (B) is bridging the ports to pipes E and H, the latter leading to exhaust. The weight of the load (in this case an ammunition cage) keeps the plain ram (F) in its retracted position through the wire running over a sheave (G) fixed to the cylinder, a second sheave (I) attached to the ram, and so to its anchor point on the underside of the cylinder itself. The ram is shown solid, but it was usually hollow for lightness' sake. This hollowing will not, of course, alter the effective surface area upon which liquid from pipe E can act.

When the external control rodding is moved to the right (C), system pressure is allowed to create flow from A to E, whilst the valve prevents a direct path from A to H. The flow causes the ram to move to the left and the load is thus raised. If the valve is partially opened, liquid can only 'leak' past it to E, the flow rate is lower and the ram will move slowly.

Discreet movement of the control rodding to the left will first close the supply from A and then gradually open the path from E to H – and, because liquid is incompressible, if the valve is set so that it blocks port D the system will stop. This device was used from the introduction of hydraulics and remained as the principal means of raising ammunition cages. Two such assemblies working in opposition were also used for shell transportation in the shell room, and a typical application is shown in the section on the British 15in Mk I.

Its application to ammunition lifts is worth examining further. The ammunition cage often had to move through a considerable vertical distance and so, to keep the maximum extension of the ram to reasonable limits, multi-sheave systems were employed. Hence a small movement of the ram resulted in a large movement of the wire attached to the load.

Anyone who has attempted to move a pulley-block system by pulling its two blocks away from each other will know that the greater the multiplicity of the sheaves, the harder it becomes so to do; however, this work was done in the plain ram by the system hydraulic supply. When the total load had diminished (in this case by the removal of the ammunition), the residue load – in other words the weight of the cage – acted upon what was, in effect, a pulley-block system at its maximum mechanical advantage, thus retracting the ram, and discharging liquid to exhaust.

A considerable force was nevertheless required to extend it on its 'work-stroke' under what might be described as 'mechanical disadvantage' conditions, and so, with a given system pressure and a given load to lift at a given speed, the requirements could be met by designing a ram of a particular diameter. This, of course, would be such that its surface area, equated to the system pressure, would provide the required force. As a result, the cage-lifting presses, as they were called, were of large diameter and were slung from compartment deckheads. When this position could not be arranged above the 'plumb line' of the hoist, the wire was led through guide sheaves as can be seen in the drawing of the 15in gunhouse arrangements.

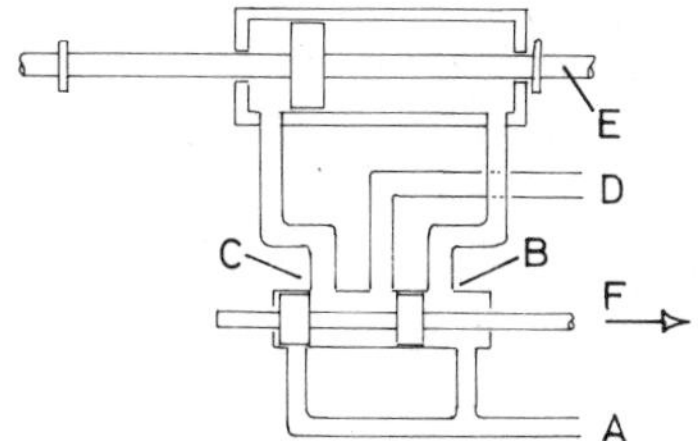

DOUBLE-ACTING PISTON

DOUBLE-ACTING PISTON

The next drawing shows a double-acting piston controlled by a piston control valve. As drawn, the system supply at A leads directly to B and the double-acting piston (E) is at its extreme leftward movement while the left-hand side of the piston head is linked to exhaust via C to D. Moving the control valve to the right (F) transposes the arrangement, and the piston now moves to the right. The linear movement of such devices could be translated to a rotating movement by machining a toothed rack on E and engaging it with a gear wheel. It was in this way, for example, that some powered breech mechanisms functioned; the same system was also employed by the Germans for their elevation arrangements.

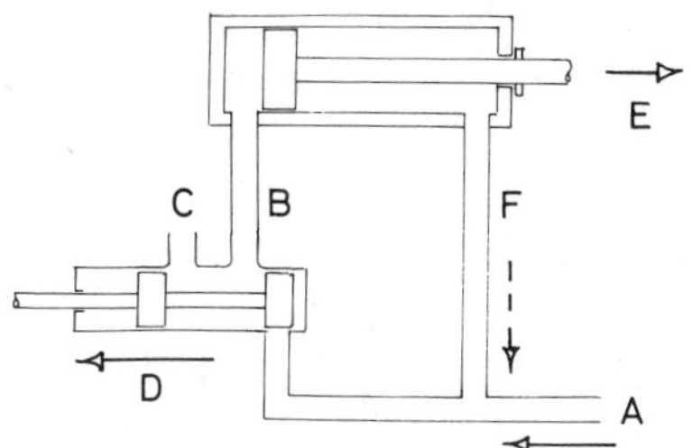

CONSTANT PRESSURE PISTON

CONSTANT PRESSURE PISTON

The third drawing of this group shows the constant pressure piston and bears out what has been said of the effect of a given pressure on a given surface area. The piston is 'uncompensated' in that its opposite surface areas differ by the cross-sectional area of the tail rod (E). System supply is constantly fed from A both to the control valve (D) and to the right-hand side of the cylinder, through pipe F. Its left-hand side is linked to exhaust by the control valve bridging B and C (exhaust) and the main piston is quiescent.

If the control valve is moved in the direction of the arrow, A is linked to B and the same pressure is applied to both sides of the piston head. However, the left-hand side has a greater effective surface area than has the right, so there is a greater force acting towards the arrow above E than against it. In consequence, the piston moves to the right and liquid at the right-hand side of its piston head simply joins up with the system supply as shown by the dotted line.

The piston head was prevented (by means not shown) from blocking the entry of F into its cylinder, so restoring the control valve to its 'as drawn' state instantly caused it to retract. Much use was made of this device in hydraulic systems because it was still double-acting, in that it 'worked' in both directions, but at the same time there were only three ports in the control valve, compared with five in the double-acting piston described previously.

HYDRAULIC TRANSFER ARRANGEMENTS

The three positions of transfer were from the ship's structure to the mounting rotating structure; from the non-elevating to the elevating structure; and from the non-recoiling to the recoiling structure. The first brought the hydraulic pressure supply on to, and the exhaust from, the mounting and, as long as its overall design remained comparatively simple, the connecting point took the form of a conventional swivel set on the centre of rotation. When, however, the turret trunk began to extend deeper and deeper into the ship, it became more convenient to arrange for the transfer to take place by 'walking pipes' set in a compartment below the working chamber. These are seen in side elevation in a number of the gun mounting drawings reproduced later in this book, and so the accompanying sketches show them in plan only.

WALKING PIPES

1 Turret trunk, in fore-and-aft position
2 One set of 'walking pipes' in line
3 Cam rail
4 Turret trunk, trained from fore-and-aft position
5 Off-mounting swivel
6 Pipe-to-pipe swivel
7 On-mounting swivel
8 Arc of circle of 6

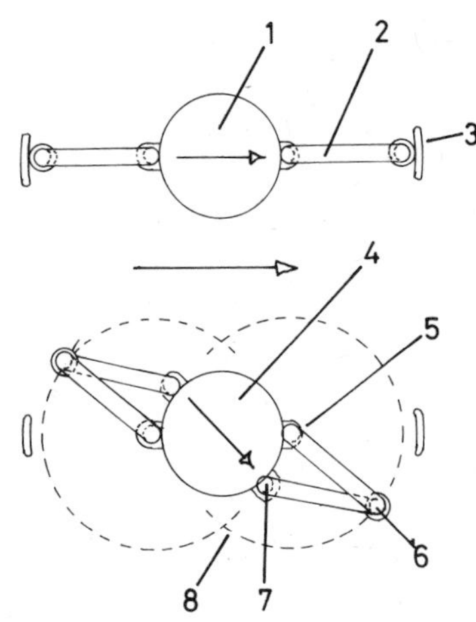

The upper sketch shows the turret trunk (1) in the fore-and-aft position with one of a pair of 'walking pipes' (2) in a lined-up position. When the mounting trained (4), the lower pipe rotated on the off-mounting swivel (5) and the upper on the on-mounting swivel (7), both pipes being mutually joined at swivel 6. This point moved on a circle (8) and as long as the 'legs' of the pipes were parted point 6 was, of course, locked. However, in the fore-and-aft position, when 5 and 7 were vertically above each other, the pair of pipes could swing freely about, so, in order to constrain them, a short cam rail (3), suspended from the deckhead, engaged with the outer swivels to hold them in position. As the upper pipe crossed the lower, when the mounting trained from one side to the other, it 'strode' around giving rise to the term 'walking pipe.'

Initially, one set of pipes was used for the incoming pressure supply and the other set for exhaust but later the pipes were made co-axial, with pressure on the inner and exhaust on the outer pipe. Both sets were retained, one as 'normal' and the other as 'alternative' supplies. The swivel connection was reintroduced by the British for their triple 16in and twin/quad 14in mountings and was commonly employed in the major equipments of other nations.

A similar arrangement was used between the non-elevating and elevating structure, in front view resembling a figure 8, with swivels at the top, centre and bottom. Transfer of supplies to, and exhaust from, the recoiling structure was made by 'sliding pipes' which functioned like telescopic tubes. Compressed air was required 'on-mounting', principally to be automatically injected into the open breech to discharge the cordite fumes from the chamber. This discharge was effected by a trip-lever on the breech mechanism and its effect can sometimes be observed in a movie film, when a small puff of smoke is seen to appear from the muzzle after gunfire, recoil and run-out. In British ships the appearance of this puff was always an indication that the breech had just been opened.

Compressed air (at about 4000psi) was usually stored in 'gas bottles' which were topped up during maintenance periods by flexible hoses coupled to the ship's high-pressure air main, but some mountings had a special high-pressure air swivel engineered co-axially with their hydraulic lead-on arrangements. 'Walking pipes' obviously limited absolute maximum training but mountings were, in general, incapable of all-round training, being conventionally sited before and abaft the ship's central superstructure.

TRAINING BASES AND ROLLERS

The drawing of the barbette mounting of 1877 in Chapter 1 shows the original style of turntable supported by comparatively few large wheels. The next development was to adopt a large number of plain rollers, each with an axial rod attached to a necklace ring which surrounded the central tube and was free to revolve about it. This resulted in a large number of shafts of considerable length all projecting radially from the necklace ring, so in later designs the ring itself was made of much greater diameter and the rollers secured to it directly by stub shafts. To locate them they were machined with flanges which prevented lateral movement between the rollers and the machined upper and lower roller paths between which they ran.

The ring was called the live roller ring and, driven by the roller's stub shafts, rotated at half the speed of the turntable. This behaviour is analagous to a track-laying vehicle, like a military tank with the large Christie-style roadwheel suspension. If it is proceeding at 20mph then, of course, so are its roadwheels and axles; the lower section of track is, in fact, stationary but the *upper* sections must be moving at 40mph.

TRAINING ENGINES AND TRAINING DRIVES

Little more need be said about the design of training engines beyond what is already detailed against the relevant drawings, except to remark on the universal joint (13) in the swashplate engine. This was of special design because it was essential that the cylinders (and therefore their pistons) constantly remained in identical alignment with the position of the rotating angled thrust-plate. The conventional universal joint will, of course, translate rotatory motion equally in terms of total revolutions input to total revolutions output, but during one rotation, the output tends to 'lag' and to 'lead' the input by a factor governed by the angle between them. The 'lag' and 'lead' effect is balanced out every 360°, but in the case of the swashplate engine constant identical alignment was imperative. Thus, a special universal joint having this ability had to be designed.

PRINCIPLES OF SWASHPLATE ENGINE

1 Pressure lead
2 Fixed valve plate
3 Left-hand kidney-shaped port
4 Cylinder block
5 High point of wedge
6 Thrust plate
7 Piston rods, extending under pressure
8 Thrust race
9 Fixed cylindrical wedge
10 Output shaft, driven by thrust plate
11 Low point of wedge
12 Piston approaching low point
13 Universal coupling
14 Cylinders discharging to exhaust
15 Top 'land' in valve plate
16 Exhaust lead

Operation
This compact and very efficient engine was described as being of the 'axial' type in that the pistons lay in the same plane as the output shaft. Pressure was led through pipe 1 to a fixed valve plate (2) in which two kidney-shaped ports were machined. They were separated by two blank 'lands' at 2 and 15. Pressure was admitted to three pistons (7) and the reaction of their thrust between the vertical plane of the cylinder block (4) and the sloping 'swash', or thrust plate (6) – into which they were anchored by ball-and-socket joints – caused them to move towards the low point of the wedge angle 17, thus rotating the thrust plate against the thrust race (8) which bore against the fixed cylindrical wedge (9).

The thrust plate was connected to the output shaft (10) and also, through universal joint 13, to the cylinder block. The cylinder block therefore revolved around the valve plate (shown 'exploded' away in the drawing, but, in fact, actually butting up against the cylinder block rear face). Piston 12 is nearing the 'low point' of the swash plate, which coincided with blank 'land' (15) and also with the maximum extension of the piston. Rotation imparted by cylinders constantly coming into line with 'kidney' port (3) caused the pistons on the opposite side to retract into their cylinders, discharging to exhaust, through the opposite port, to pipe 16. The maximum retraction of a piston occurred at point 2, when it transferred from exhaust to pressure to continue the rotary motion. There was always an uneven number of cylinders, equal numbers being linked to pressure and exhaust and the odd one changing from one to the other. Transposing the pressure and exhaust lines to the fixed valve plate, by a control valve, gave reversal of motion and also infinitely variable speed control.

This fundamental design had many variants, including the 'swashplate pump'. In this device, a prime mover in the form of an electric motor drive shaft 10, and the same piston movements drew liquid from supply at 1, and discharged it through 16 into the hydraulic system mains. Such pumps were sometimes automatic in that the 'swashplate' was carried in a lateral trunnion assembly and its angle of 'tilt' could be altered. A spring acting at its 'low point' was counterbalanced by a piston rod, reflecting system pressure, anchored to the 'high point'. Calibrating the spring to match the required system pressure – say 1000psi – resulted in an automatic pump, for when system pressure fell, the spring tilted the swashplate, putting the piston 'on stroke', but when the pressure level was reached, the swashplate tilted to the vertical and the pistons no longer oscillated in an out.

A further development was the pump whose trunnioned swashplate could be angled in either direction from the vertical 'no-swash' position, giving the facility of infinitely controllable flow rates and at the same time, flow in either direction.

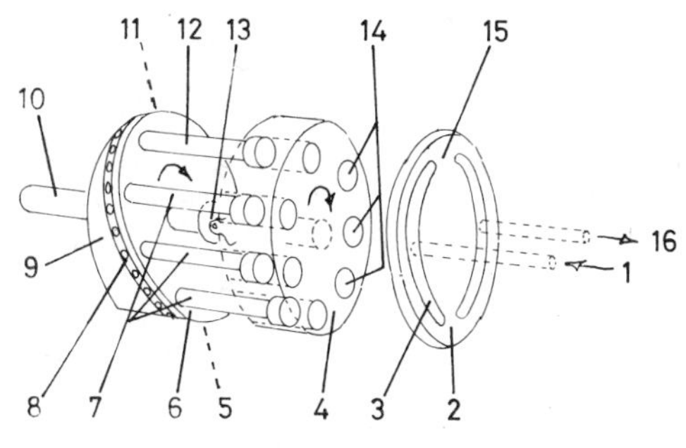

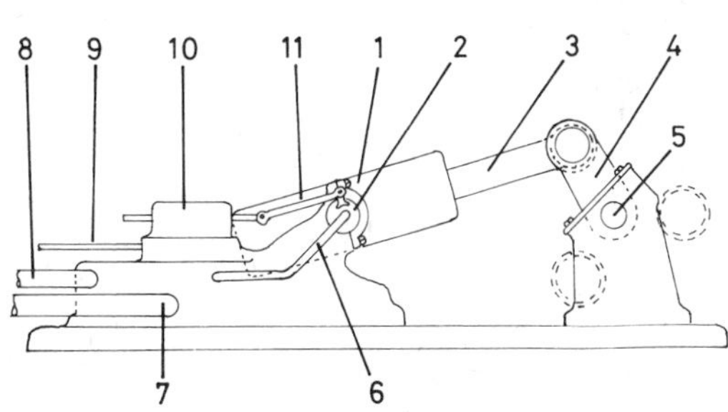

THREE-CYLINDER TRAINING ENGINE

1 Oscillating cylinder
2 Cylinder trunnion pin
3 Piston rod
4 Crank
5 Three-throw crankshaft, connected to training drive
6 Alternate pressure and exhaust pipe
7 Exhaust pipe
8 Pressure pipe
9 Reversing valve link-rod
10 Slide valve
11 Slide valve connecting-rod, attached to oscillating trunnion-pin

Operation
Main system pressure was constantly led to the slide valve (10) which directed it, via pipe 6, through a swivel connection on the cylinder trunnion axis (2) into the cylinder (1). Piston rod (3) drove through the crankshaft (5) and at the same time the cylinder oscillated, shifting the position of the slide valve through the connecting rod (11). Motion from the other pistons retracted piston (3) into its cylinder, discharging liquid within it to exhaust, via pipes 6 and 7.

The 'reversing valve', coupled to 9, was also the control valve for both speed and direction. Centrally, it closed off the pressure supply to the slide valve and thus the engine remained stationary. Opened discreetly, it controlled the speed to train either right or left.

This was the normal type of training engine fitted in Victorian and Edwardian power-operated mountings and depending on the training power drive routeing, might be mounted either vertically or horizontally. Apart from a few 'private venture' hydraulic devices, it was totally superseded by the much more compact and efficient 'swashplate' engine.

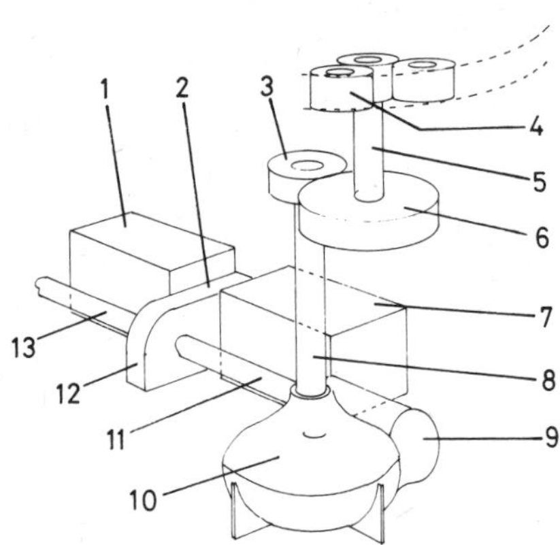

TYPICAL TRAINING DRIVE

1 Left-hand training engine
2 Engine selector clutch box
3 Wormwheel shaft pinion
4 Training pinions in engagement with fixed internal training rack
5 Drive pinion shaft
6 Intermediate pinion
7 Right-hand training engine
8 Wormwheel shaft
9 Worm gear case
10 Wormwheel gear case
11 Drive shaft
12 Drive gearbox
13 Drive shaft to left-hand training gear
(Note: Only one engine could be clutched into engagement at any time, but either drove through 12 to both 11 and 13, and so to the twin training pinions on each side.)

ELEVATING ARRANGEMENTS

A: 13.5in Elswick mounting (Royal Sovereign class)
1 Slide
2 Ball-ended link
3 Ram
4 Hydraulic lead to cylinder
In these, and contemporary mountings, the gun was breech-heavy about the trunnion axis and it was elevated by allowing liquid in the cylinder to escape to exhaust by the layer's elevation control valve. The gun was depressed by admitting pressure to the cylinder

B: 13.5in Mk II mounting (Orion class)
1 Lug on underside of cradle
2 Cross-lead
3 Cross-lead link
4 Elevating cylinder, mounted horizontally
5 Elevating piston tail-rod
This elevation arrangement was introduced when guns became balanced about their trunnion axis, but was unsuitable for high elevations.

C: 13.5in Mk III (Benbow)**
1 Lug on underside of cradle
2 Elevating cylinder trunnion axis and hydraulic swivel connection to upper surface of piston head
3 Hydrulic lead to underside of piston-head from opposite trunnion
4 Elevating piston tail-rod
5 Oscillating elevation cylinder
This arrangement became common in most mountings in the Royal Navy and was adopted for the 15in, 16in and 14in weapons

D: Typical American 'screw-jack' arrangement
1 Lug on underside of cradle
2 Threaded elevation shaft
3 Worm and wormwheel drive
The Americans devised several means of driving the gears operating the 'screw-jack' but the principle remained the same

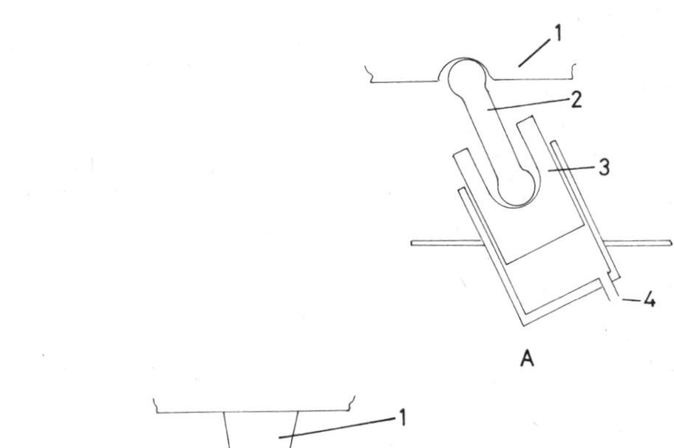

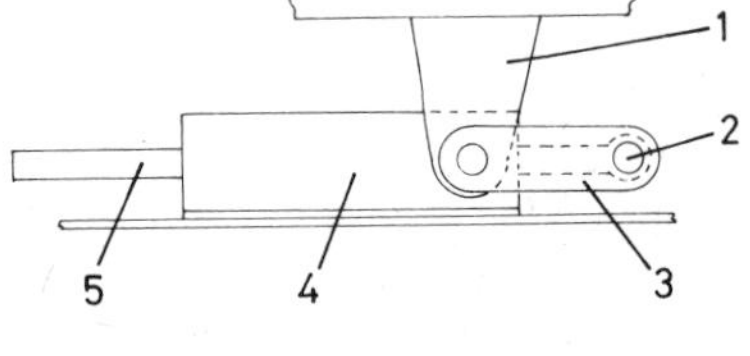

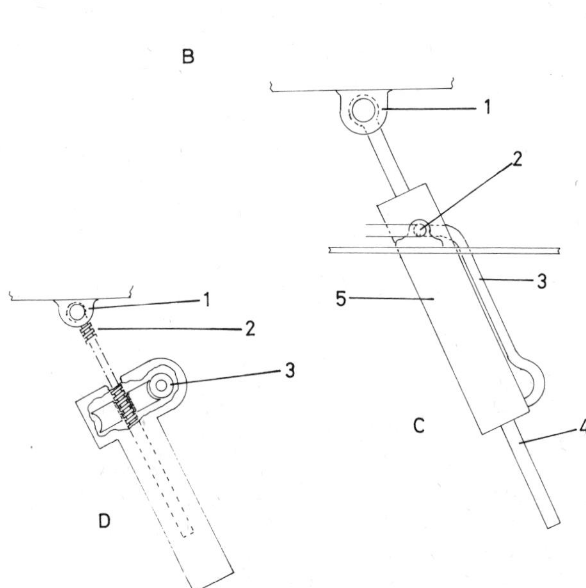

Early training drives were quite simple and usually employed a three-cylinder engine mounted so that its output shaft was upright. It drove through a straightforward spur wheel reduction gear to the training pinion shaft. Later, on-mounting engines tended to be set horizontally, in their own trunk compartment, and the translation of motion from horizontal to vertical almost always employed a worm and wormwheel. By its very nature, such a device provided a compact and considerable gear reduction while the principal alternative, bevel wheels, which inherently conformed to normal gear wheel reduction principles, would have required much more space.

ELEVATING ARRANGEMENTS

The five drawings show a variety of elevating arrangements and no further descriptive elaboration is necessary, save perhaps to say that although the Americans soon reverted to individual 'screw-jack' elevation for their heavy calibre ordnance, in medium calibre 8in and 6in cruisers they retained the single-screw, common-cradle idea for multiple barrels.

RECOIL AND RUN-OUT ARRANGEMENTS

During the period when guns remained in the 'run-in' condition for loading, the arrest of the gun in recoil and its eventual return to the firing or 'run-out' position was effected by a single hydraulic piston and cylinder. This was known as the Class I arrangement, Class II being applied to later mountings where the recoil and run-out cylinders were separate entities and Class III to those with run-out springs.

The accompanying drawing shows the arrangement in the 13.5in barbette mounting of the *Royal Sovereign* class battleships (1889).

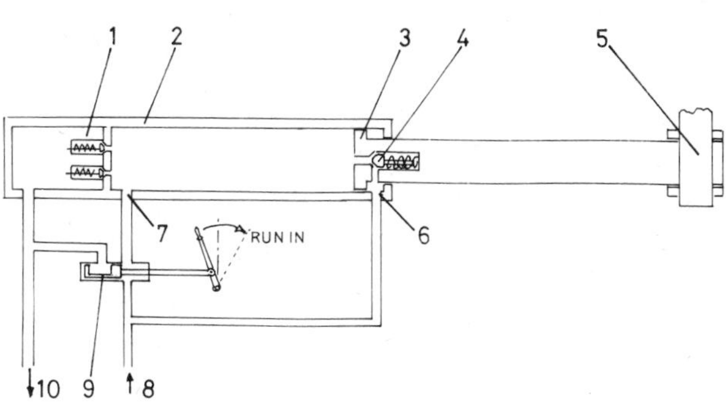

RECOIL AND RUN-OUT ARRANGEMENTS (*ROYAL SOVEREIGN* CLASS)

The cylinder (2) was fixed to the underside of the slide, and the piston (3), attached to a lug (5) on the underside of the recoiling cradle, moved into it on gunfire. The increased pressure lifted eight spring-loaded, non-return recoil valves (1), set into a bulkhead within the cylinder, allowing the liquid in the cylinder to flow to exhaust via the main exhaust line (10). To prevent dangerous over-pressures, a second 'piston' non-return valve 4 was set into the piston and this, too, lifted. As the piston head (3) moved into the cylinder an annular space was created on its right-hand side, but the liquid passing 4 was of insufficient volume totally to fill it. A pressure lead (6) from the main pressure supply line (8) was therefore taken to the front of the cylinder to make up the volume (and to obviate a vacuum effect). At this time, the control lever, in its upright position, set the 'D' slide valve (9) in such a way that incoming pressure from 8 was isolated from the entry port (7).

When the gun had been loaded, the control lever was put to 'run-out' (as drawn) when pressure through port 7 forced the gun back into the firing position because the area of the left-hand side of the piston head was much greater than the right-hand. Operating the lever to the 'run-in' position, for inspection and maintenance, linked entry (7) to exhaust (10) via 9 and pressure from 8 and 6 moved the gun to the rear; and by centralising the control valve, the gun could be stopped and held stationary at any intermediate position. Normal recoil length was 5ft and 5ft 1½in, metal to metal.

Most early guns were later adapted for cordite charges, instead of powder, and their recoil valves were redesigned. Typically in the 13.5s of *Royal Sovereign* the valve-lift settings were as follows:

Setting	**Recoil valves (lb)**	**Piston non-return valve (lb)**
Powder charge	2580	2705
Cordite charge	1550	1480

This arrangement, dictated by the run-in condition of the gun, was soon to be superseded in the Royal Navy but Norman Friedman, in his book *Battleship Design and Development 1905-1945*, has some intriguing things to say about the US mountings of the Second World War. Writing on the subject of loading angles he says that USN heavy calibre weapons were 'designed to load at a fixed angle, effort being expended. . .on powerful electric motors to move the guns into and out of the desired firing elevation after and before loading. The operation of these motors is quite evident in films of American ships firing: the guns fire, then depress as they recoil to be loaded; and then they elevate as they run out again after loading. It all seems so smooth that the period of loading itself is not very visible.'

The implications of this statement indicate a most unusual sequence, with the guns depressing as they recoil, remaining run-in during loading, and then elevating at the same time that they run out. The best rate of fire of any heavy calibre weapon – almost totally a matter of the loading cycle – was about 2 rounds per minute; but Norman Friedman based his statement on film record, and the 'not very visible' loading period may well be accounted for by judicious clipping of the film to give the appearance of a higher rate of fire than was actually obtained.

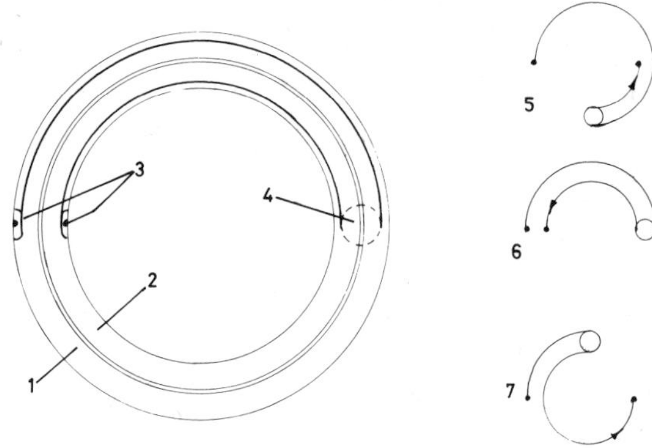

CABLE PLATFORM (SCHEMATIC)

1 Outer platform, fixed to barbette
2 Inner platform, attached to rotating trunk
3 Cable terminations
4 Cable-winding pulley
5 Turret at 180°, training left
6 Turret at 0°, training left
7 Turret at 180°, trained left (Note: In the 'train right' direction (7, 6, 5) the gearing to the pulley preserved the cable tension.)

In the Royal Navy, from the BII mounting onwards, heavy guns were arranged to run out immediately after recoil had ceased, and details of how this was effected are given later in this book. The final type of recoil and run-out system employed a compressed air cylinder (the recuperator) to run the gun out, and this required a special type of recoil cylinder. Previously it had arrested recoil but played no part in controlling run-out because this was achieved by the hydraulic run-out gear. In the recuperator-fitted mountings (for example, the British 14in quadruple) the recoil cylinder was arranged to control both recoil and run-out speeds.

Subsidiary mechanisms included buffer stops (at the limits of movement), locking bolts (often hydraulically operated) and various styles of cut-off gear. This usually took the form of a cam-operated valve that was closed towards the limit of a machine's movement, and so firstly 'throttled' and finally closed off the hydraulic supply.

ELECTRICAL ARRANGEMENTS

The almost exclusive reliance placed upon hydraulic powering by British gun mounting designers meant that there was no need to provide the rotating structure with other than comparatively modest electric cabling – for such services as fire-control transmissions (for gun orders to the gun receivers), firing circuits, communications, lighting, heating and ventilation fans. The standard mains supply in British ships was set at 220v direct current (DC) and remained so until after the Second World War, when 440v alternating current (AC) was adopted. Fire control transmissions functioned from a 24v DC supply for many decades until, again, superseded by AC systems – although the latter were originally introduced in the mid-1930s. Firing circuits were always of the 'earth return' type (rather like the electrics of a motor car) where the circuit was passed through to the electric firing 'tube' in the breech by cable and returned to its source through the ship's structure. Most big mountings had emergency supply sources, fed from hydraulic motors or impellers driving small generators, for lighting, firing circuits and local fire control transmissions.

The transfer of supplies (all combined together in a main cable loom) was effected by 'cable platforms'. They took the form of two large flat rings, the outer fixed around the inside of the barbette (usually just below the training rack) and the inner, level with the first, fixed to the periphery of the mounting trunk. The cable was fixed to the ship's structure at one end, led around the outer platform and then turned in a 'U' form and doubled back upon itself along the inner platform to an entry point on the rotating trunk. Sufficient cable was provided for the full arc of training of the mounting and, as it moved, the 'U' bend rolled around the platforms. Like the duplication of hydraulic supplies, the electrics were given two routes – 'main' and 'alternative' – whose terminal points on the platforms were 180° apart. To assist in maintaining the 'U' bend 'cable winding gear' was often employed. This consisted of a deeply grooved pulley wheel at the 'U' bend of the cable, geared to revolve at the appropriate speed to control the loom and prevent any twisting or buckling.

Only in their electrically powered 12in twin BXI and BXII mountings did the British employ the 'slip-ring' principle of electric transference from ship's to rotating structure, although this method was frequently used by other nations. The slip-ring consisted of a drum-shaped stack of contact rings (each alternating with an insulated disc) against which spring-loaded contact brushes ran, the whole assembly being on the centre of rotation of the lowest point of the turret trunk. Its advantages were that it occupied little space and inherently gave all-round 'indefinite' training, but the latter was rarely required and, while cabling clearly gives a direct connection between one point and another, the brushes of a slip-ring are subject to wear and also to jumping out of contact under shock conditions. When the triple 16in and the twin and quadruple 14in mountings were developed for the Royal Navy between the wars, the space which might have been occupied by a slip-ring had, in any case, already been taken up by the very heavy hydraulic swivel connection that had replaced the earlier 'walking pipes'.

FIRE CONTROL TRANSMISSIONS

As has been mentioned, the earliest fire control transmissions employed by the Royal Navy were fed from a 24v DC supply. The system was known as the 'M' type and consisted of a transmitter driven either by a handle or, in fire control tables, by a motor which might be electric, pneumatic or hydraulic, depending upon the period. The transmitter consisted of a drum-shaped commutator with contact plates on its periphery at displaced angles. As it revolved, it sent pulses of DC along wires connected to a small motor which moved around in sympathy. The latter was geared to the 'electric' pointer in, for example, the training receiver, which stepped around a dial calibrated in degrees and minutes of arc. There was usually a 'coarse' and 'fine' dial, the former (and smaller) showing 360° and the latter 10°, sub-divided into units of 6 or 2 minutes of arc, depending upon the accuracy required. A mechanical shaft drive, taken from the mounting motion to a second pair of pointers set (like the hour and minute hands of a clock) co-axially with the 'electric' pointers, showed the actual position of the mounting in degrees annd minutes 'red' (port) or 'green' (starboard) about the centreline of the ship. By 'matching' pointers, the gun was moved to the correct position.

Elevation transmissions were identical – except that the coarse dial did not cover so great an arc – but range and deflection were transmitted for quarters firing to counterdrum displays similar to motor car mileage indicators.

The advantages of the 'M' type system were that it was inexpensive, could be battery-powered in emergencies and that its 'M' type motors were powerful enough to drive small mechanisms. The three disadvantages were firstly that it moved around in steps (it was also called 'step-by-step' transmission) and thus gun-pointing accuracy was related to the magnitude (in minutes of arc) of the step itself. Secondly, it had a critical speed of rotation, called the 'slipping speed', beyond which the receiver lagged farther and farther behind the initiating transmission. Thirdly, because of the likelihood of 'slip', it became necessary to provide a means of lining up all instruments. For this purpose banks of circuit-breakers, fitted in the transmitting station (TS), were arranged to open up all the 24v DC transmission circuits so that, on initially 'closing up', all the outlying positions could manually set their 'electric' pointers to a predetermined datum point. All positions then had to report back to the TS in turn, and when all receivers were lined up the circuits were closed. All positions were then required to 'check receivers' and, if any had 'jumped' out of alignment (as they sometimes did), the lining-up process had to be repeated.

An AC system was experimentally introduced by the British in 1935 and its smooth follow and inherent characteristic of never becoming misaligned proved, despite its greater expense, to be far superior, and thereafter it gradually superseded the systems for 'indicator' transmissions. The same AC principle was later developed for remote power control (RPC) to give automatic gun-follow but, in the Royal Navy's capital ships, only *Vanguard*'s 15in mountings had this very desirable refinement – and then solely for the training motion.

3 Ballistics

The three major factors affecting the theoretical range of a gun are firstly, and fairly clearly, the size of the propellant charge in relation to the weight of the shell; secondly, the length of the barrel; and thirdly, the elevation of the gun in its trunnions. In order to achieve stability in flight, the ratio of projectile length to diameter is approximately the same for any size – and the limits of cartridge mass are dictated by the practical dimensions and structural strength of the breech block and chamber.

Because cordite is, by definition, a 'low' explosive which, upon ignition, takes a measurable time to expand in gaseous form (as distinct from a 'high' explosive the expansion rate of which on detonation is virtually instantaneous), it will continue to expand behind the shell for about half the barrel's length. In simple terms this means that the longer the barrel is made, the greater will be the muzzle velocity (MV) of the emerging projectile, with a consequent increase in range.

Barrel length is limited by its stiffness as a tube structure. If too great, 'droop' will occur, and thus, for heavy ordnance, a barrel the total bore length of which falls between 40 and 50 calibres becomes an optimum size. The smaller the calibre the easier it is to increase the proportionate barrel length: a rifle, for example, may be very long-barrelled indeed and out-range a pistol firing identical ammunition by many hundreds of yards.

The battleship *Royal Sovereign* fires her 15in guns during gunnery exercises during the latter part of World War I. *Conway Picture Library*

For comparative purposes, bore length, calibre and muzzle velocity of some twentieth century battleship guns are given in the accompanying table. Quite apart from the structural problems of building a long-barrelled gun, an attendant consideration is that of barrel life. A high MV creates greater wear – and relining a big gun may be a protracted and expensive exercise. In peacetime, expense is usually the deciding factor; in war, time is all-important.

BORE LENGTH, CALIBRE AND MUZZLE VELOCITY OF SOME TYPICAL BATTLESHIP GUNS

Country of origin	Gun	Length of bore (calibres)	Nominal MV (fs)
GB	15in Mk I	42	2450
GB	13.5in Mk V	45	2582
USA	14in Mk IV	50	2800
USA	14in Mk I	45	2600

The battleship *Nelson* firing a broadside from her nine 16in Mk I guns during the Second World War. *Imperial War Museum*

It will be well worth while to fringe upon the complex science of external ballistics at this point, the better to understand the real significance of a surface weapon's maximum elevation, and to start by saying that the *theoretical* range of any missile – be it shell from a gun or stone from a catapult (though not, of course, a powered rocket) – is governed by a formula which is finally multiplied by the trigonometrical term *sine of twice the angle of elevation*.

Now the sine of zero degrees is zero and increases to unity at 90°, thereafter diminishing to zero at 180°. Plotted graphically against a horizontal axis calibrated in angles, this produces the familiar 'sine wave', with a crest at 90° and a trough at 270°. The formula employs twice the angle of elevation (θ), so when this angle reaches 45°:

$$\begin{aligned}\text{Sin } 2\theta &= \sin(2 \times 45)^\circ \\ &= \sin 90^\circ \\ &= 1 \text{ (and maximum)}\end{aligned}$$

If, however, the angle of elevation is 40°, then the natural sine law will show that the sine of twice the angle is

$$\text{Sin } 80 = 0.9848$$

Hence if the maximum range for 45° is, say, 30,000yds, then at 40° it will be

$$30{,}000 \times 0.9848 = 29{,}544\text{yds}$$

It will be observed how small is the increase in range between 40° and 45°. Evidently, as 45° is approached, the less is the range increased per degree. The engineering problems involved in building a mounting capable of 45° elevation as against one having a maximum of 40° are very great – and for little benefit. It will be noticed also, from the accompanying table showing progressive ranges for a gun with a maximum of 30,000yds (an arbitrary figure but deliberately chosen), that whilst 15° elevation gives 15,000yds, the elevation must increase threefold to double this range.

PROGRESSIVE RANGES FOR A GUN OF 30,000yds MAXIMUM RANGE

Elevation (degrees)	Range (yds)		
5	5209	30	25,980
10	10,261	35	28,191
15	15,000	40	29,544
20	19,283	45	30,000
25	22,981		

The formula referred to above is

$$R = \frac{MV^2 \times \sin 2\theta}{3g}$$

where R = range in yards, MV = muzzle velocity in feet per second and g = gravitational effect in feet per second squared. The figure '3' in the denominator merely translates the result into yards. It should be noted that, in a vacuum, the size, weight and shape of the projectile do not enter into the formula – only the muzzle velocity and the angle of elevation are significant.

Further laws of physics show that the momentum of a body – or its resistance to being stopped once it has been set in motion – is related to its mass and to its velocity; and the weight of a shell of established proportions is given fairly accurately by the formula

$$\frac{C^3}{2},$$

where C = calibre in inches. Thus an 8in shell weighed

USS *Texas* fires a broadside. She and her sister-ship *New York* were fitted with ten 14in/45cal Mk 8 guns firing a 1500lb shell at a muzzle velocity of 2600 feet per second. This is a 1940s photo, taken after the ship's main armament had been modified to increase elevation by 15°, although her guns are something short of the maximum angle here. *Conway Picture Library*

roughly 250lb, while a 16in projectile weighed about 2000lb, or eight times more. Once these two shells become subjected to the constraints of the atmosphere, their ability to pass through it takes on significance – an ability heavily influenced by their cross-sectional area. In the case of the 16in shell this area will be approximately 200sq in but in the case of the 8in only about 50sq in. Therefore, the larger shell has four times the cross-sectional area of the smaller to force through the atmosphere's retarding effects but, at the same time, has eight times its momentum. However, the total surface area of the larger projectile will be much in excess of that of the smaller so the former will feel proportionately higher friction effects. When all these factors have been equated, together with the nose contour shapes of the individual missiles, the result is always that the larger shell travels much the further. It is difficult accurately to compare the British 16in with the 8in, because the muzzle velocities were so different, but justification of the foregoing may be seen from the accompanying extracts from the range tables for the two guns.

EXTRACTS FROM RANGE TABLES FOR BRITISH 16in AND 8in GUNS

Gun	MV (fs)	Elevation	Range (yds)
16in	2525	41° 31′	38,000
8in	2725	41° 28′	29,000

The atmospheric effects on a shell in flight produce an interesting phenomenon in that, even though the physical formula shows that 45° elevation will give the absolute maximum range, because at higher elevations the shell's trajectory will pass through more and more rarified air the resistive effect throughout the total flight time is lessened, so in practice most heavy guns would achieve maximum range at about 50° elevation. Because its ballistic shape will also affect the shell's behaviour in the atmosphere, the range of any given gun will immediately be increased if, within the limits of its stability in flight, the projectile profile is improved. The table in the section on projectiles gives a typical example.

An examination of the laws of trigonometry shows that the sine of 88° is the same as the sine of 92° and there are thus *two* elevations for any given range equally set about 45°. For example, 30° and 60° will give the same theoretical range. Firing against targets at elevations above 45° is known as upper register firing and is used by such weapons as mortars and howitzers. The former may be useful in dropping a projectile *into* something – like a trench – and the latter would be ideal if heavy 'plunging' fire were required at a comparatively short range. Equally, it could be used in undulating terrain to lob shells over a hilltop. Neither weapon, however, is of much practical use at sea (although some river gunboats were fitted with 3.7in howitzers) because the object of naval gunnery is to get the shell to the target as quickly as possible, and not waste precious seconds by firing it at an unnecessarily high trajectory. In passing, it should be noted that there is a distinct difference between upper register firing and the high-angle firing employed against aircraft.

In the theoretical case, the path followed by the projectile will be exactly symmetrical about its highest point and its angle of impact, the same as the elevation at which the gun was set. In practice, the external terrestrial influences cause the shell to describe an asymmetrical curve, the descent being increasingly steeper than the upward climb. This, again, is borne out by the table in the section dealing with projectiles.

PROJECTILES

Hand in hand with the improvements implemented in guns, breech mechanisms and gun mountings generally, went parallel improvements in the nature and fillings of shells, as well as a very radical change in the type of propellant charge employed. This latter was initiated by the French, who introduced the first 'smokeless powder' (so called because unlike gunpowder, which produced dense clouds of smoke, it was almost completely combusted on firing) in the mid-1880s. This was a nitro-cellulose powder, later adopted by the US and Russian Navies, which had very good ballistic qualities but suffered from instability. This necessitated great care in storage if the powder's qualities, and indeed safety, were to be maintained, and initially involved the provision of refrigerated magazines to prevent decomposition at high temperatures. Subsequent developments, including the addition of stabilising agents, greatly improved the powder's qualities and few problems were encountered with its use after World War I. The remaining major naval powers adopted the British nitro-glycerine powder-cordite – which was introduced in the Royal Navy in 1890. Cordite was more stable than pure nitro-cellulose powder, provided it had been properly manufactured and had not been subject to long-term decomposition, but it was not as good ballistically. The original cordite adopted by the Royal Navy – called, not surprisingly, Mk I – was found to be detrimental to the gun barrels and caused very rapid wear. The proportions of nitro-glycerine and nitro-cellulose that formed the two main constituents were revised, and a much more efficient propellant, designated Cordite MD, was produced. A 25 per cent increase in weight of MD over Mk I gave the same ballistic results but doubled the life of the gun.

Initially, the projectiles themselves were a solid elongation of the old cannon-ball, were made of iron, and were simply known as 'shot'. The expression 'shot hoist' continued to be used, in fact, even after the introduction of 'shell', which very name implied that they were hollow and contained something.

The earliest form of shell, called common shell, had a filling of gunpowder specially prepared into a form known as pebble mixture for the most efficient explosive effect. Its purpose was to explode into splinters on impact and to create damage by these, together with blast and fire. However, the actual weight of explosive within it was only some 5–7 per cent of its total weight – and gunpowder at that – which perhaps puts a slightly different complexion on the projectiles of that day.

The armour-piercing (AP) shell contained even less actual explosive – between 3 and 5 per cent of the total weight – and was initially made from cast steel. To improve its penetrative powers in the face of tougher ship armour, it was manufactured from forged steel and then went through a heat-treatment process to harden its point while retaining a resilient body. The intention was for the body of the shell to resist breaking up on impact so as to drive the hard point into the enemy armour while, at the same time, an inertia-activated fuze, in the base of the shell, set off the explosive filling. Hence, one sees that the sheer velocity of impact was not, in itself, enough: the shell had to penetrate and then explode at the optimum time after contact. When fired against a 'thin-skinned' target an armour-piercing shell would more than likely pass straight through it without exploding at all, a situation which spurred the development of the semi-armour-piercing (SAP) shell, designed for use against less heavily protected targets. Thus did the race between ship armour and armour-piercing shell develop, each, in turn, overhauling the other. Next came the 'capping' of AP shell with a special steel cap which assisted in armour penetration by pre-stressing the area of impact before the hardened point entered – shells so fitted being designated 'armour piercing capped' (APC).

Longer, 'ballistic' caps, constructed of thin mild steel, were also added to improve the contours, or ballistic shape, of shells although this innovation was restricted by the need to keep the overall length within the confines of gun mounting shell cages and loading arrangements generally. As the ranging qualities of a projectile depend substantially on its shape and the radius at which its head is struck, these are very important points. Formerly this was not allowed for and, in consequence, different shapes of shell ranged differently from the same gun. Initially projectile correctors were introduced to allow for such differences; later, however, these were done away with and, instead, all shells and caps were struck with the same 'calibre radius head' (crh) so as to range uniformly. The British found the best results were given with the cap struck to 4crh (known as the 'A' class) and all shells of this class had 'A' stencilled on the shoulder after the calibre and mark of shell markings. Between the wars, sharper heads were adopted to improve the aerodynamics and the effect on the range of the British 15in gun, by replacing 4crh shells with 6crh shells, can be seen in the accompanying table.

TYPICAL BALLISTICS OF BRITISH 15in Mk I GUN

Elevation (degrees)	Range at 4crh (yds)*	Approx angle of entry (degrees)	Approx armour penetration (in)	Range at 6crh (yds)*
1	1920	1		1939
5	8629	6	16	8939
10	14,853	13	12	15,823
15	19,707	21	11	21,210
20	23,734	29	9	25,621

*Ranges at 2400fs MV, 1920lb shell, 428lb cordite MD charge weight.

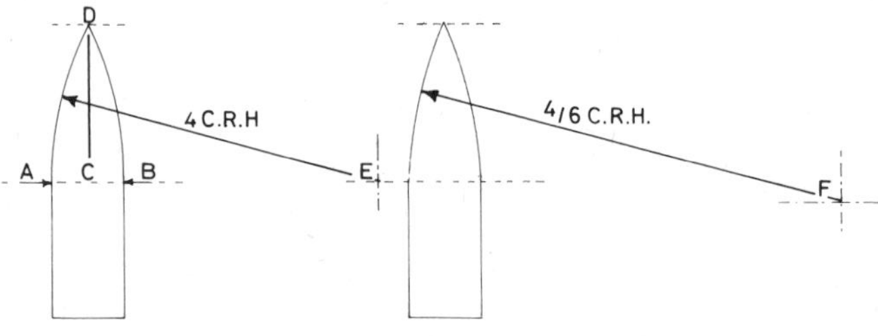

OGIVAL SHELL HEAD

CALIBRE RADIUS HEAD

This, abbreviated to crh, was the relationship between the contour of the nose and the calibre of the shell. In the accompanying drawing of the 4crh shell, AB is the 'shoulder', which is the start point of the nose and, of course, its calibre. Striking an arc equal to four times this dimension (from point E) gives a shape known as an ogive, and such shells are described as being 'ogival headed', which experiments proved to be superior to any plain conic form. The vertical distance CD was known as the ballistic length and was the most important factor in the design of a shell for stability in flight. In order to preserve this and yet achieve an element of latitude in the design of the contour, the method by which the head was struck was modified by giving a fractional definition to the crh number. Thus, while a 4crh gave one shape, a 4/6crh meant that CD – the ballistic length – was still equal to 4 calibres but that the striking arc was centred at a point (F) which was 6 calibres distant.

4 Dreadnought and Pre-Dreadnought

By the end of the 1880s the development of heavy gun mountings had resolved itself into a choice between the barbette and turret systems. The former had the advantage of allowing guns to be mounted high up, where they had good arcs of fire and were less affected by weather conditions. The turret, on the other hand, was heavy and, for reasons of stability, had to be mounted low down, which required a ship of low freeboard and therefore affected the performance of both the mounting and the ship in heavy weather. The barbette was open at the top and therefore vulnerable to shells which might detonate against the guns, while the turret provided complete protection for both the guns and their machinery.

The British built example of both types until 1889 when the barbette mounting was adopted for the last time in the *Royal Sovereign* class – the disadvantages in armament protection were considered less important than overall seaworthiness. In the next major battleship group, the *Majestic* class, the problem was solved by adding an armoured gunhouse to the top of the barbette and this subsequently became the standard arrangement not only for British but eventually for all battleship heavy mountings.

FRENCH MOUNTINGS

The only country to continue turret development for any length of time was France, somewhat surprisingly as she had both introduced and been one of the major developers of the barbette system. All her pre-dreadnoughts were fitted with turrets and the change to the barbette/gunhouse arrangement was not made until the adoption of the dreadnought type with the *Courbet* class. Similar comments apply to Russia, whose warship designs during this period were largely based on French technology.

The Russian *Pobieda*, a pre-dreadnought of typical French style with high freeboard, pronounced tumblehome and turret-mounted main armament. *Imperial War Museum*

The US pre-dreadnought *Georgia*, of the *Virginia* class, which carried four 12in guns in two Mk 5 barbette mountings. An unusual feature of this class, and of the earlier turret ships *Kearsarge* and *Kentucky*, was the fitting of a twin 8in gunhouse on the roofs of the main gunhouses. *Musée de la Marine*

The French turret differed from the barbette gunhouse in that it carried its guns much higher, accommodated most of the gun operating machinery and was, therefore, larger and heavier. On the other hand, the armoured tube protecting the ammunition hoist was of much smaller diameter and consequently lighter than the barbette. The overall effect showed little difference in weight but its distribution was such that the turret mounting, with its high centre of gravity, presented problems with regard to ship stability. It was also limited in development for as guns and their machinery became larger and more complex, it became less and less feasible to fit all the necessary equipment into a turret of reasonable dimensions.

French pre-dreadnought gun mountings possessed some intriguing design features, including a hydraulic pivot which supported the rotating structure when it was training. On gunfire the whole mounting 'sat down' on an upper seating.

The *Republique* and *Liberté* classes mounted the 12in 40cal (1893) gun and by then earlier hydraulic systems were abandoned and all powering was electric with spring run-out. The five-funnelled *Danton* class (with a mixed armament of two 12in twins and six 9.4in twins, rather like the British *Lord Nelson* class) were similar.

US MOUNTINGS

The USA also continued to employ the turret in her early pre-dreadnoughts but changed to the barbette system in the mid-1890s. In general, American nineteenth century design philosophy ran parallel with that of Europe but it was soon to diverge in several fundamental ways. Apart from some early mountings, US breech mechanisms came to be hinged horizontally and to open downwards, below and behind the mass of the gun-rear. Again, after the early years, they settled for the 'Asbury' breech mechanism, the geometry of which differed from British practice (although, exceptionally, the Royal Navy used a very similar type for its cruiser 6in Mk XXIII gun of the 1930s and it proved to be highly successful). Obturation was by the de Bange style of obturator pad and power for breech closing was mostly provided by compressed air.

In some of the mountings, multiple barrels were contained in a common elevating structure, while in others individual elevation was provided. To define precisely the two styles, 'twin' implied the former and 'two-gun' the latter. In point of fact, the Americans only once ventured into the 'common cradle' design for battleship mountings, although it was extensively employed for cruiser-calibre weapons.

Both steam and conventional hydraulics were used in early ships, followed by direct electrical powering in some instances, but independent systems for each major mounting function were later introduced. They consisted of an electric motor as prime mover, driving a hydraulic 'A' end, linked by pipework to a 'B' end. The former defined a pump and the latter a motor or engine.

The British had always made extensive use of the ram or piston/cylinder arrangement to effect elevation, but the Americans adopted a powered drive, and instead of employing the established gearwheel and toothed arc configuration, they elected to revolve a 'lead screw' which literally screwed the elevating mass up and down. In simply-drawn profile the device resembled the piston/cylinder combination but the 'piston' was, in fact, a screwed shaft secured to a lug beneath the cradle and the 'cylinder' merely a casing into which the shaft descended as the gun elevated. At the upper end of this casing (which was free to oscillate in trunnions to suit the geometry of the elevation position) a large nut-like device was set, through which the screwed shaft passed. The nut was rotated by a motor set nearby, so altering the elevation. While on the one hand a screwed shaft is not the most rapid way of moving a mass of any kind (compare, for example, a screw and a hydraulic automobile jack), it nevertheless inherently provides a rigid self-locking characteristic and was a viable design, given that some kind of geared, rather than hydraulic, device was required in the first instance.

The trunnions of the 'naturally' balanced guns were set close to the front of the gunhouse whose flat and sharply angled face, together with voluminous blast-bags, were to become typical of the American heavy gun mounting.

GERMAN MOUNTINGS

The navies of Italy, Austro-Hungary and Germany had all opted for the barbette system at an early date and their subsequent adoption of the British barbette/gunhouse configuration was little more than a natural extension of what they were already developing. In fact, in all three cases the protection of the guns by revolving hoods, either open-backed or completely enclosed, became standard practice well before the *Majestic* class battleships were designed. These early forms of gunhouse were, however, usually constructed of light or medium thickness plates and were intended to give defence against splinters and light/medium calibre weapons, whereas the later British gunhouse was fully armoured against heavy calibre guns and formed an integral part of the mounting – and was much more than just a splinter cover.

The early German barbette ships were all coast defence vessels, but in the early 1890s they laid down their first pre-dreadnoughts (the *Brandenburg* class) heralding Germany's rapid rise to a first class naval power. Details of the mountings in these pre-dreadnoughts are sketchy. The

The German pre dreadnought *Schlesien*, launched in 1906, survived until 1945 when she was mined; the wreck was broken up in the early 1950s. In these ships, and their early dreadnoughts, the Germans showed a preferences for smaller calibre weapons by adopting the 11in gun while most other navies were employing 12in guns. They did, however, compensate for this to a large extent by aiming for higher relative performance. *Conway Picture Library*

The Italian battleship *Sardegna*, built by the Royal Arsenal at Spezia in 1885–95. She carried four 13.5in/30 Armstrong guns weighing 69 tons each. The mountings were of the barbette type, but the guns were given the additional protection of splinter hoods. *Conway Picture Library*

11in L/40 and L/35 in the Drh LC/1892 mounting (*Brandenburg* class) probably had the contemporary fixed loading position common elsewhere and had a surprisingly high maximum elevation of 25°. Both elevation and training were hydraulically powered, with alternative hand drives, and the turntable was supported on a ball race. The use of this latter device, as distinct from the more generally employed tapered roller, became a regular feature of German mountings, even including the twin 15in in *Bismarck*. This somewhat surprised the Allied mission to Germany after the end of the Second World War; but the Germans were past masters in the production of ball-races and, having established this principle at the outset of their battleship building programme, saw no good reason to change to rollers, even in the knowledge that others were using them. Apart from the usual post-machining annealing, neither the steel balls nor the ball races were hardened or otherwise heat-treated. In the *Brandenburg*s, a screwed breech was employed and the usual bagged cordite formed the charge. The guns themselves were fitted with old-style trunnions and recoiled 'uphill', on inclined slides, on gunfire.

In their last pre-dreadnoughts, the *Braunschweig* and *Deutschland* classes, armed with the 11in SKL/40 in the Drh LC/1901 mounting, another special feature of German heavy weapon engineering was introduced in that a sliding 'wedge' breech was employed instead of the stepped-thread variety. In principle, this Krupp-designed device functioned in the same manner as the sliding breech block commonly employed in the (later) quick-fire and semi-automatic guns of other nations. The particular style of breech is distinguished by referring either to the breech *screw* (for the threaded type) or to the breech *block* (for the other). In British parlance, both types operated in a breech-ring, a term derived from the truly ring-shaped female-threaded component of the screw breech but also used by them to describe what was, in fact, its roughly cube-shaped counterpart. The latter was slotted either horizontally or vertically to form the breech 'mortice' in which the block moved to open and close the chamber.

In wedge breech mechanisms, obturation – or the sealing of the rear from the escape of the charge gases – was effected by a cased cartridge which was usually of brass but sometimes of steel. The cartridge body was slightly tapered towards the muzzle end and expanded on gunfire, so forming the seal. In order firmly to seat the case into the chamber the breech block was tapered so that, as it moved across behind the rear of the case, it wedged it into position. Extractors, like steel index fingers, were incorporated in the breech design and taken under the cartridge-case rim. When the breech was opened after gunfire the movement of the block operated them to unseat the case and throw it rearwards in much the same way as in small arms. (Oddly, these cartridge-cases are nearly always referred to as 'shell-cases' by the layman, who also seems prone to describe mortar bombs as 'shells', or even simply as 'mortars'.)

The dimensions of German heavy ordnance breech blocks were, naturally, quite considerable, as were those of their charges. Other nations tended to restrict charge weight to about 100lb (for ease of handling in magazines) and merely used them in multiple, depending on the gun calibre. The Germans, on the other hand, only use two charges, even for their heaviest guns, making each of them, individually, extremely weighty. The 'fore' charge was of the conventional cordite bag style, while the 'main' charge was contained in the case referred to above. As will be seen in the later detailed descriptions of their mountings, the two were often carried in individual charge-cage compartments and were sometimes loaded separately. Like their adherence to training ball races, they adopted these breech and charge principles at the outset and saw no reason to change them thereafter. Indeed, some advantages accrued, for part, at least, of the stowed cordite in magazines and in ready-use positions was cased and thus well protected from fire and action damage. In addition the general configuration of the wedge breech mechanism was simple and easy to manufacture when compared with the stepped Welin breech, its associated lock-and-box slide and its obturator pad.

The Drh LC/1901 mounting again had hydraulic powering with steam pumps as prime movers. There was no working chamber, and hydraulic pusher hoists, loaded with an alternating column of shell and charge, ran directly to the rear of each gun, where a tilting tray swung over to form a loading tray. An auxiliary hoist delivered ammunition to the outside of the guns, whence it was transferred on rails to the breech. The guns themselves were housed in cradles; run-out was pneumatic; and the breech mechanisms were hand-worked as was ramming. The elevating cylinder was connected by rodding to the cradle, and maximum elevation was 30°.

JAPANESE AND ITALIAN MOUNTINGS

Early Japanese mountings closely resembled their Royal Navy counterparts. Thus the 12in 40cal mounting of the *Fuji* class was based on the BII; the 12in 40cal of the *Shikishima* class was like the BIV; and the 12in 45cal of the *Kashima*, *Tsukubu* and *Kurama* classes generally resembled the BVII(S). Like Japan, Italy also relied heavily on British-built mountings throughout the pre-dreadnought and dreadnought era and, again, successive installations resembled contemporary Royal Navy weapons.

The *Re Umberto* class 13.5in 30cal twin turret was based on the BIII in *Caesar*, with hand elevation but hydraulic powering elsewhere. The Italian version was an early example of the all-round loading facility. The 12in 50cal *Brin* class twin mountings resembled the BVI, as did the 12in 40cal singles in the *Vittorio Emanuele* class. The latter, however, were electrically powered, run-out was by springs, and elevation was by arc and pinion.

The Italian dreadnoughts were armed with 12in 46cal guns in triple mountings sited at 'A', 'Q' and 'Y' positions and in superfiring twins at 'B' and 'X'. The contracts for these were divided between the Elswick Ordnance Company and Vickers, Son and Maxim (VSM), the former building all the mountings for *Dante*, *Cesare* and *Duilio* and VSM building those for *Cavour*, *Leonardo* and *Doria*. The triples were very similar (although at 670 tons the Vickers mountings were about 25 tons heavier than Armstrong's) and all were hydraulic with any-angle loading between limits of 20° elevation and 5° depression.

Throughout the pre-dreadnought and early dreadnought period the 12in calibre gun was, by far, the most popular battleship weapon. The choice was due most probably to the fact that it provided a good balance of gun qualities and weight, a larger weapon necessarily being heavier and therefore requiring a heavier mounting and consequently either a larger ship or a ship in which some other quality – such as protection, speed or number of guns – was sacrificed. Moreover, earlier large calibre guns, such as the British 16.25in, had not proved greatly superior to lighter weapons owing to their slow rate of fire and various other difficulties encountered in their manufacture and operation. There were of course exceptions – the USA built several 13in gun ships while the Germans showed a preference for the 11in gun until well into her dreadnought building programme – but generally speaking the 12in gun reigned supreme for a period of about 15 years. Its ultimate supersession by larger guns was inevitable with the acceptance of larger (dreadnought) battleships, the development of improved manufacturing techniques and the acceleration of international naval rivalry. The resulting 'calibre race' is, however, the subject of the next chapter. The following sections describe the principal naval mountings of the pre-dreadnought and early dreadnought period.

THE BRITISH 12in Mk VIII GUN ON THE BII (ELSWICK) MOUNTING

The 12in guns of this mounting were carried on a revolving turntable totally enclosed by an armoured shield, the complete revolving structure being referred to as a 'mounting'. It was surrounded by a pear-shaped armoured barbette (called a redoubt in the handbook) and the gun-house, with its sloping sides and pronounced overhang at the rear, set a pattern that was to last for several decades.

The reduction in calibre from the 13.5in of the *Royal Sovereign* class to 12in in the *Majestic* class was more than compensated for by greatly improved gun construction and a superior breech mechanism. The gun itself was 35½ calibres long, weighed 46 tons and was wire-wound. This last process, which continued to be employed for many years, was the method adopted to literally bind the internal tubes which formed part of the complete gun barrel, thus giving the necessary strength to prevent the gun from bursting under the pressures set up by the cordite in the chamber. A second and very important benefit was gained by the introduction of cordite as a propellant because, as it was so much more powerful than gunpowder, the actual weight of the charge was considerably reduced: the old 13.5in was 30 calibres long and used a charge of 630lb of powder for its 1250lb projectile, whereas in the later 13.5in Mk V gun of 45 calibres length the charge was only 293lb of cordite for the same weight of shell.

The bore of the 12in was, of course, rifled but the rifling was somewhat unusual in that the 48 grooves ran straight for the first 6ft and then spiralled with a gradually increasing twist towards the muzzle. This scheme allowed the projectile to accelerate rapidly without turning as it started, and then to be 'flicked' on its spin axis as it left the gun.

The *Majestic* class battleship *Jupiter*, which carried a main armament of four 12in Mk VIII guns in twin BII mountings. *Molland*

BRITISH TWIN 12in BII MOUNTING

1 Sighting hood
2 'Single-lever' control
3 Sights
4 Ready-use shell
5 Elevation cylinder
6 Training roller
7 Training limit buffer
8 Hydraulic swivel on centre of rotation
9 Hand training crank
10 3cyl training engine
11 Control shafting to training engine
12 Training hand-power dog clutch
13 Lower position of ammunition cage
14 Emergency shell hoist
15 Ammunition hoist hydraulic press
16 Training pinion
17 Off-mounting rammer
18 Gunhouse loading rammer
19 Rammer control lever
20 Control officer's hood

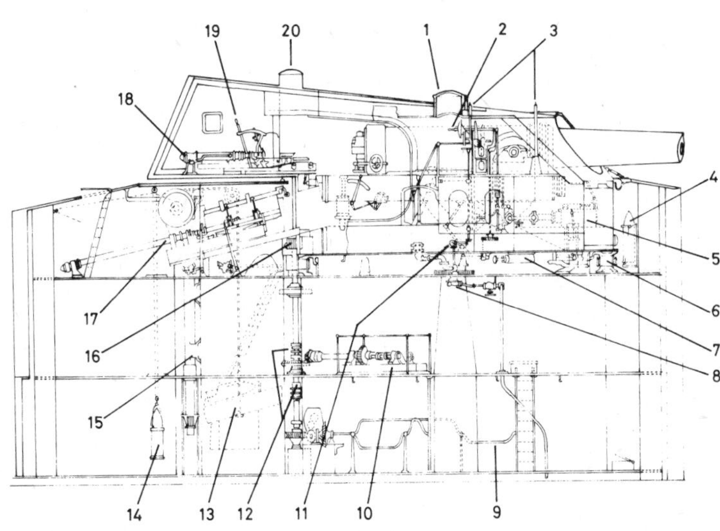

BRITISH 12in BL Mk VIII BREECH MECHANISM

1 Breech-ring
2 Upper pivot shaft
3 Bevel
4 Carrier
5 Lower shaft bevel
6 Lower pivot shaft
7 Upper lug
8 Part-toothed pinion
9 Lower lug
10 Hand drive
11 Hand-power clutch lever
12 Power drive pinion
13 Dog clutch
14 Carrier ring
15 Toothed rack on
16 Breech-screw lever
17 Cam slot
18 Breech unscrewing crank and roller

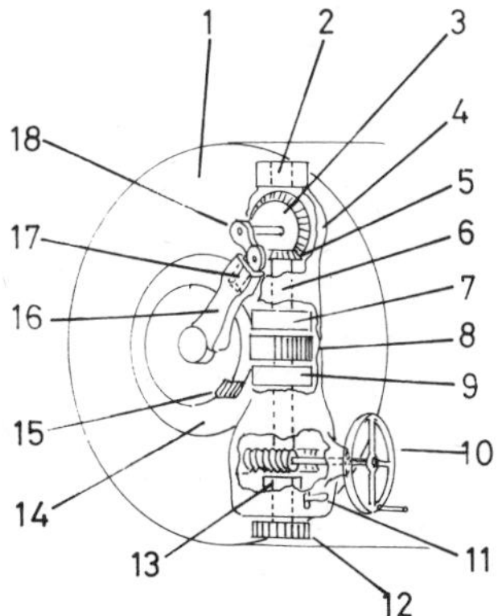

The right 12in Mk VIII gun in one of the BIII mountings of HMS *Illustrious*, showing the breech open. *By courtesy of John Roberts*

The principles of the 12in Mk VIII breech mechanism can be seen from the relevant diagram from which, for clarity's sake, the lock embracing the firing mechanism has been omitted. This lock was, in essence, a miniature breech mounted on the rear of the breech screw to hold the tube, whose detonation either by percussion or by an electric circuit ignited the cordite in the chamber. Safety devices ensured that it was inoperative until the breech was fully closed.

The main components of the breech mechanism were the breech screw, of the plain cylindrical type having six interuptions; the ring-shaped carrier, pivoted on an upper and lower shaft; and the gears on the lower shaft itself. Turning the handwheel drove through the worm and wormwheel to revolve the lower shaft and thus the lower bevel wheel. This, in engagement with the upper bevel wheel, turned the crank to unlock the breech screw. A pinion, on the lower shaft, with gear teeth cut on about two-thirds of its surface, also revolved and, as the unlocking action described above was completed, the pinion teeth engaged in a toothed rack machined on the side of the breech-screw. Continuing to turn the handwheel now withdrew the breech-screw into the carrier ring until the pinion locked on the end of the rack, at which point the drive caused the carrier to swing outwards, door-like. A clutch beneath the wormwheel gearbox either connected in the hand drive or, in its opposite position, introduced (in some mountings) an alternative power drive. The complete sequence was reversed to close the breech. First, the carrier swung to the gun, then the screw was entered by the rack and pinion, and finally the bevel wheels and crank locked the screw.

Built-in safety arrangements included the automatic isolation of the percussion/electric fitting arrangements before the breech-screw started to revolve; the locking of the carrier until the breech-screw had withdrawn; and the locking of the breech-screw within the carrier when the breech was open. Although still rather cumbersome (by later standards) the device as a whole was clearly a great advance on the old mechanism, and it was this, coupled with the improved gun construction and the introduction of cordite, that made the 12in Mk VIII gun so much better than the 13.5in of the *Royal Sovereign* class.

Now that the breech mechanism was carried totally on the elevating structure, it became possible to provide an alternative loading position and this, the upper loading position in the gunhouse, became a regular feature in succeeding mountings. The ring style of carrier was to be superseded quite soon by a heavier type in which the breech screw was carried on a pintle, but the Elswick works seem to have favoured the ring pattern and re-introduced it for their private venture 14in Mk I for the Chilean Government (see Chapter 5). Among the claimed benefits of what was later to be called the short-arm breech mechanism were that the breech-screw entered directly and 'sweetly' into the gun, and that less space was taken up by the complete mechanism in the open position than with other types.

Because these guns (and most other big pieces) were carried in twin mountings, the breech mechanisms were 'handed' to the left or right and opened towards the sides of the gunhouse. In the case of the 12in Mk VIII, the gun and breech mechanism were designed in such a way that a complete assembly could be mounted as a right-hand gun or, by turning it over, as a left-hand. They were, however, normally manufactured and assembled as a right- or left-hand and were kept as such.

An important change in the positioning of the guns on the revolving structure took place with the emergence of the BII mounting. For the first time, the total training mass was balanced about the centre of rotation and, at the same time, the elevating mass was balanced (in the 'run-out' condition) about the trunnion – or in other words the elevation – axis. This immediately allowed a secondary hand drive to be incorporated in both motions, which had been impossible hitherto. It also made changes necessary in the hydraulic elevating gear because, whereas in early guns their tail-heaviness was utilised to elevate them and pressure was admitted to a ram to depress them, with a balanced arrangement a piston in a cylinder had to be used, to enable pressure to be directed to act on either side of the piston head (the opposite side being linked to the exhaust line). The elevating cylinder was carried horizontally beneath the slide, and its piston was connected by a cross-head to a large lug formed on the slide itself. All mountings had a hand pump which could be connected to various hydraulic circuits for maintenance and testing purposes; and in some there was a small supplementary pump driven by an electric motor supplied off the lighting circuits.

The adoption of the new style of breech mechanism, and the balanced condition of the gun in the run-out position, brought sweeping changes to the basic concept of the mounting as a whole. As there was no longer any need to remove the breech-screw completely and literally put it to one side for loading (and because it was obviously an advantage to keep the gun balanced at all times), the recoil and run-out arrangements were revised to allow the gun to recoil on gunfire and then automatically return to the run-out position immediately afterwards. This is now quite accepted practice, but at the time was novel to the 12in Mk VIII.

There was now a separate recoil piston working in its own cylinder and an independent run-out cylinder and ram. The recoil piston was fixed but its cylinder was attached to the recoiling mass and was thus drawn over the piston head. A valve key, tapered in depth, was fixed inside the cylinder and passed through a calibrated slot cut in the piston head. The clearance between the key and slot was at a maximum in the fully run-out condition but, because of the taper on the key, diminished the further the gun recoiled. Hence the flow of water from one side of the piston head to the other was gradually throttled and the recoiling mass was finally brought to rest after about 36in of movement.

The energy of recoil was in fact transferred into heat, the latter generated by the friction effect of the water passing through an ever-diminishing orifice in the piston head. At the same time, the run-out ram was being forced into a fixed cylinder, over-pressure exhausting through a relief valve. Once recoil had been halted, the mounting's hydraulic system pressure forced the ram out and so returned the gun to its firing position. By suitably changing over the appropriate stop valves, system pressure could be used to artificially run the gun in for maintenance and inspection purposes. The basic features of these arrangements remained largely unchanged in all succeeding British heavy guns up to and including the 15in Mk I.

The hydraulic systems of this new generation of mountings showed little change. A steam engine still drove a pumping unit in the ship; water was used as the pressure medium; and the same family of piston, rams and turning engine as before formed the power devices. An important side effect of the improvements introduced in the 12in Mk BII mounting was the change that was made in the ammunition routeing and it was in this area more than any other that further improvements were to be seen in later classes.

The need to bring the guns to a fixed elevation and the whole of the rotating structure into alignment with the ship's structure in order to reload had been accepted previously, not only with muzzle-loaders but also with breech-loading guns up to and including the 13.5s of the *Royal Sovereign* class. In this group the rate of fire was approximately one round every two minutes – and re-phrased as 30 rounds per hour it sounds very slow indeed. Several factors (some already mentioned) created the time lag between successive firings, among them the fact that the ammunition cage had to move from magazine and shell room to the rear of the gun and remain there until loading had been completed. Only then could it be sent back to be recharged.

In the *Majestic* class battleships (which introduced the 12in Mk BII) the old arrangements were continued, to provide what was known as the fixed loading position. This required the mounting to be trained fore and aft, and the guns laid at 13½° elevation much as before, but the cages bringing up shell and cartridge from below were arranged to terminate beside the rammers in the ship instead of in line with them. When the cage reached the top of its trunk, it automatically tipped its contents out sideways on to a 9° sloping ramp leading to a bogie in line with the rammer, whereupon the cage could immediately return to the lower quarters.

The first movement of the rammer control advanced the bogie (now carrying shell and cartridge) so that it not only bridged the gap between the ship's structure and the mounting but also served as a locking bolt for both elevation and training. A tray then extended from the bogie to cover the threads of the breech and finally the rammer proper advanced to ram the round. On retracting, the complete sequence was reversed, with the bogie retracting

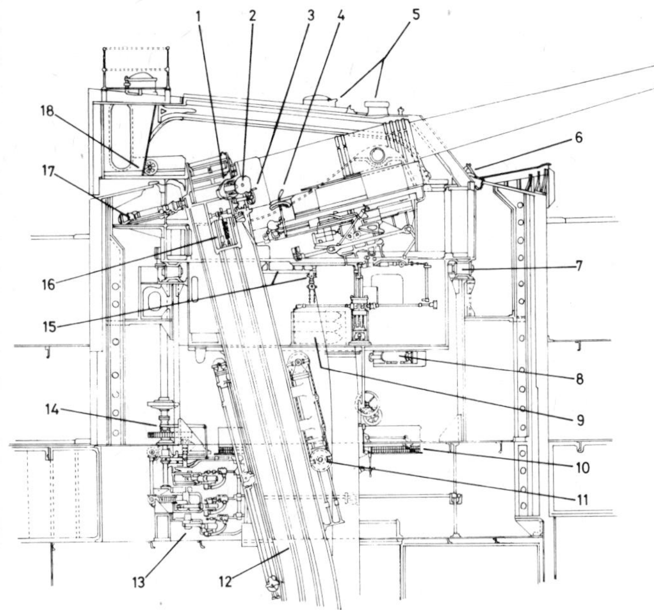

BRITISH TWIN 12in BIII MOUNTING

1 Breech carrier ring
2 Breech block, extracted and open
3 Breech mechanism hand wheel
4 Run-in and run-out control lever
5 Sighting hoods
6 Weathering
7 Training roller
8 Training limit buffer
9 Shell stowage
10 'Fixed' and 'moving' control racks
11 Hoist hydraulic press
12 Cage trunk
13 3cyl training engine
14 Hand-power training drive clutch
15 Secondary shell supply overhead rail and purchase
16 Ammunition cage
17 Off-mounting rammer
18 On-mounting shell bogie

last, by which time the cage had been reloaded below and was ready to come up. A second position, called the 'all-round loading position', was also provided and was regarded as the more important of the two, for obvious reasons.

Up to 18 shells could be stowed on racks in the revolving structure and these provided ready-use projectiles in the gunhouse. A rammer and bogie (for each gun) were mounted on the deck of the turret rear overhang, both functioning in the same manner as those at the fixed loading position. Hydraulic gear was provided for handling these shells, and special provision was made for lifting shells up into the gunhouse, through doors cut in the floor of the overhang, to recharge the ready-use stock. The guns still had to be brought to a fixed loading angle, of 1° elevation, but at least the mounting could remain trained on the firing bearing – as long as the ready-use stock lasted. Extra shells were also stowed at the fixed loading position to permit rapid 'topping up' to the gunhouse.

The supply of cartridges to the all-round loading position showed a very significant change for, although the 12in BII had no revolving trunk, it did revolve around a fixed trunk which terminated between the guns. This trunk contained two cages, connected together by a wire and driven by a drum such that when one cage was at gunhouse level the other was at magazine level. The cages carried charges which could be supplied to the gunhouse irrespective of its position relative to the ship, and the rate of fire, using all-round loading procedure, was improved to about one round per minute. This, allied to the better ballistics of the 12in, made it altogether a great step forward.

THE BRITISH 12in Mk VIII GUN ON THE BIII MOUNTING

This mounting, designed by Whitworth, was fitted in the battleships *Caesar* and *Illustrious* of the *Majestic* class and *Canopus*, *Goliath* and *Ocean* of the *Canopus* class. The old method of delivering ammunition to a position in rear of the revolving structure was abandoned in favour of a larger trunking set around the centre of rotation, which meant a circular barbette could be used instead of the pear shape of the BII, saving both space and weight. The trunking did not itself rotate but terminated in a revolving compartment, called the shell (or working) chamber, attached below the gunhouse floor. It contained three independent cartridge cages, a central access ladderway, two shell hoists (still referred to as 'shot hoists' at this time) and the hydraulic presses or rams employed to lift the cordite cages. The shell hoists consisted of a bucket in which the shell was raised vertically by similar presses, while the cordite hoists had double-compartment cages to hold two half-charges.

On its arrival at working chamber level, the shell was lifted vertically by a hydraulic hoist, picked up by a hydraulic crane and transferred, in a horizontal attitude, to a waiting tray abreast the foot of a loading hoist. The latter ran on slanting beams between the working chamber and the gunhouse and carried shell and cartridges upwards to the loading position, arranged at 13½° gun elevation. A lever, operated in the working chamber, allowed the shell to roll sideways from the waiting tray on to a loading tray, whence it was rammed into the loading cage. In the gunhouse a three-throw telescope rammer, linked to a tray that extended to cover the breech threads, completed the loading cycle.

Again, an alternative upper loading position was provided, but only three rounds per gun were stowed in the gunhouse and loading and ramming at this level could only be carried out by hand. There were, in addition, 24 rounds per gun stowed in bays in the working chamber, and the cranes could fill the loading hoists from the bays, or fill the loading hoists from the trunk, or top up the bays from the trunk. When the upper loading position was employed, the cartridges were passed up to the gunhouse through hand-up hatches in the working chamber roof. It was generally conceded that the arrangements in the main loading positions of *Caesar* and *Illustrious* were a great improvement on those in the earlier *Majestic* class ships so long as the shells could be provided from the working chamber bins, but that direct provision from the shell room made for a slow loading cycle and that the upper loading position of the BII mounting was superior while its shell supply lasted.

In the three *Canopus* class ships the ammunition supply arrangements were revised. The central trunk held two main cages, each capable of holding a shell on top of a double compartment for two half-charges. The arrangements in the working chambers were similar to those in *Caesar* and *Illustrious* but shell and cartridges for each gun came up together rather than in individual hoists.

BRITISH 12in BIV MOUNTING

1 Breech block
2 Auxiliary hoist
3 Recoil cylinder
4 Control position
5 Sights
6 Elevation cross-head link
7 Weathering
8 Elevation cylinder
9 Training roller
10 Overhead rail purchase
11 Central-pivot hydraulic swivel
12 Cordite cage in upper position
13 Hand training crank
14 Cordite loading door
15 Cordite cage in lower position
16 Shell lifting head
17 Shell tilting lever
18 Overhead shell grab
19 Shell bins
20 Shell traverser press
21 Emergency shell hoist winch
22 Ammunition hoist hydraulic press
23 3cyl training engine
24 Shell lifting head in upper position
25 Gunloading hoist alternative hand-drive
26 Shell in gunloading hoist
27 Hoist hydraulic press
28 Overhead shell grab
29 Shell traverse press
30 Gunloading cage cordite tubes
31 Off-mouting rammer
32 Auxiliary shell hand winch
33 On-mounting shell bogie.

HMS *Illustrious* during practice firing of her main armament. *Molland*
Inset The right 12in Mk VII gun of a BIII mounting on board *Caesar*, showing the breech closed. *By courtesy of John Roberts*

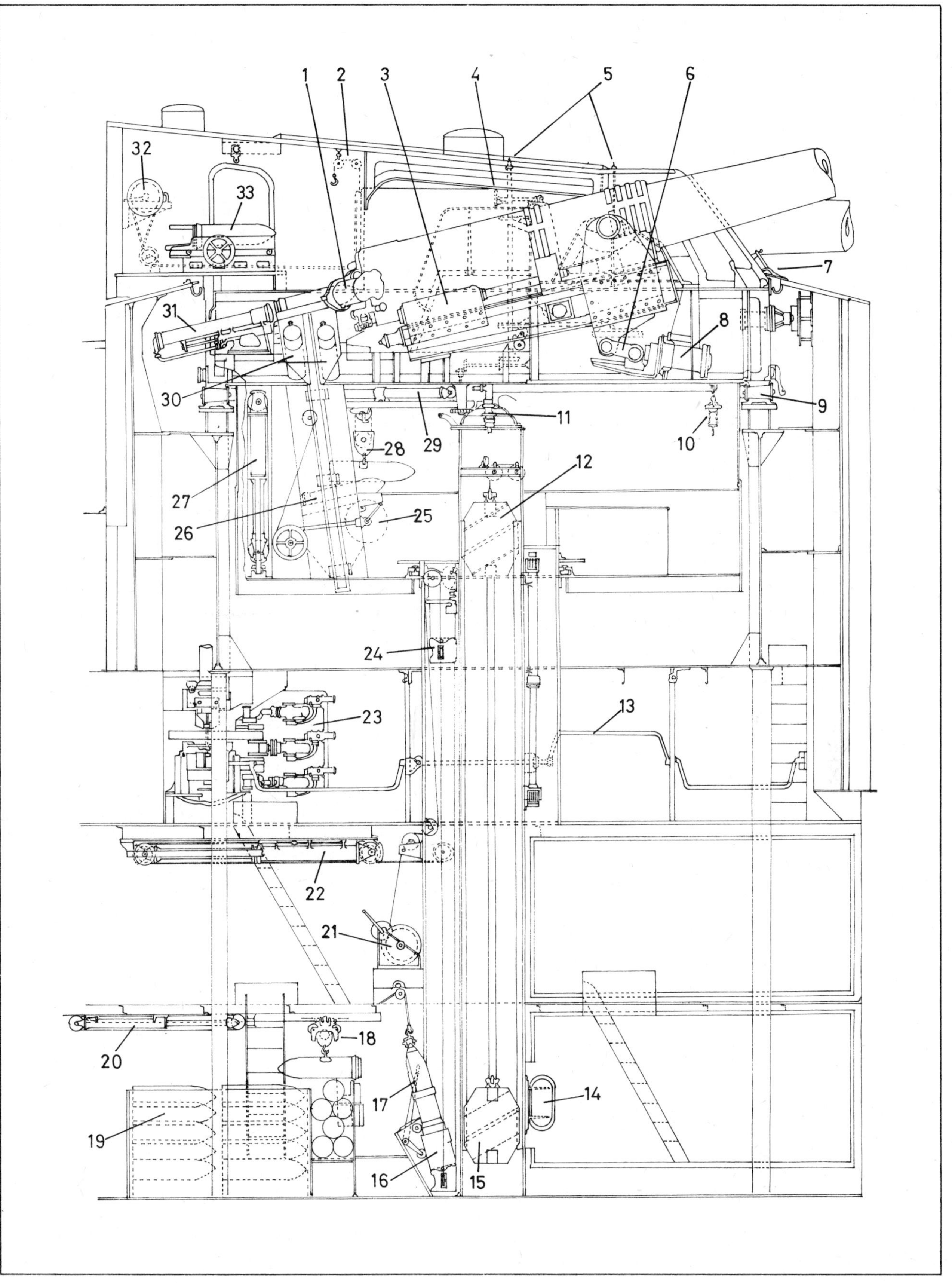
1
2
3
4
5
6
7
8
9
10
11
12
13
14
15
16
17
18
19
20
21
22
23
24
25
26
27
28
29
30
31
32
33

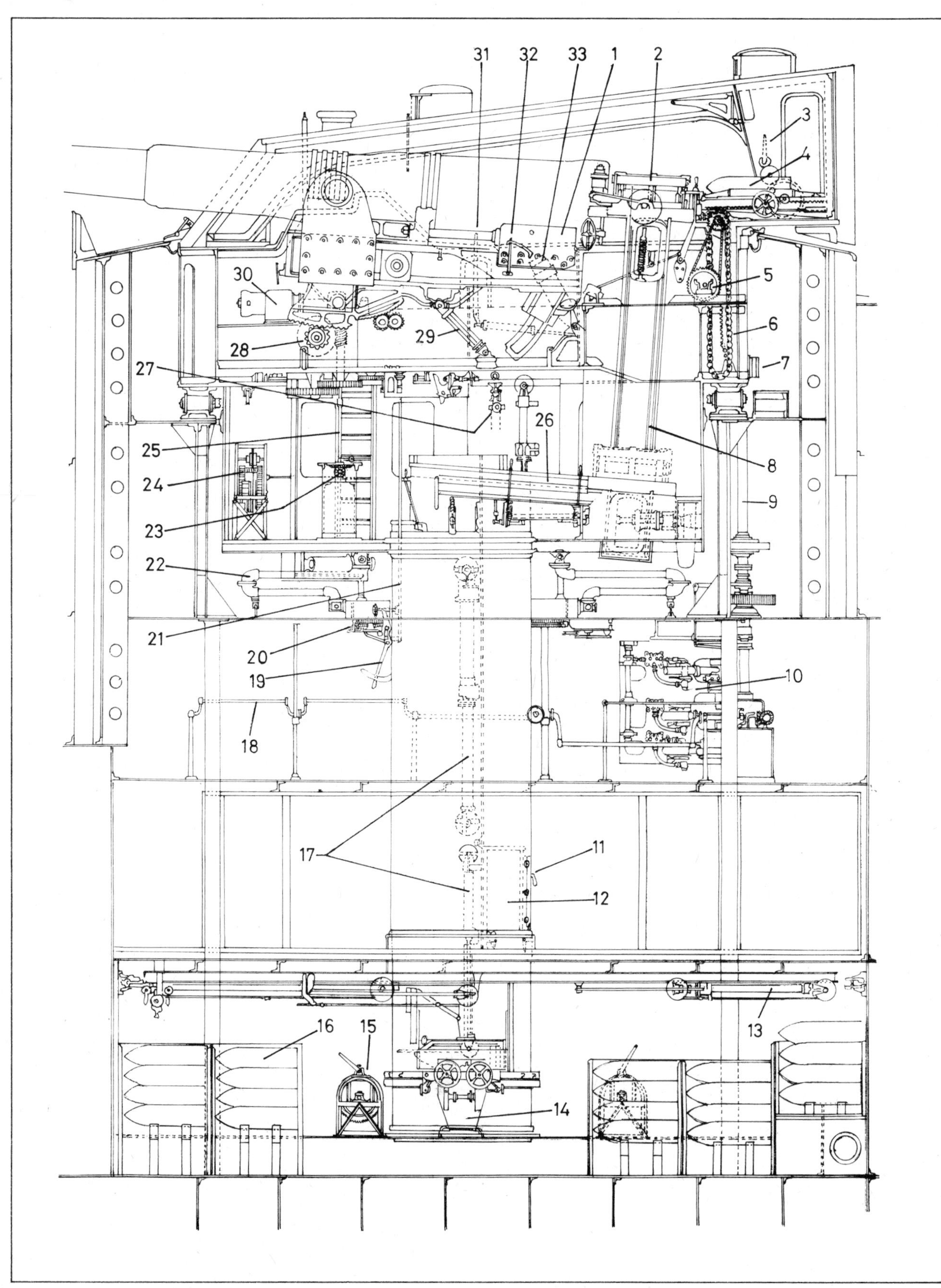
31
32
33
1
2
3
4
5
6
7
8
9
10
11
12
13
14
15
16
17
18
19
20
21
22
23
24
25
26
27
28
29
30

BRITISH 12in BVI MOUNTING

1 Recoil loader
2 Gun loading cage
3 Hand-loading crank
4 Shell on loading bogie
5 Power drive sprocket to chain rammer
6 Chain rammer
7 Training rack
8 Gun loading cage track rails
9 Training shaft
10 Three-cylinder training engine
11 Cordite loading door
12 Cordite cage
13 Overhead hydraulic press
14 Shell bogie
15 Auxiliary hand winch
16 Shell bin
17 Ammunition hoist hydraulic presses
18 Hand-training crank
19 'Local' power training handle, operating 'moving' rack
20 'Fixed' and 'moving' training control racks
21 Linkage to control racks
22 'Walking pipe' swivel
23 Hand elevation drive
24 Hand auxiliary ammunition winch
25 Hand elevation gear shaft
26 Ammunition transfer tray
27 Auxiliary overhead shell purchase
28 Alternative hand elevation gearing
29 Telescopic hydraulic transfer pipes
30 Elevation cylinder
31 Cordite 'bucket' tilting lever
32 Run-in and run-out control lever
33 Cordite tilting bucket

THE BRITISH 12in Mk VIII GUN ON THE BIV MOUNTING

Building steadily on the knowledge and experience gained from earlier ammunition supply arrangements, the Elswick works produced the BIV mounting for the *Albion* and *Glory* of the *Canopus* class. The configuration of the gunhouse, the guns, their breeches and the hydraulic machines remained virtually unchanged but a great step forward was taken by the adoption of a revolving trunk extending from gunhouse to magazine and shell room level. It ran vertically in its lower part, then angled backwards and terminated behind the breech end of the guns. The cages (for each gun) each held a shell, with two charges carried in compartments above it. When the gun was brought to the fixed loading angle of 13½° the cage stopped with the shell in alignment between the open breech and a floor-mounted hydraulic rammer – necessarily angled upwards at 13½°. Once the shell had been rammed and the rammer retracted, operating a lever on the cage itself allowed the charges to drop, in sequence, to the lowest position and thus themselves be in line for ramming. The obvious advantage of the system was that ammunition could be passed from the lower quarters directly to the gunhouse, but there were still some drawbacks.

Assuming that the gun was already loaded but had not fired, a freshly recharged cage at magazine level could only rise as far as a 'waiting position', in the shell chamber beneath the gunhouse, where it automatically came to rest against spring-loaded stops. Interlocks prevented it from moving any further until the gun had fired, been laid at 13½° and its breech opened. When reloading had been completed the cage then had to descend all the way to magazine/shell room level and if the gun fired immediately there was an inevitable delay before the cage was again ready – although under these circumstances it could move directly to the loading position (provided that the breech was open).

In addition to the main cages, the trunk contained two alternative shell hoists and an access passage up which shell could be triced if all else failed. Alternative loading was carried out at 1° elevation, the projectiles arriving nose downwards in the alternative hoists. They were conveyed in a bucket, which could be tilted to the horizontal by a hand lever, then lifted by a derrick and purchase, placed on a hand-loading bogie and finally hand-rammed. A secondary cartridge route was provided by a small axial hoist running from the lower quarters to a position between the guns. Three rounds per gun were stowed in the upper loading position with a further eight rounds per gun in the shell chamber. When required, these rounds could be loaded into the alternative hoists through doors in its trunk and were thus delivered to the upper loading position. Equally, the shell chamber stowages could be replenished by the alternative hoists, shells being worked by blocks running on overhead rails.

The fact that the trunk revolved meant that in order to load its cages at shell room level some link had to be provided between the overhead conveyors, which brought the projectiles from their stowages, and the foot of the shell hoist. This was provided by a turntable surrounding the trunk on which two diametrically opposite trays (one for left and one for right gun) were carried. It was powered by a small hydraulic engine and through a system of levers and clutches could be locked to the trunk (when it would move if the turret trained) or independently slewed around the trunk so as to place the trays beneath the shell room overhead conveyors. The trays were arranged to roll the shell through a port cut in the main trunk directly on to the shell tray of the main loading cage.

Cordite handling was considerably simpler because the charge was deliberately split into half-charges whose independent weight came within the bounds of manhandlability. These were simply placed by hand in their respective positions in the cage.

The lower parts of the rotating structure were protected by a fixed armoured cylindrical barbette extending below the load waterline, where its protective duties were taken over by the ship's side armour. The barbette thickness varied from 10 to 12in.

THE BRITISH 12in Mk VIII GUN ON THE BV MOUNTING

Vickers took a hand in the proceedings in designing the BV mounting for HMS *Vengeance*, the last ship of the *Canopus* class. The mounting was closely akin to the BVII – again built by Vickers – and was in any case special to *Vengeance* alone. It shared the same handbook as the BVII and so can be conveniently disregarded at this stage.

THE BRITISH 12in Mk IX GUN ON THE BVI (ELSWICK) MOUNTING

The first improvement in the BVI was the new mark of 12in gun. The barrel itself was bigger all round and at 40 calibres long came out at 50 tons. Again the rifling started

HMS *Vengeance* as completed. She was the only ship to carry the 12in BV mounting. *Conway Picture Library*

'straight' but this length was reduced to the first 4ft of the bore after which it spiralled gradually to one turn in 30 calibres at the muzzle. A new style of breech mechanism was introduced with this, the 12in Mk IX gun which differed from the Mk VIII in that the breech-screw revolved on a pintle, or stem, which formed part of the carrier. To enable the breech-screw to be swung clear for loading, the axis of the carrier hinge had to be set further from the gun and, in consequence, the arc through which the carrier moved was of greater radius.

The key to the difference in carrier design lies in the form that the breech-screw took. In the Mk VIII, it was of the cylindrical pattern with alternate threaded and plain portions and, because this gave only half locking power – since half the surface was unthreaded – the necessary strength was provided by the length of the screw along the axis of the bore, but this in turn made it necessary to withdraw the screw directly from the breech before it could be swung to one side, in the same way that a key can only be withdrawn directly from a lock. With the 'stepped' threads of the Welin pattern screw employed on the Mk IX gun, however, the locking power was increased to three-quarters, and this allowed for a relatively shorter breech screw. The actual geometry of its swinging movement in fact meant that the threads in the breech closest to the carrier had to be machined down, so as not to foul as did some of the threads on the breech-screw. Having thus undercut the tips of the threads – an interesting exercise in engineering in itself – the breech-screw could now swing to and from the closed position. Thus with the Mk VIII gun, the opening action was, sequentially, unlock, withdraw, swing out, whilst with the Mk IX it was unlock, swing out. A complete movement was eliminated leading to a speeding-up of the breech machanism cycle.

The operation of the mechanism was as follows. The handwheel drove through the worm and wormwheel gears to revolve the hinge bolt to which a partially toothed hinge-bolt pinion was keyed. This in turn meshed with an intermediate pinion part of which had plain spur gear teeth, part was untoothed and part had skew gear teeth. The latter meshed with a 90° skew gear pinion extended in the form of a link (it was, in fact, called the link pinion) and to which was attached a plate with a cam slot machined in it. A cam follower stud, attached to a bar, was constrained to run in the cam slot, the other end of the bar being connected to the lock in the box slide. A heavier bar connected the link pinion to the breech-screw and, as the gears rotated, the arm of the link pinion turned counter-clockwise, turning the breech-screw to unlock and at the same time opening the lock. When this action was completed, the stop tooth on the hinge bolt pinion came against a stop face inside the carrier, so continuing to revolve the shaft and pinion caused the carrier itself to swing open. A wheel-operated clutch engaged either hand or hydraulic drive.

Internally, the lock rather resembled a shotgun chamber and had simple extractors which ejected the spent tube. One of the gun's crew inserted a new tube – again,

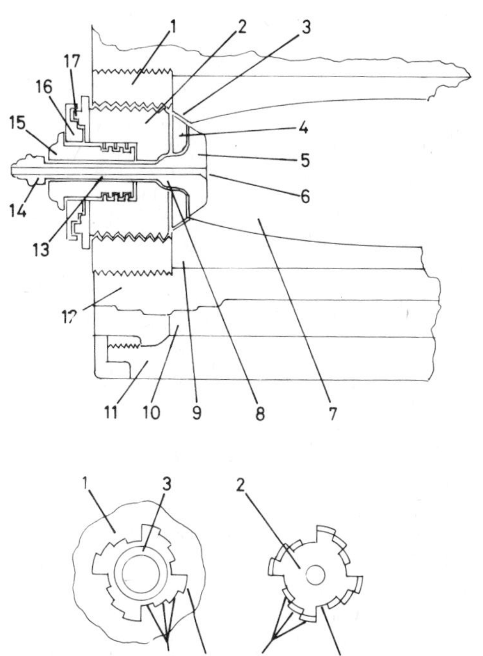

BL BREECH COMPONENTS

1 Breech bush
2 Breech screw
3 Seating
4 Obturator pad
5 'Mushroom head'
6 Vent
7 Chamber
8 Vent axial
9 Inner 'A' tube
10 Wire
11 Jacket
12 'A' tube
13 Vent stalk
14 Lock and box slide
15 Carrier pintle
16 Breech screw lever
17 Breech screw stud
18 Stepped internal 'V' threads
19 Undercut
20 Stepped external 'V' threads
21 Undercut

(Note: Highest point of 20 passes through the appropriate undercut in breech bush. Rotation through 22½ degrees engages the threads, giving three-quarters locking power.)

rather resembling a shotgun cartridge – while reloading was in progress and usually wore a bandolier of tubes around his waist. Percussion tubes had a normal percussion cap, while electric tubes had a fuse which ruptured when the firing circuit passed through it.

The term 'lock' for the firing mechanism is a very ancient one, with origins in such familiar mechanisms as the 'flintlock', and because it moved, or slid, sideways in a box-shaped miniature breech, this part of the assembly became known as the box slide. It was located by collars on the vent stalk and each gun had its own pattern of slide with a distinguishing letter, although some were interchangeable between calibres. Box slide A, for example, would fit certain 12in, 9.2in and 7.5in guns. Locks were similarly designated, and in some guns a percussion or an electric lock could be fitted.

In the case of the 12in Mk IX the lock was a combined electric/percussion device, in which the firing pin also functioned as an electric firing needle, but, whatever style was used, the same safety arrangement was included. This was that, as the lock moved sideways in the box slide, the firing needle/striker was retracted and held back on all occasions when the breech was not fully closed.

The accompanying drawing shows the principle of the Welin 'stepped' thread which gave three-quarters locking power, and also a section through a typical BL wire-wound gun. The breech-screw could revolve on the carrier pintle on which it was located by interrupted square threads. Passing through the centre of the pintle was the steel vent axial with its 'mushroom-head' at the chamber end and the lock and box slide for the firing tube at the other. Immediately behind the mushroom-head was the obturator pad which acted as a washer to seal the chamber. Closing the breech and turning the breech-screw caused it to move forwards slightly along the lead of the threads and to press the obturator against the cone seating machined on the inner 'A' tube. On firing the tube, a flame would run up the vent into the chamber to ignite the main charge. The chamber gas pressure acting on the mushroom-head tended to squeeze the obturator pad (which was really a heat-proof washer made from asbestor fibre) against the seat and around the vent stalk to prevent the escape of gases to the rear. The interruptions on the square thread of the pintle were arranged so as to retain the breech-screw throughout its turning arc in the breech, but permitted its complete removal when required. Apart from improvements to the actual breech opening mechanism, and to the quality and composition of the obturator pad, this style of screw breech remained unchanged thenceforth.

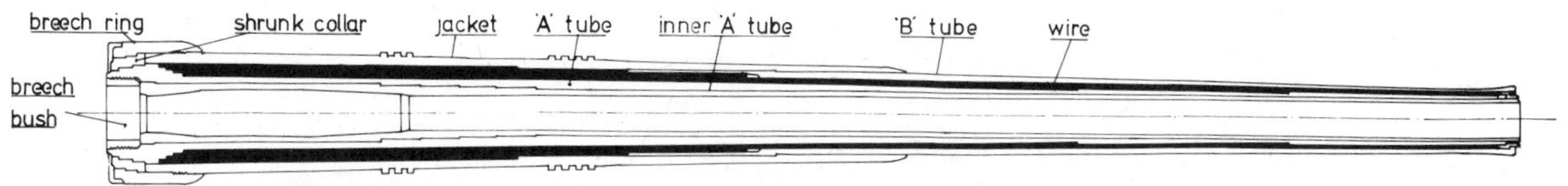

Drawing by John Roberts

SECTION THROUGH TYPICAL BL GUN

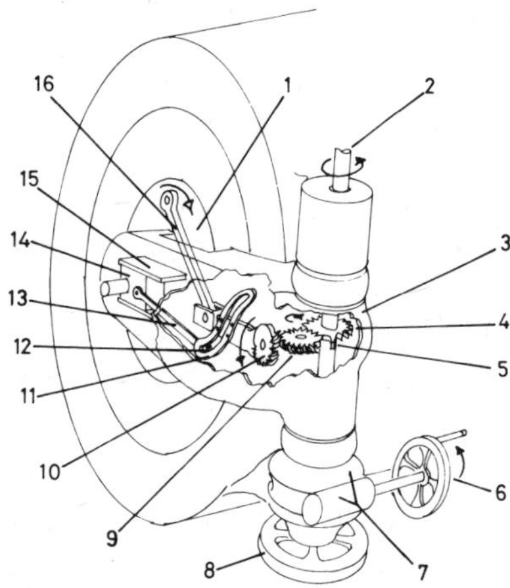

12in BL Mk IX BREECH MECHANISM

1 Breech screw
2 Power-drive shaft
3 Carrier
4 Hinge bolt pinion
5 Stop-tooth
6 Hand drive
7 Worm and wormwheel driving hinge-bolt
8 Hand-power clutch wheel
9 Intermediate pinion with plain and skew teeth
10 Skew-tooth link pinion
11 Cam
12 Cam follower
13 Link actuating lock
14 Firing lock
15 Box slide
16 Breech screw link

In the BVI mounting the primary supply route for ammunition was split. The rotating trunk contained two shell hoists, two cordite hoists and an access passage which doubled as an auxiliary route for both shell and cordite in the event of a power failure. It ran between the shell room (now one deck lower than the magazine) and the working chamber. At this point, the shell was tipped out of the main shell cage on to a tray and then pushed by hand on to a second hoist running from the working chamber to the gunhouse. Cordite was again manhandled between the hoists. The main loading angle was at 4½° elevation but, instead of a telescope rammer, a chain rammer was employed. A secondary hand-loading bogie was fitted at the rear of the gun, aligned to 1° gun elevation. Two ready-use rounds per gun were stowed in the gunhouse (later increased to five) and a further eight per gun in the working chamber, all handled by a winch in the gunhouse in the event of a breakdown.

At the foot of the trunk, in the shell room, the transfer of projectiles from their stowage bins to the shell cages was similar in principle to the method employed in the BIV mounting except that instead of a revolving platform two independent shell bogies were arranged to run around the trunk on rails. Each had a locking bolt to secure the bogie to the trunk or to the ship, and when disengaged from both the bogie could be pushed around. Not surprisingly, a 'bogie' was difficult to control in a seaway when carrying a shell weighing 850lb.

A 1912 photograph of *Prince of Wales*. She was one of five ships equipped with the twin 12in BVII mounting. *Imperial War Museum*

The split-hoist principle allowed the main cages to be sent back to magazine and shell room as soon as they had deposited their contents in the working chamber, so that as soon as the loading cage had completed the loading cycle and had been returned to the working chamber another shell and charge were already waiting there. To this end, the tray between the top of the main shell cage and the foot of the loading cage could accept two shells in tandem, so to speak, prevented from bumping nose to base by a removable stop bolt. Once established, the split hoist scheme was employed in all future British heavy calibre gun mountings with the exception of the triple 16in Mk I mounting (see Chapter 6).

THE BRITISH 12in Mk IX GUN ON THE BVII MOUNTING

After their BV mounting in *Vengeance* (which might be regarded as a prototype), Vickers came back with the BVII for a group of five ships – *Irresistible*, *Venerable*, *Albemarle*, *Exmouth* and *Prince of Wales*. The big advance in the design of these mountings was the curved trackway for the loading hoists and the extension of the slide to the rear of the breech to enable the chain rammer to be mounted on the elevating mass. The curved trackway was arranged to follow the sweep of the breech end as it elevated or depressed and, at last, loading at any angle of elevation between the limits of 5° depression and 13½° elevation was achieved.

Since the chain rammer was carried on an extension of the slide it was, obviously, always in line with the breech. The loading tray rose until it reached the extension, or loading arm as it was called, wherever it might be in elevation. An auxiliary hand-loading bogie was provided in the gunhouse, and the transfer arrangements in the working chamber were much the same as those of the BVI mounting. In the shell room, however, improvements were made to the shell bogies around the trunking by the inclusion of geared rings. One was bolted to the trunk, the other to the ship's structure, and the bogies were given a clutchable handwheel drive to work them around the trunk under the control of gearing. This became a standard arrangement and its application in the 15in can be seen in detail in the drawing in Chapter 5.

With the exception of the old *Hood* all the 12in and 13.5in gun mountings of this period had training engines sited off the mounting. Thus all the training gear was carried within the ship's structure and terminated in a training pinion meshed to a geared ring bolted to the mounting. As long as there was no working chamber and revolving trunk beneath the turntable, the control of the engine from a position on the mounting was reasonably easily provided by rod gearing passing through the centre of rotation, but this became increasingly difficult as the trunks extended deeper and deeper into the ship.

The means devised to effect the control of off-mounting training engines in the presence of a trunk was quite ingenious and is shown in the accompanying drawing. The scheme employed two curved racks and a gear train of three pinions. The upper rack (1) was fixed rigidly inside the ship's structure surrounding the working chamber and beneath it was a second rack (3) also carried on the ship's structure but capable of moving through a limited arc. Links were attached to this 'live' rack as it was called, themselves connected to the reversing valve of the training engine. The three pinions 2, 4 and 5 were all carried on the mounting, 2 in mesh with 1, 4 in mesh with 3, and 5 in mesh with 2 and 4. The deep pinion (5) was carried on a sliding plate (7), and by moving the control arrangements within the mounting, 6 was moved either towards or away from the twin racks. Assuming the mounting was stationary, all the gears would be at rest, but moving the training control to push 7, say, towards the racks caused 5 to revolve over a small arc (since 2 was stationary). Hence 4 revolved over the same small arc and altered the relative positions of the two racks. The movement of 3 via its links opened the reversing valve and the mounting began to rotate. Now, pinion 2 simply 'walked around' the fixed rack, revolving 5 and 4 as it did so, so that 4 similarly 'walked around' the displaced rack (3) without changing the rack's relative position. Reversing the direction of movement to 7 revolved 5, 4 and 3 in the opposite direction to stop the mounting, and further movement outwards reversed the direction of training.

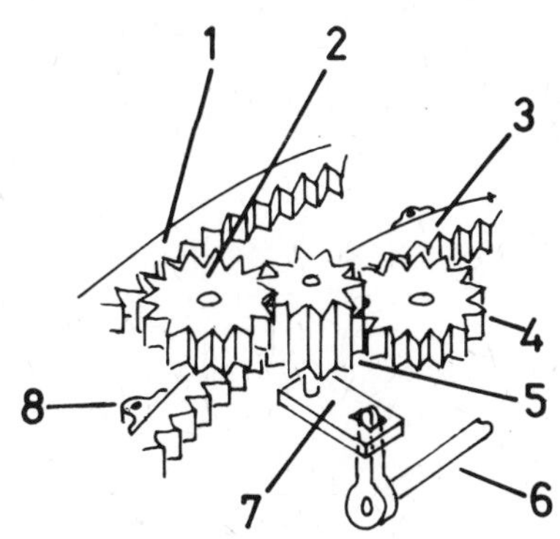

BRITISH TRAINING ENGINE CONTROL GEAR (*FORMIDABLE*)

1 Fixed training rack, engaged by training pinion (elsewhere)
2 Pinion in engagement with 1
3 'Moving' rack
4 Pinion in engagement with 3, and of equal size to 2
5 Double-depth pinion in engagement with 2 and 4
6 Shaft from training control lever
7 Laterally sliding mounting plate, carrying 5
8 Lug for linkage to training engine reversing valve

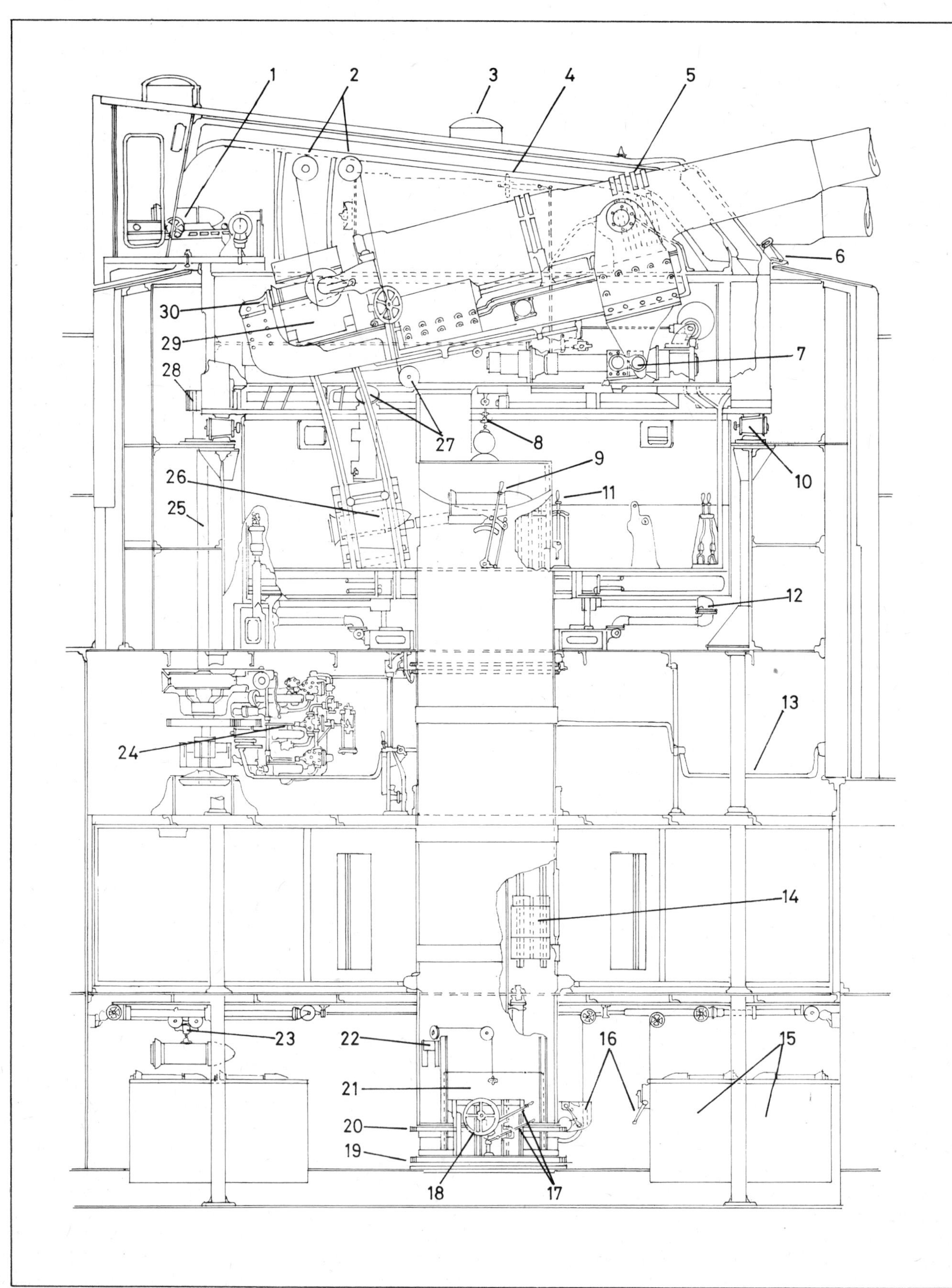
1
2
3
4
5
6
7
8
9
10
11
12
13
14
15
16
17
18
19
20
21
22
23
24
25
26
27
28
29
30

BRITISH 12in BV AND BVII MOUNTING

1 Shell bogie and rammer
2 Gunloading cage lifting wire sheaves
3 Sighting hood
4 Control lever
5 Front locating collars
6 Weathering
7 Elevation cross-head
8 Secondary shell supply grab
9 Shell tilting lever
10 Training roller
11 Cage control lever
12 'Walking' pipes
13 Hand training crank
14 Cordite cage
15 Shell bins
16 Secondary shell lifting and traversing hand winches
17 Shell bogie clutch and locking levers
18 Shell bogie traversing hand wheel
19 'Fixed' training control rack on ship's structure
20 'Moving' rack
21 Shell door
22 Door counterbalance weight
23 Shell traveller
24 3cyl training engine
25 Training shaft
26 Left gunloading cage
27 Guide sheaves
28 Training pinion
29 Right gunloading cage
30 Rammer

In fact, the whole assembly was a differential drive and, ingenious though it was, it was rather a cumbersome method of control. There had some merit in siting the engine off-mounting in the older ships, simply to reduce the weight and the size of the training mass, but, once the idea of a revolving trunk had taken a firm hold, it became more practical to put the training engine (or more properly engines, since there were two) within the mounting. This very much simplified the control arrangements (and also relieved the considerable backlash problems), and the training power drive now terminated in a pinion engaged in a fixed training rack with internal teeth bolted inside the barbette.

In passing, it is interesting to observe that in the handbook of the day the precise definition of 'mounting', 'turret' and 'barbette' had by no means become firmly established. The book for the *Formidable* class is headed 'Elswick Mountings', and on the first page speaks of the 'armoured shield', and mentions that the 'barbette can be trained by hand as well as by hydraulic power', while the first plate is headed 'General Arrangement of Turret and Mounting for a Pair of 12 inch 50 ton guns', and shows that the rotating structure is surrounded by a fixed armoured barbette. The accepted definitions are now:

Mounting: The complete rotating structure

Barbette: The fixed armoured ring around the trunk of the mounting

Turret: The armoured shield visible above the barbette

Ring bulkhead: 'Gunhouse' term describing an unarmoured barbette-style bulkhead

All handbooks always refer to 'mountings' but it has now become accepted that one refers to a *turret* if one speaks of a totally enclosed gunhouse or a *mounting* if one speaks of a gun with an open shield. The handbook for the BVII (Vickers) mounting made the observation that it was also applicable to the BV in *Vengeance* but pointed out that the latter had the 12in Mk VIII gun.

THE BRITISH 12in Mk IX GUN ON THE BVII(S) (VICKERS) MOUNTING AND THE 12in Mk X GUN ON THE BVIII (VICKERS) MOUNTING

The basic concept of the British heavy calibre twin gun mounting had now crystallised and there were to be few more major changes. The *King Edward VII* class introduced a variant of the BVII mounting, designated the BVII(S) – again built by Vickers. It was very similar to the earlier BVII but the two training engines were carried on the rotating structure and drove training pinions in engagement with an 'internal' circular rack fixed to the ship's structure inside the barbette armour.

New geared telescope gunsights were fitted in place of the older front-and-back sight and were protected by prominent sighting hoods on each side and between the guns. Single lever control was provided at all three positions for power operation, allowing the left or right gunlayer to elevate his own gun and train the mounting; alternatively, either gun could be worked from the central position. The facility for power operation of the 12in Mk IX breech was added, and two hand pumps in the working chambers (manned by ten men) provided the alternative power arrangements.

What has been described as the 'pre-dreadnought era' came to a close in the Royal Navy with the battleships *Lord Nelson* and *Agamemnon*, both with the now familiarly sited twin 12in mounting forward and aft, but with a two-calibre main armament made up by four twin and two single 9.2in. This calibre does not concern us, and it is sufficient to say that the two ships had new 12in Mk X 45 calibre guns in BVIII (Vickers) mountings. Their principal difference was in the transfer arrangements of ammunition of working chamber level. In the BVIII (also mounted in *Dreadnought*, *Inflexible* and *Indomitable*) shell and charges were rammed directly from the main cage into the gunloading cage without any form of 'tip-out' into an intermediate or waiting position. This made for a 'clean' transfer but a time penalty had to be accepted because the main cage could not descend until the gunloading cage had received the ammunition.

THE BRITISH 12in Mk X GUN ON THE BIX AND BX MOUNTING

The same situation obtained in these two remarkable mountings, fitted only in the battlecruiser *Invincible* (later to be lost at Jutland). They were designed by the Elswick Works and Vickers, Elswick producing the BX and their rivals the BIX.

The mountings were totally electric powered and were fed with 200v from four 200kW steam generators and two 100kW oil motor/generators within the ship. The revolving structure received its own electricity supplies through a slip ring unit at the bottom of the trunk. The training motors, fitted off-mounting, were regarded as part of the ship's structure rather than of the mounting itself. Speed control was effected by the Ward Leonard system which varied the field current of the electric training motors and gave a maximum training rate of about 4° per second.

BRITISH 12in TWIN BVII(S) MOUNTING

1 Radial crane
2 Breech power-opening cylinder
3 Sighting hood
4 Geared telescopic gunsight
5 Anti-torpedo-boat 3pdr QF
6 Guardrail stanchion
7 Front collars
8 Elevating cylinder
9 Elevating 'walking pipes'
10 Slide locking bolt housing
11 Vertical on-mounting 3cyl training engine
12 Ammunition transfer arrangements
13 Walking pipes (end view in section)
14 Trunk guide roller
15 Hand shell-traversing winch
16 Shell bogie clutch lever
17 Shell bogie traversing hand wheel
18 Hand shell-lifting winch
19 Shell door counterbalance weight
20 Cordite cage at magazine level
21 Training limit buffer
22 Gunloading cage rails
23 Manual breech-operating hand wheel
24 Loading-arm rammer
25 Manual gunhouse shell loading bogie
26 Gunloading cage

The original 12in BVIII mountings for the *Lord Nelson* (shown here) and her sister *Agamemnon* were appropriated for the battleship *Dreadnought*, in order to speed the latter's completion. New mountings had to be constructed and these ships, the last of Britain's pre-dreadnoughts, did not enter service until 1908. *Conway Picture Library*

Other electrical machinery included the winch for the ammunition cages, the transfer rammers in the working chamber, the rammer motor on the loading arm and the breech mechanism motor. Elevation was by a motor-driven 'lead-screw' about 5in in diameter which literally screwed the gun up and down through worm gearing. To absorb the shock of gunfire the complete screw was allowed to float about ½in against a spring and oil buffer.

Gun trials revealed a number of shortcomings. The 10hp elevating motor was found to be difficult to control because it took time to develop sufficient torque for rapid response of the elevating mass, and the general configuration of the lead-screw assembly was insufficiently robust. The Americans had a similar system in the *Connecticut* and British visitors to that ship privately noted that the lead-screw arrangements were very much more heavily constructed.

In the absence of main hydraulic power, a new run-out system was necessary because, as has been mentioned, it was normally hydraulic main pressure that was utilised to move the gun back to the run-out position after its recoil had been absorbed by the recoil buffer arrangements. Vickers chose to use run-out springs (of considerable proportions), while Elswick went for pneumatic arrangements which were later to be adopted in almost all types of mountings.

A mechanically improved breech mechanism was designed for the new 12in Mk X gun and was also fitted to a variant of the Mk IX called the Mk IXA. Changes were made to the gearing within the carrier, and also the means by which the breech-screw itself was revolved. The rather complex skew gearing of the Mk IX was superseded by a pair of bevel wheels, the second having a spur tooth pinion on a common stub shaft. The single link, by which the Mk IX breech-screw was revolved, was replaced by a more efficient breech-screw lever. Studs, projecting rearwards from the breech-screw, engaged in square blocks set diametrically opposite each other in the breech-screw lever, giving a much more positive and powerful revolving action. In terms of mechanics, it was as near as possible a pure couple and mechanisms of this kind were designated as such. This was initially done simply to distinguish them from earlier styles but, with the general acceptance of the method, the expression began to be omitted from descriptions of later breech mechanisms; indeed, so similar were they to the 12in Mk X that this was taken as the

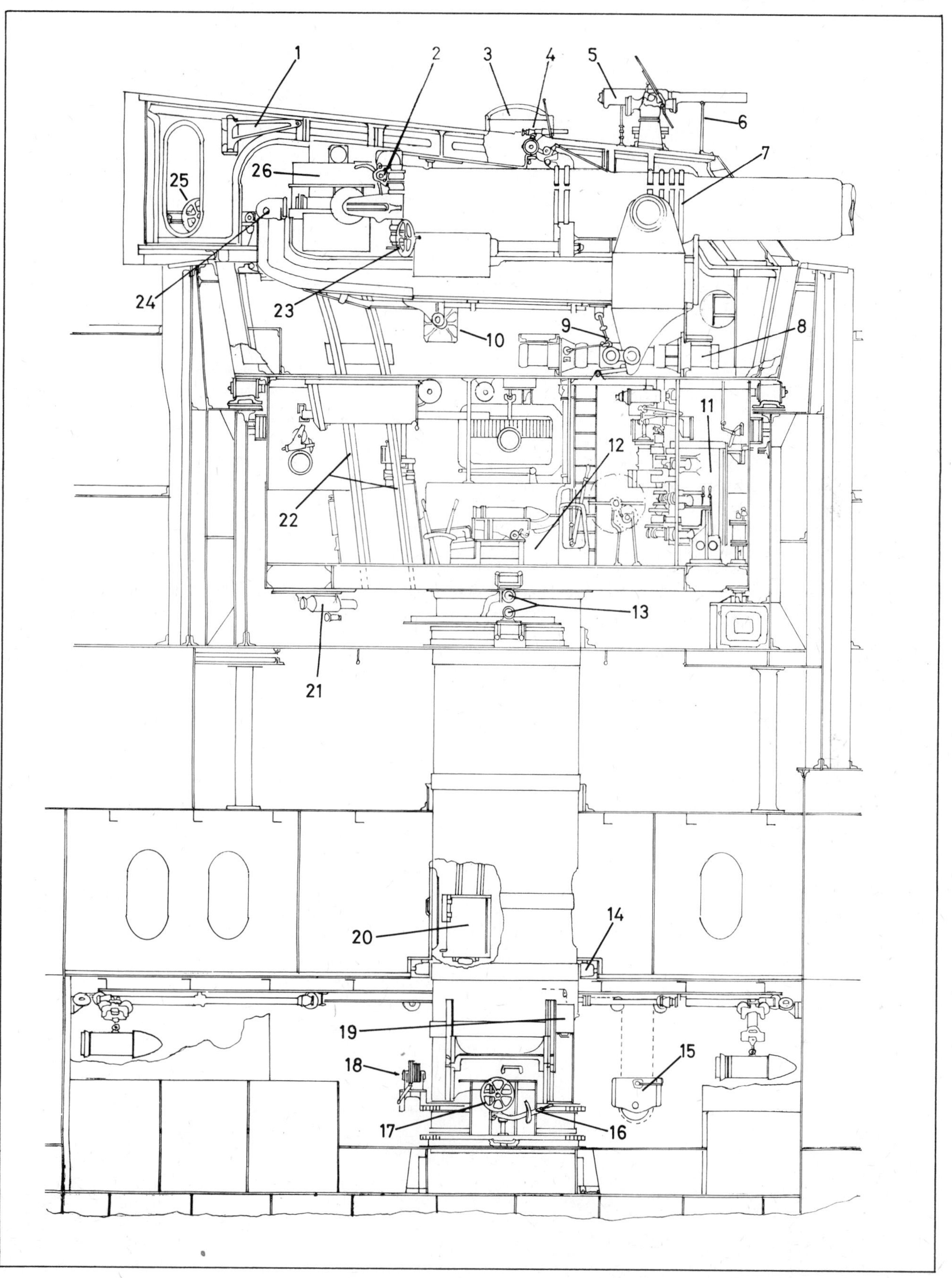
1
2
3
4
5
6
7
8
9
10
11
12
13
14
15
16
17
18
19
20
21
22
23
24
25
26

standard and only small mechanical differences were later made. The same sort of design improvements were implemented across the board, and so one saw similar changes in, for example, contemporary 9.2in and 7.5in guns. The unsatisfactory performance of these two electric-powered 12in mountings led to their being converted to hydraulic power before the First World War.

THE BRITISH 12in Mk XI AND XII GUN ON THE BXI MOUNTINGS

These mountings were the last of the British 12in family and used the final 'stretch' of the 12in gun to 50 calibre length. The BXI first appeared in the *St Vincent* class, completed in 1910, and mounted the Mk XI gun, followed by the similarly fitted *Neptune* in 1911. The final BXIs came with the arrival of *Colossus* and *Hercules* in the same year, the latter ship having the BXII gun. Both had swash-plate training engines, which made them unique among the British 12in-gunned ships. The Mk XI gun breech mechanism was powered by a 3-cylinder hydraulic motor (instead of a piston-rack assembly) and these turrets reverted to 'tip-out' arrangements in the working chamber.

As a more or less private venture, Elswick produced a special 12in twin mounting (with a 12in Mk XIII gun of 45 calibres length) for the Brazilian battleship that was in due course to become HMS *Agincourt*. Little is known of the detail of the mounting except that it had a fixed loading angle of 5°; it had overhead rail loading arrangements in the shell room as distinct from revolving shell bogies; and although nominally a 'hydraulic' mounting, it had an electric training system. Other details can be imagined when one learns of the layout of the Elswick 14in Mk I which is dealt with in Chapter 5.

The problems of smooth mounting control in elevation and training during the 12in era were quite severe. The single-lever control linkages introduced considerable backlash, and were finally abandoned in the later classes in favour of a wheel control. The old 3-cylinder oscillating training engines were superseded for a short time by the Elswick-designed 6-cylinder unit but, with the advent of the very efficient swashplate machine, together with finer toleranced control valves, a 'sweetness' of control was finally achieved.

THE US 12in Mk I MOUNTING

This mounting, fitted in the battleship *Texas* (1889), was typical of the period and was designed with a fixed loading position although this was later modified to 'all-round'. The breech had interrupted threads and, like most of its contemporaries, was hand-worked and opened sideways.

The battleship *Vanguard* (1909) carried ten 12in Mk XI guns in five twin BXI mountings. These guns were 50 calibres long and represented the ultimate development of the British 12in, but they did not prove successful in service. *Conway Picture Library*

HMS *Agincourt* mounted more turrets than any other battleship. Originally laid down for Brazil, she was taken over by the Royal Navy on the outbreak of the First World War. Her main armament, of fourteen guns in seven twin turrets, was given the British designation Mk XIII in 12in 'Special' mountings. *Conway Picture Library*

THE US 12in Mk 2 AND 13in Mk 1 AND 2 MOUNTINGS

The 12in Mk 2 was fitted in the monitors *Monterey* and *Puritan* and the 13in mountings in the battleships of the *Indiana* class. All except *Oregon* had steam training engines (*Oregon*'s were hydraulic), with hydraulic elevation, run-out and ramming. All-round loading was available at a 10° loading angle, the elevation limit being 15° and the depression limit 5°. Ammunition was supplied by central hoists running directly from the lower quarters to the gunhouse and these too were hydraulic.

THE US 12in Mk 3 MOUNTING

The recently adopted hydraulic training was repeated in this mounting, fitted in the battleship *Iowa* (1893), but elevation was by hand only and, while the hoists remained hydraulic, run-out springs replaced the previous system. Ramming was by hand or electric motor. The all-round loading facility had by now become standard, although the actual elevation loading angle varied from one mounting to another; in this case it was 3°, the elevation limit being 14° and the depression limit 5°.

The US 13in Mk 3 MOUNTING

This, the last of the US turret type mountings, was fitted in the *Kearsarge* class battleships. The 13in firmly established the electric powering principle in having two 50hp training motors, as well as electric elevation (with alternative hand), hoists and chain-driven telescopic rammers. The guns were carried in cradles and had combined recoil and run-out spring cylinders.

THE US 13in Mk 4 MOUNTING

These mountings, fitted in the battleships of the *Alabama* class, were the first 'British style' barbette mountings employed by the USN. However, in other respects the mounting was of the same general design as the 13in Mk 3, with electric power and direct hoists.

THE US 12in Mk 4 MOUNTING

The 12in Mk 4 was of similar design to the 13in Mks 3 and 4, adopting the barbette arrangement of the latter; however, being a lighter weapon, it had slightly less powerful electric motors. The elevation limit for all three mountings (13in Mk 3 and 4 and 12in Mk 4) was 15° and the depression limit 5°. The fixed loading angle was 2° and, in the 12in mounting only, a second loading position was provided at 0°. The 12in Mk 4 was fitted in the battleship *Maine* and the monitors of the *Ozark* class.

THE US 12in Mk 5 MOUNTING

Fitted in the battleships of the *Virginia* class, this mounting had wider elevation limits, between 20° elevation and 7° depression. Gun loading was at 0° and electric hoists provided ammunition to each gun in 90 seconds, the shell tipping into an automatic loading tray. There were combined recoil cylinders and run-out springs and the usual electric training and elevation.

THE US 12in Mk 5 GUN ON THE Mk 6 MOUNTING

The 12in Mk 6 mounting was carried by the *Connecticut*, *Idaho* and *Kansas* class battleships (except *New Hampshire* which is believed to have been fitted with 12in Mk 7 mountings; see below). It was similar to the Mk 5 and had endless chain hoists. Like all US pre-dreadnoughts, the hoists were direct from the lower quarters and, running on unenclosed rails, were completely open. This practice was followed until an accident in *Missouri* in April 1904, when a flame-back from the turret went straight to the handing room; thereafter automatic shutters were introduced between the two extremities. In 1905, exposed switch-gear to the rear of a breech in one of *Kearsarge*'s 13in mountings also caused an accident, and between 1907 and 1908 all electrical equipment that might present a spark hazard was removed and dividing bulkheads were fitted in the gunhouse, separating individual guns.

USS *Florida*, which carried ten 12in Mk 6 guns in five twin Mk 8 mountings. *Conway Picture Library*

THE US 12in Mk 5 GUN ON THE Mk 7 MOUNTING

The 12in Mk 7 mounting was fitted in the first two American dreadnought types, the *South Carolina* and *Delaware* classes. Their 12in guns were separated by dividing bulkheads and fitted into cradles with a recoil buffer and four run-out spring boxes. Training was by two 25hp motors and elevation by a 15hp motor (for each gun) driving a lead-screw between the limits of 15° elevation and 5° depression. Loading was possible from any elevation within these limits and was powered by a 10hp motor driving a chain rammer on an extension of the cradle – the loading arm in British parlance. The hoists, too, were electric, and were split between a lower hoist reaching the working chamber and an upper hoist delivering ammunition to the gunhouse. All electric motor applications were duplicated by alternative hand drives. In the working chamber, ammunition was transferred between hoists by a 10hp electrically powered rammer.

The hoists for the *South Carolina* class were engineered by the Washington Navy Yard and those of the *Delaware* class by Bethlehem Steel, but the latter proved to be quite unsatisfactory in service and were removed. Improvised fittings, in the form of rope whips, were installed in their stead, the need for which must have been a disappointment since the concept of two-stage ammunition hoists and a working chamber beneath the gunhouse had been introduced for the first time to the USN with these two classes. The 12in Mk 8 mounting (*Utah* class) was generally similar to the Mk 7.

So unsatisfactory were the ammunition supply arrangements in the bulk of these early dreadnought period mountings that they were converted to hand-loading. The existing cages and rammers were dispensed with, shells were hoisted vertically in a tube, powder charges were passed up by hand and even wooden hand rammers were used to load the guns. However, when the 14in mounting of the *Texas* class was introduced, as related in the next chapter, the loading arrangements of the two-stage mountings were redesigned and power hoists and power ramming was re-introduced.

THE US 12in 50 Mk 7 GUN ON THE TWO-GUN MOUNTING

These mountings were fitted in the *Arkansas* class and introduced the final 'stretch' of the 12in gun to a 50 calibre length – a design procedure that has been met with elsewhere. Again, all powering was electric and ammunition supply was two-stage. Powder was conveyed vertically in hoists, set forward of the centre of rotation of the turret, and then passed by hand, via a 'passing box', upwards to the gunhouse. In the lower shell hoists, projectiles were raised in a vertical position by winch and cable and then transferred to upper pusher hoists. A particular aspect of American design philosophy began to manifest itself in this mounting in that a proportion of the projectile outfit was carried on the rotating structure. A chain rammer was fitted for loading but, unlike the contemporary British practice, the chain trunking was taken upwards towards the gunhouse roof. The maximum elevation of the gun was 15° and the depression limit 5°. The all-up weight of the rotating mass (which when referred to hereinafter does not include on-mounting stowed ammunition) was 491 tons.

THE GERMAN 11in SKL/45 IN THE DRH LC/1906 MOUNTING

Fitted in the battleships of the *Westfalen* class (wing turrets only in the *Posen* and *Rheinland*), these mountings introduced electric powering to the German Navy for both training and elevation – each with auxiliary hand drives. A conventional pinion/toothed-arc arrangement for the elevation drive gave limits of 20° elevation to 6° depression. The breech mechanisms and rammers were hand worked only and run-out was pneumatic. The turntable revolved on the usual ball race and the all-up weight was about 400 tonnes.

The working chamber, below the gunhouse, was fixed and supplied with ammunition from the lower quarters by electric lower hoists. The shell hoists, which were separate, raised the projectiles in a vertical position and there were individual hoists for the (bagged) fore charge and the (cased) main charge. In the working chamber, the shells were moved to a transfer tray on transfer beds and thence by tackle to the loading tray of the main upper hoist. The main charges were moved in 'U' shaped troughs, on castors, to the loading trays of the main upper hoist, but the fore charges were passed by hand. There was stowage for about eight ready-use rounds in the working chamber – the shells on a roller track near its ring bulkhead, the cased charges against the bulkhead and the fore charges in containers under the shells.

The two main upper hoists were electric powered and delivered the ammunition, in a horizontal position, between the breech ends of the guns. The main hoist cage had three compartments, carrying, in sequence from top to bottom, main charge, shell and fore charge. Auxiliary hoists were also fitted, running from the working chamber to the rear of the gunhouse. On arrival in the gunhouse, the triple shell/charge group was transferred from the main cage to a loading rack by a trio of electrically-powered chain rammers. The loading rack itself was placed immediately behind the main hoists, so that the ammunition was now set inboard but to the rear of the breech. It was now necessary to move first the shell, then the fore charge and, lastly, the after charge in a lateral direction on to a moving loading tray, ready for ramming. The shell was transferred first, and as a drill event two fore charges were initially provided in line with their chain rammer head. A portable extension of the fore charge loading rack trough thus received one charge, it having been 'shunted' by the other when the transfer rammer was extended. Once the shell had been rammed into the chamber, this 'available' fore charge was handed on to the loading tray and was similarly loaded. Finally, the main charge (whose loading rack was pivoted on its long axis) was tipped sideways on to the loading tray.

Probably for reasons of ship stability, the shell rooms were above the magazines for the centreline turrets but below them in the wings.

THE GERMAN 11in SKL/45 IN THE DRH LC/1907 MOUNTING AND THE 11in SKL/50 IN THE DRH LC/1908 AND LC/1910 MOUNTINGS

These mountings were the last of the 11in type to be fitted in Germany's First World War battlefleet and were generally similar to each other. The 45cal gun was found in their first true battlecruiser, *Von der Tann*, as well as in the fore and aft mountings of *Posen* and *Rheinland*. The 50cal 1908 model was fitted in *Moltke* and *Goeben* and the 50cal 1910 model (with heavier armour) in the *Seydlitz*.

Training was electric but elevation (which included the facility of coupling the two cradles) was hydraulic, utilising the piston/cylinder configuration –

The German battlecruiser *Goeben* as completed. She carried ten 1908 Model 11in/50 guns in five twin mountings. *Conway Picture Library*

repeated in the later 12in and 15in calibre mountings. The designed elevation limit of the 50cal guns was 13.5° but was later increased to 16° and finally in *Goeben* only, to 22.5°. Ramming and breech mechanisms were hand worked, alternative hand drives were provided for the two mounting motions, and run-out was by the now well-established compressed air medium.

The shell rooms were below the magazines in all these mountings and separate electric shell and cartridge hoists brought the ammunition thence to the working chamber. Here it was transferred to the upper hoists, shell arriving between and in rear of the guns and cartridges on their outboard sides, near the mounting centre of rotation. A hand operated loading tray, spring-loaded to return, was supplied from each shell hoist and moved on the arc of a circle, while the two charges moved on slides from their own hoist to the rear of the gun and then on their own loading trays.

GERMAN 12in MOUNTINGS

The Germans went straight to a 50 calibre gun for their 12in and fitted it thereafter in a succession of five warship classes. This, the 12in SKL/50, appeared in the Drh LC/1908 mounting (*Ostfriesland* class); the 1909 mounting (*Kaiser* class); the 1911 mounting (*König* class); the 1912 mounting (*Derfflinger* and *Lutzow*); and the 1913 mounting (*Hindenburg* only). The first three classes were battleships and the last three ships (which collectively comprised a class) were battlecruisers. The five mountings were similar in many respects and are most easily described in reverse chronological order.

THE GERMAN 12in SKL/50 IN THE DRH LC/1913 MOUNTING

Mixed powering media were used in this mounting in that training (both main and auxiliary) was electric, giving a maximum speed of 3° per second; elevation was hydraulic, with limits of 16° elevation and 5½° depression; and run-out was by compressed air. The gun cradles could be coupled to elevate as a pair, although both elevating cylinders were still needed, working in parallel. The shell hoists were electric; the cartridge hoists were electric or hand; and the breech mechanisms, telescopic loading rammers and transfer rammers were hydraulic or hand. The total weight of the mounting varied between 543 and 558 tonnes, depending on its trunk depth.

The shell rooms were positioned below the magazines but in 'B' and 'X' mountings there was an additional shell depot room above them which provided an alternative shell hoist loading level. The shell hoists themselves were continuous from shell room to gunhouse, where they emerged between the guns, just to the rear of the mounting centre of rotation. A transfer rammer thrust the projectile backwards to a waiting tray, whence it was moved to a loading tray for ramming.

Cartridge supply was two-stage. The lower hoists, set outside the continuous shell hoists, ran to the working chamber, where the charges were placed in a transfer car. The latter was driven by gearing and pinions engaging in top and bottom racks and carried a main and fore charge. The upper cartridge hoists arrived outboard of their respective guns on about the mounting centre of rotation. The fore charge moved down a slide to a waiting tray, followed by the main charge – the latter having its own tilting tray. Both shell and cartridge loading trays (which were hand operated, spring-return) swung on the arc of a circle at right angles to the axis of the bore. Loading speeds were impressive. Individual hoist delivery rates averaged one shell or charge in 5 seconds and the complete loading cycle was only 20 seconds.

THE GERMAN 12in SKL/50 IN THE DRH LC/1912 MOUNTING

This mounting differed from its successors in that in 'A', 'B' and 'X' positions the magazines were below the shell rooms while in 'Y' position they were above them. In addition, the shell supply was two-stage and there were no shell depot rooms. In the working chamber shells were transferred between hoists by hand on an inclined roller-chain and charges on a sloping roller track. Training and all hoists were electrically powered, elevation was hydraulic and, like most of these earlier 12in mountings, the designed maximum elevation of 13½° was later modified to 16°. All weighed about 550 tonnes and none prior to the Drh LC/1912 differed significantly from it, except that in the battleship mountings the armour was more substantial. In passing it is worth remarking that the *Kaiser* class mountings were reported to have had an overall ammunition supply speed of three rounds in 48 seconds, including all transfers.

BRITISH 10in BATTLESHIP MOUNTINGS

During the last decade of the nineteenth century and the first of the twentieth, a 10in gun was mounted in some specialised ships of the Royal Navy. The old *Thunderer* and *Devastation* were re-gunned with twin 10in Vavasseur mountings in, respectively, the 'Turret Mk I' and the 'Turret Mk II', and in the mid-1890s three ships, *Renown*, *Barfleur* and *Centurion*, were given an interim mounting bridging the 'barbette' and the enclosed gunhouse of the *Majestic* and following classes. This, designated the Barbette Mk III, was described as being 'hooded'. It followed the pattern in contemporary ships with their guns *en barbette* but had a shield fitted to the turntable that enclosed the twin guns, save for its rear face which was open.

The three ships were designed for deployment to foreign stations and their overall design reflected this intention in having hulls sheathed in wood and copper; a greater proportional space for fuel and ammunition stowage; and a shallow draught to enable them to negotiate the Suez Canal. The 10in guns were of 32 calibre length and, following the trend of the day, were supplemented by ten 6in, twelve

12pdrs, eight 3pdrs and two Maxim machine guns. An even heavier subsidiary armament was mounted in the only two other 10in-armed battleships to serve under the White Ensign.

THE BRITISH 10in Mk VI AND Mk VII GUNS

In 1906 two ships originally laid down as coast defence vessels for the Chilean Government joined the British Fleet. These were *Swiftsure* and *Triumph* and both had a main armament of twin 10in guns in the conventional fore and aft positions. Neither the guns themselves nor their mountings were absolutely identical, in what were nominally sister-ships, and a special handbook was produced covering not only both types of 10in but also the other calibre weapons, the torpedo tubes and the ships' electrical installations. It seems probable that this comprehensive volume was produced for the benefit of the original South American customer.

An element of muddle is evident within the text in the descriptions of *Swiftsure*'s 10in compared – later in the book – to *Triumph*'s. The section on the former ship is headed '10 inch BL guns on Barbette Mountings', and goes on to describe a 'turntable rotating inside a redoubt'. The associated plate, on the other hand, is headed 'Mounting in Armoured Turret to take two 10 inch 45 calibre guns', while the plate on the gun barrel is headed '10 inch 50 calibre gun'. The compiler of the text was not, it seems, concerned with the fetish of exact terminology which so bedevils us today. *Triumph*'s 10in are described simply as 'mountings' revolving inside a 'barbette' – which, of course, became the accepted terms. Perhaps the two sections of the composite volume were prepared in the first instance by the weapon contractors, who chose different terms to describe the same thing.

Switfsure carried the Mk VI and *Triumph* the Mk VII gun. Both styles used 146lb of cordite as the propellant for their 500lb shell, and both were of wire-wound construction following the fashion of the day. The principal difference between the two lay in the design of the breech mechanisms. *Swiftsure*'s had a cylindrical breech-screw (as distinct from the stepped Welin thread) with four interruptions and unlocked after rotating 45°, reflecting the very set ideas of the Armstrong Whitworth company.

Power operation for the two breeches was most unusual and consisted of one 3-cylinder radial hydraulic engine, mounted in the gunwell, driving shafting and gears to the two mechanisms. Splined shafts were incorporated in the drives to take account of varying gun elevations and recoil – because the hydraulic motor was fixed to the mounting and not to the elevating portions. The power drive to each breech was engaged by a friction clutch, worked by a lever; alternatively, the mechanism could be operated by fitting a removable handwheel. Owing to the arrangement of the ammunition supply, the breeches had axes on the inner side of the breech-ring and thus opened back-to-back.

The second class battleship HMS *Renown*, which carried a main armament of four 10in guns. *National Maritime Museum*

The elevating arrangements and cradle design closely followed those of the contemporary British 9.2in mountings. Power operation, by a hydraulic piston-cylinder assembly, was supplemented by an alternative hand drive through gearing to a toothed rack under the cradle, and incorporated an automatic friction coupling linked to the hydraulic system. Its effect was to disengage the hand drive when hydraulic power was on, and vice versa. A conventional recoil buffer was fitted but run-out springs replaced the hydraulic run-in and run-out cylinder.

A working chamber (described as a hanging chamber in the handbook) was bolted to the underside of the turntable floor and contained the hydraulic training engine and the alternative hand training gear. Beneath this compartment, a revolving trunk extended down to shell room level, where it was constrained by a central pivot through which hydraulic pressure and exhaust pipes led to the pumping unit.

The size and weight of the 10in ammunition allowed for a much simpler – and more efficient – ammunition supply system than was the case with the 12in mountings. The tracks for the two gunloading cages lay close together in the lower quarters but then spread outwards (in the form of a letter Y), to emerge on the outboard side of each gun. A cage held a shell in the upper tray and four quarter-charges of cordite in compartments below. On arrival at gunhouse level, the shell tray automatically came to rest level with an intermediate tray on to which the projectile was pushed, and from this tray it was moved on to the loading tray. The latter was pivoted in such a way that it could be swung round to place the round ready for ramming. The rammers were telescopic and could be locked upright in the event of a power failure, when hand ramming was resorted to. Rather unusually, a wire, attached by one end to the rammer body and by the other to the elevating mass, kept the rammer in line with the chamber for loading at any angle between 3° depression and 5° elevation. In the shell room, the usual type of overhead rails and grabs were fitted to supply the cages from the shell bins but the cages themselves were hoisted by winch rather than by hydraulic press.

The circular redoubt (or barbette) was 10in thick over the front half and 8in thick in the rear. The 10-sided gunhouse had 9in front plates, 8in rear plates and a 2in roof. Eighteen ready-use rounds were carried in the rear of the gunhouse but, even when loading directly from the lower quarters, a rate of fire of four rounds per gun per minute could be achieved.

The twin 10in in *Triumph* followed the broad principle of her sister-ship's mounting but differed in several details. The gun, at nearly 31 tons, was some seven tons lighter than *Swiftsure*'s and was fitted with a Vickers breech mechanism identical to that of the 12in Mk IX. Thus it had the stepped Welin pattern breech-screw with power operation from a simple piston and cylinder assembly, mounted on the breech-ring itself. Chain, instead of telescopic, rammers were employed in the gunhouse, and hydraulic presses rather than a winch were used to power the loading cages. The gunhouse was again 10-sided, but unlike *Swiftsure*'s its roof was absolutely flat.

Both variants of the 10in were attractive and neat in their layout, but were little known in the Royal Navy since they were unique to the two ships. They were complemented by fourteen 7.5in, fourteen 14pdrs, two 12pdrs, four 6pdrs and four Maxim machine guns.

HMS *Swiftsure* was one of two ships taken into Royal Navy service in 1906 but actually designed for Chile. She and *Triumph* were hybrid vessels carrying an armament of four 10in, fourteen 7.5in, fourteen 14pdr, two 12pdr and four 6pdr guns. *Molland*

5 The Calibre Race

In an attempt to keep pace with the development of armour of improved quality and thickness, the penetrating power of the 12in gun had been steadily improved during its years as the standard battleship weapon. In Britain all the 12in guns from the Mk VIII onwards fired an 850lb projectile but the propellant charge, and necessarily the length, of successive designs had been increased from 200lb in the 35.5cal Mk VIII to 307lb in the 50cal Mks XI and XII, thereby increasing the muzzle velocity from 2350 to 2825fs. With the high-velocity 50-calibre designs the British 12in had reached the limit of its development, and with the gun versus armour race still accelerating apace and the prospect of even thicker armour, perhaps tougher armour, or even both, there was no alternative but to go for a larger calibre gun. In effect it became necessary to increase shell weight rather than shell velocity, to improve penetrating power which is basically a function of these two factors. Thus for the battleships of the 1909 Programme, the *Orion* class, the Admiralty decided to reintroduce the 13.5in gun to British service.

The provision of a shell of larger volume had the additional advantage of providing a larger bursting charge which, combined with the greater mass of metal, greatly increased its destructive effect. The function of the armour-piercing (AP) shell – as distinct from the straight high-explosive (HE) type – is initially to penetrate enemy armour, and then to explode. To achieve these ends, the AP projectile needs to be constructed in such a way that it will not shatter on impact but rely on its mass and velocity to smash through a considerable thickness of steel. It must be of tough construction with thick walls and therefore, within the same shell profile, the AP type can only accept a reduced payload of explosive compared with the HE shell. However, if it does penetrate armour, a highly potent result is achieved by its filling detonating inwards in a cone, giving a combination of blast and splinter effects. The 'delay' in detonation is achieved by fitting an inertia-actuated fuze in the base of the shell rather than, as in the HE shell, the nose.

Soon after the British adopted the 13.5in gun the USA and Japan advanced a stage further by providing for 14in guns in their latest dreadnought designs, to which Britain replied with the 15in. At this point the outbreak of the First World War brought the calibre race to a halt but it was soon clear that the situation would renew itself at the end of hostilities. Apart from the production of the hybrid 18in gun, Britain had little time for the development of new heavy guns and mountings but in 1916 both the USA and Japan jumped another calibre by authorising the construction of ships armed with 16in guns. The war delayed work on these programmes, however, and it was not until 1919 that their full effect began to be felt. Eventually the naval race which naturally developed, including British replies in the shape of 16in and 18in-gunned ships, was brought to a halt by the Washington Conference of 1922. In the end the only 16in gun vessels of First World War origin to complete were the Japanese *Nagato* and *Mutsu* in 1920 and 1921 and the three US battleships of the *Colorado* class in 1921 and 1923.

The European reaction to the calibre race was much less dramatic. In 1912 the French introduced the 13.4in (340mm) gun for the three battleships of the *Bretagne* class and in subsequent designs, the *Normandie* and *Lyon* classes, all of which were later cancelled, went for increased numbers of guns rather than larger calibres by adopting a quadruple turret. The other European naval powers progressed no further than the 12in gun with the exception of Germany which initially continued to develop the high velocity 12in but then made a major jump to the 15in gun for the four battleships of the *Baden* class, of which only *Baden* and *Bayern* were completed. They also ordered four battlecruisers armed with 14in guns and three armed with 15in guns but only two of these vessels were launched and none was completed.

The Germans always showed a preference for high-velocity guns, which may partially explain their continued use of the 12in gun after Britain had changed over to the 13.5in. In addition to improved penetrating power, three advantages accrue from high velocity, the first being that the initial trajectory remains flat for a longer period, giving more accurate shooting at shorter ranges. The second is that the shell reaches its target quickly (an obvious advantage against a moving object) and the third is that the absolute maximum range is improved. However, the great disadvantage of a high-velocity gun is that it tends to wear more rapidly than a lower velocity piece, with all-round diminution of performance. Even the comparatively low velocity 13.5 Mk V, which had a range of 23,500yds at 20° with a new gun muzzle velocity of 2500fs, was, when worn and due for replacement, reduced to a muzzle velocity of 2100fs giving a maximum range of 17,700yds at 20°.

THE BRITISH 13.5in Mk V GUN

The gun had a bore length of 45 calibres, weighed 76 tons and was sometimes suffixed as Mk V(L) and Mk V(H). This signified the weight of the projectile it fired – in the former case the original 1250lb (light) shell and in the latter the 1400lb (heavy) shell. With the original projectile a slightly lighter cordite charge of 293lb (compared with that of the 12in Mk XIII) gave improved wear-rate characteristics and, at the same time, the much greater weight and consequent penetrating power of the projectile put it in a class of its own – a situation still further enhanced by the introduction of the 1400lb projectile. All the 'unstarred' marks of 13.5in mounting were fitted with Mk V(L) guns and the 'starred' with Mk V(H) guns.

THE BRITISH 13.5in Mk II, Mk II* and Mk II** MOUNTINGS

The Mk II version was fitted in the battleships *Orion*, *Monarch* and *Thunderer* and the battlecruisers *Lion* and *Princess Royal*, and the Mk II* (a slightly modified Mk II) in the battleships *King George V*, *Centurion* and *Audacious* and the battlecruiser *Queen Mary*. The opening statement in the mounting handbook describes the 13.5in mounting as being very similar to the 12in BXI mounting of the *St Vincent* class, from which one can judge how that calibre had progressed since the BVIII. The listed differences include a necessarily stronger slide to support the heavier gun, a maximum elevation of 20° and the provision of a small turbo-generator, called a Pelton wheel, for the gun-firing circuits. The latter produced 20v at 5amps and was supplied by a take-off pipe connected to the hydraulic pressure main on the revolving structure. So far as the hydraulics are concerned, these mountings are of interest in that they employed the newly invented swashplate engine as the means of training. It had already been fitted, in fact, in *Hercules* and *Colossus*, and was by no means a special attribute of the 15in as is sometimes believed.

In order not to increase the overall physical size of the gunhouse and trunk, their dimensions were kept approximately the same as those of the 12in BXI and, in consequence, space was at a premium in the gunhouse – so much so that the alternative supply trunks for cordite, which previously emerged between the guns, had to be suppressed. They were replaced by secondary cages (which also carried shell) running from the working chamber to a position outboard of the guns. Radial overhead cranes in the working chamber were employed to place the shells on the secondary hoist trays.

In the trunking, the main cordite and shell cages were combined together so that, at their lowest level, they were in line with the shell bogies in the shell room and the cordite hoppers in the magazine above. However, the increased length of the 13.5in projectile in a trunk of dimensions comparable to those of the 12in made it necessary to cant the main cages upwards as they rose and return them to the horizontal position at the limits of their travel.

On arrival at the working chamber, the shell and cartridges were automatically tipped outwards on to reception trays placed between the gunloading cage and a set of telescopic power rammers. When extended, these rammers transferred the shell and the four cordite charges directly into the gunloading cage. This additional power operation replaced the earlier hand- or gravity-assisted procedures at this point in the supply route.

The Japanese 14in-gun dreadnought *Hiei*. *Conway Picture Library*

Stowage for eight rounds per gun was provided in the gunhouse, with two power-worked derricks to lift the shell and place them on special hand-loading trays. The derricks were also arranged to serve the shell trays of the secondary hoists mentioned earlier. Bins for six rounds per gun were arranged in the working chamber, served by power-worked radial cranes, and an emergency shell and cordite supply route was built into the main trunk.

In battleship mountings, the gunhouse armour thickness was 11in on the front, sides and rear, 4in on the roof and 3in on the floor but in the battlecruisers it was thinned down to 9in front and sides, 8in rear and 3¼in roof.

There seems to be an impression that British heavy calibre gun mountings were devoid of any anti-flash arrangements prior to the disasters at Jutland but this is not the case. In this particular 13.5in mounting there were automatic flash doors between the top of the trunk and the reception trays, and on the entry ports of cordite compartments of the gunloading cage. In addition, a large flash door closed over the gunloading cage as it reached working chamber level to seal that compartment from the gunhouse. These arrangements may have been sadly inadequate, but it is wrong to suppose that they did not exist at all.

Additional minor modifications were made to the 13.5in Mk II* mountings, when an additional 'star' was added after the basic mark number. The Mk II** variants were fitted in the battleships *Iron Duke*, *Marlborough* and *Emperor of India* and the battlecruiser *Tiger*.

The 13.5in Mk II mounting in 'Q' position on the battlecruiser *Lion*, showing the front roof plate removed following damage received during the Battle of Jutland in 1916. *Conway Picture Library*

The forward 13.5in Mk III* mountings of the battleship *Ajax* in 1918. *By courtesy of John Roberts*

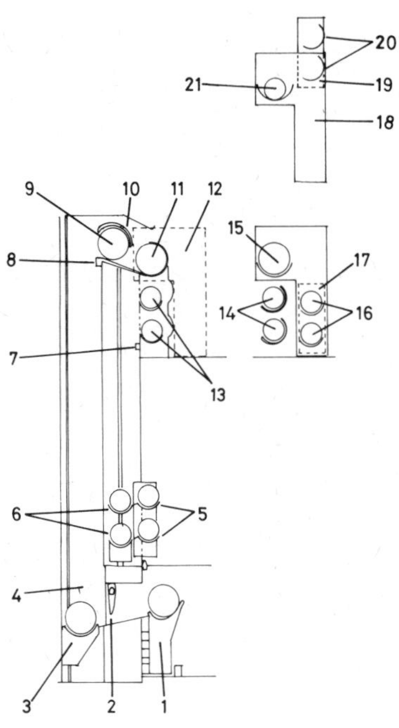

BRITISH 13.5in Mk III (SERIES) MOUNTINGS – AMMUNITION SUPPLY ARRANGEMENTS

1 Revolving shell bogie in shell room
2 Spring-loaded flap-door
3 Shell cage with tilting tray
4 Shell cage trunk
5 Cordite hopper tilting tray in magazine
6 Cordite cage tilting trays
7 Cordite cage trunk stop, actuating cage tilting trays
8 Shell cage trunk stop, actuating shell cage tilting tray
9 Discharged position of shell
10 Hand-operated shell release dog
11 Shell in 'waiting' position
12 Relative position of gunloading cage
13 Cordite tipped to 'waiting' position

Insets

14 Cordite rammed into tilting trays
15 Shell rammed into gunloading cage, in alignment for gunloading rammer
16 Cordite tipped into gunloading cage tilting trays from 14
17 Internal cordite compartment (rises by action of counterbalance weight)
18 Loading cage in upper position, shell and first pair of quarter-charges rammed into gun chamber
19 Cordite compartment in final position
20 Compartment trays tilted by cage hand-lever
21 Final cordite charges discharged to ramming position

THE BRITISH 13.5in Mk III, Mk III* and Mk III** MOUNTINGS

These three mountings were fitted in the battleships *Conqueror*, *Ajax* and *Benbow* respectively and shared a common handbook giving details of their individual differences. They were the first mountings to be designed by the Coventry Ordnance Works and were noticeably different from Vickers and Elswick types. This firm chose a new elevation piston and cylinder configuration, reverted to 7-cylinder training engines instead of swashplate machines, and produced a different style of ammunition caging. Externally, the gunhouse side plates were curved instead of being flat and rangefinder hoods were fitted in *Conqueror*'s 'Q' turret and in all the turrets of *Ajax* and *Benbow*.

One unusual feature of these mountings was the position of the elevating cylinder. To maintain the geometry of the arrangement the cylinder was pivoted so that it followed the gun as it moved between its limits of 5° depression and 20° elevation. The maximum elevating speed in *Ajax* was 3° per second, but this was improved to 5° per second in the other two ships.

The ammunition supply arrangements conceived by the Coventry works were peculiar and are, perhaps, indicative of their inexperience in such matters. It goes almost without saying that they would have gained little in the way of advice from either Vickers or Elswick. The outline arrangements show that there were separate shell and cordite cages in the main trunk but that, although the shell room was below the magazine, the relative position of projectile and charges had become transposed at working chamber level. The projectile rolled out on to its own waiting tray as did the cordite, ready for ramming, but when the upper unit of a triple-headed rammer advanced to push the shell into the gunloading cage the lower units merely moved the cordite on to tilting trays alongside it. Tilting these inwards caused the charges to roll into the cage, so that they were now below and to one side of the shell. They were, in fact, carried in a small lift within the cage itself, which was arranged to rise as the cage ascended. The motive power for the independent movement of the lift within the cage was provided by a weight connected to it by a wire or a chain.

As the cage moved upwards towards the gunloading arm, the lift partially rose until it came against a stop which left the upper cordite tray still well below the level of the shell tray. When the shell had been rammed, four successive movements of a lever on the cage (tallied with the legend 'Pull lever and let go'):

1 brought the first charges up to a level just below the shell tray;
2 moved them up level and tipped them out;
3 brought the second charges up as in 1; and
4 discharged them as in 2.

This left the lift in the upper position, but when the descending, empty, loading cage neared the floor of the working chamber a projection took against the weight and so allowed the lift to drop to its start point.

It was altogether a very odd arrangement, and although the cordite lift was an ingenious device the designers had really made a rod for their own backs in adopting the style of main cage they did. Their claim, in fact, was that by so doing, the heavier shell hoists were concentrated as close as possible to the centre of rotation of the mounting. In other respects the mounting resembled its contemporaries. The 13.5in series mountings were followed into service by the 15in Mk I and so closely did the general arrangement of the latter follow its immediate predessor that a detailed drawing of the 13.5in twin is made superfluous.

THE US 14in/45 TWO-GUN MOUNTING

Following the European trend towards larger calibre guns, the Americans introduced a 14in/45 calibre gun for the battleships *Texas* and *New York*, laid down in 1911. Five twin mountings were fitted in each of these ships and two twin mountings, of the same type, were fitted in the battleships *Oklahoma* and *Nevada*, laid down in the following year (these latter also carried two triples which are described in the next section). Electric power gave a maximum elevation speed of 4° per second and a training speed of 100° per minute. Elevation limits remained as in the earlier 12in mountings at 15° elevation and 5° depression, but all-up weight rose to 532 tons in the *Texas* class and to 618 tons in the *Oklahoma* class, which had thicker gunhouse armour. Shells appear to have been stowed point-down; they were certainly hoisted in this position, and are shown entirely on the rotating structure. Power-operated two-stage ammunition supply and loading arrangements were reintroduced in the twin 14in following redesign work on the unsuccessful system employed in earlier (12in) mountings. The powder hoists were endless chains terminating below the gunhouse floor, where the charges were passed upwards by hand through a scuttle. The lower shell hoists consisted of a winch and whip (hooked to an eye-ring in the shell nose) and the upper shell hoists, running in rear of the centre of rotation, were inclined 'pusher hoists'.

THE US 14in/45 TRIPLE MOUNTING

The *Oklahoma* class carried two of these mountings, in 'A' and 'Y' positions, but in the following *Pennsylvania* class, *Pennsylvania* and *Arizona*, all four mountings were triple, thus increasing the broadside on each ship from ten to twelve 14in guns. This mounting was novel in that all three

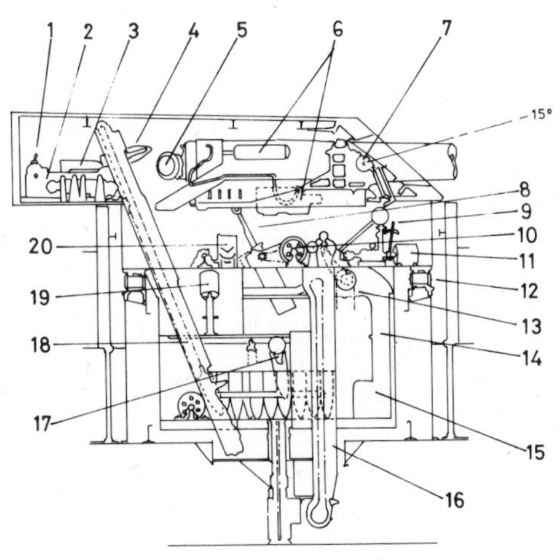

US 14in/45 TWIN MOUNTING (*NEW YORK*)

1 Rammer control lever
2 Chain rammer casing
3 Shell in 'waiting' position
4 Tilting shell bucket
5 Breech (open)
6 Recoil and run-out cylinders
7 Trunnion
8 Elevation screw drive
9 Hand/power clutch lever
10 Elevation drive
11 Electric motor
12 Training roller
13 Alternative hand chain-drive to powder hoist
14 Vent trunking
15 Blower casing
16 Powder hoist
17 Lower projectile hoist
18 Upper projectile hoist
19 Powder scuttle
20 Powder chute

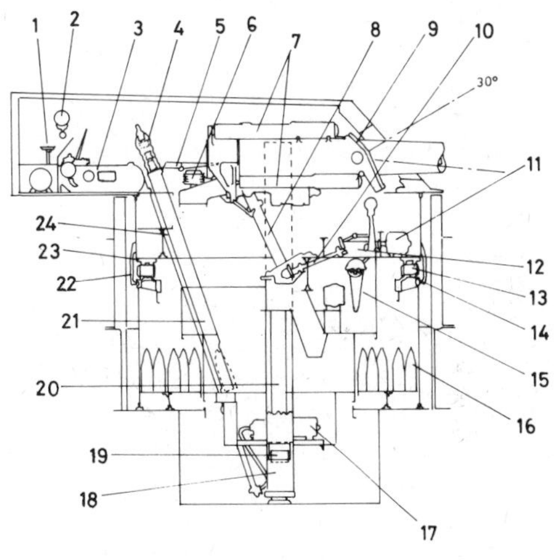

US 14in/45 TRIPLE MOUNTING (*NEVADA*)

1 Rangetaker's seat
2 Rangefinder
3 Rammer casing
4 Tilting shell bucket
5 Loading tray
6 Breech block
7 Recoil and run-out cylinders
8 Elevation screw for common triple gun cradle
9 Mantlet plate
10 Elevation power drive
11 Elevation motor
12 Elevation gearbox
13 Training roller
14 Lower roller path
15 Auxiliary hand chain-drive to elevation gear
16 On-mounting shell stowage
17 Hoist motor
18 Powder hoist
19 Powder charge
20 Central cable conduit tube
21 Projectile hoist
22 Jumping clip
23 Upper roller path
24 Auxiliary projectile hoist

The after triple 14in turrets of the USS *Pennsylvania*. *Conway Picture Library*

barrels were carried in a common elevating cradle, necessitating a massive 'lead-screw' and a 40hp elevating motor. In the *Pennsylvania* class the shell hoists were powered by a single 60hp motor but in the *Oklahoma* class there were two separate 30hp units. The all-up weight was about 720 tons in *Pennsylvania* and 748 tons in the *Oklahoma*.

It would seem that the triple design was in many ways experimental and it must have presented engineering problems in the first instance and tactical problems thereafter. With the common cradle conventional salvo fire, with some barrels loading while others were laid to the firing elevation, was obviously not possible (although in the *Oklahoma* class it could still be conducted by the two-gun mountings in 'B' and 'X' positions). At the same time the trunnion load rose from, typically, about 950,000lb for a single gun at maximum elevation to nearly 2,500,000lb for three guns fired simultaneously. The elevation limit was 15°.

The general arrangement of the mounting can be seen from the drawing but what cannot be shown in this view is how closely the gun bores were set towards each other. The by now well-established downward-opening breech block, although taking up space in rear of the gun, did not, of course, obstruct an adjacent gun, and thus American mountings tended to be longer and narrower than their European counterparts. At the same time, their style of ammunition stowage and supply tended to make the 'turret trunk' proportionately squatter than the British equivalent.

THE US 14in/50 THREE-GUN MOUNTING

The practice of 'stretching' an existing calibre was again followed in this mounting, designed for the battleships of the *New Mexico* class (*Idaho, Mississippi* and *New Mexico*) for which the guns were increased in length to 50 calibres. The common cradle of the previous 14in mountings was abandoned in favour of independent elevation drives which allowed, once again, for a maximum elevation of 15°. Shells were stowed vertically at one level but were distributed both on and off the mounting. Shell hoists were direct from handing room to gunhouse but powder supplies were two-stage, both upper and lower hoists being of the endless chain type. The all-up weight was 897 tons and the gun bores were again in close proximity to each other.

The final group of US battleships to employ the 14in gun was the *California* class (*California* and *Tennessee*) authorised in 1915. They carried a modified version of the *New Mexico* triple mounting, with similar 50-calibre guns but maximum elevation increased to 30°. In addition, light dividing bulkheads were fitted between the guns. The internal barbette diameter was comparatively small at 31ft, but, despite this, the all-up weight was 958 tons. Shell stowage was arranged on one level as in the previous mounting.

THE BRITISH 14in Mk I GUN ON THE TWIN Mk I MOUNTING

This very interesting weapon was produced by the Elswick works for the Chilean battleship *Almirante Latorre* which was subsequently purchased by the British government and renamed HMS *Canada*. The gun and its mounting were unique to that ship and had certain features that made them similar to the 'special' 12in mountings in the ex-Brazilian, ex-Turkish, battleship that was to become HMS *Agincourt*, which also had Elswick-designed mountings. Despite the fact that the 14in mounting entered service after the 15in it was, in fact, of earlier design. It was very much a 'dark horse' in the Royal Navy; HMS *Canada* was sold back to the Chilean Government in 1920 and comparatively few knew the details of her mountings.

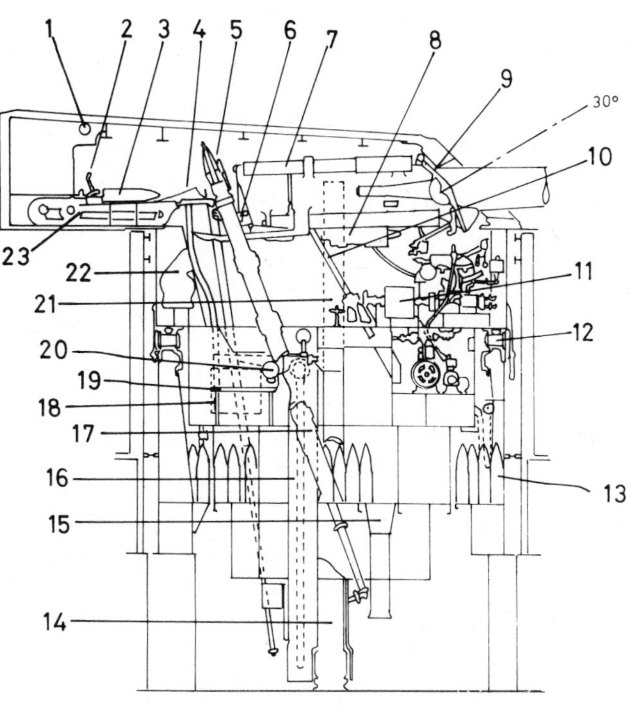

US 14in/50 TRIPLE MOUNTING (*TENNESSEE*)

1 Rangefinder
2 Rammer control lever
3 Shell in ramming position
4 Shell trough
5 Shell tilting bucket
6 Breech block (open)
7 Recuperator cylinder
8 Recoil buffer
9 Mantlet plate
10 Elevating screw
11 Elevating motor
12 Training roller
13 'Off mounting' shell stowage
14 Cabling duct
15 Shell tube
16 Lower right gun powder hoist
17 Right gun shell hoist
18 Upper right gun powder car
19 Powder transfer tray
20 Powder bag
21 Auxiliary shell hoist
22 Ventilation fan
23 Chain rammer casing

The 14in Mk I gun was 45 calibres long, weighed nearly 85 tons and employed a charge of 344lb of cordite as the propellant for the 1586lb projectile. The barrel itself was of conventional wire-wound construction but it had the 'short-arm' type of breech mechanism favoured by the Elswick Ordnance Company, who claimed that its advantages over exisiting types were that there was no 'slam' on the breech closing; that a simpler type of obturator could be employed; and that less space was taken

The USS *Idaho*, which carried twelve 14in/50 Mk 5 guns. *Conway Picture Library*

up in the gunhouse when the breech was opened. Power-opening was by a small hydraulic motor (with the usual alternative hand drive) and the whole mechanism was, in effect, the 'carrier-ring' of the old 12in Mk VIII but with the stepped-thread breech-screw.

Elswick's claims were not idle boasts, for the scheme had much merit and, indeed, early design reports indicate that this style of breech was chosen for the 15in Mk I. However, the 'A' tube of the second, experimental, 15in gun (E597) failed, and to save rebuilding time the Vickers 'carrier-arm' type was substituted. The other main differences in this mounting from the others so far discussed are best dealt with by tracing the path of ammunition from its source in the shell room and magazine to its loading position in the gunhouse.

No bogies were fitted around the foot of the trunking in the shell room; instead an overhead rail, fixed to the deckhead and carrying four travellers with shell grabs, encompassed it. Two doors ('Kenyon doors') gave access to the hoists and each had a waiting tray attached to the trunk outside them. Shells were lifted from their bins and conveyed towards the circular rail in the usual way, transferred to the travellers, run around the trunk into coincidence with the waiting trays, and then lowered on to them. The provision of four travellers allowed two to be serving the trays while the other two were being replenished from the bins.

As far as the shell room machinery was concerned, the scheme had some merit in its simplicity but, on the other hand, a shell suspended from the circular overhead rail had to 'chase' the waiting tray around should the mounting (and thus, of course, the trunk) train. A drawing of the 'Kenyon door' arrangements – readopted in the 15in Mk I* mounting – is included later in this book.

In the magazine, above the shell room, cordite was loaded into its cage through hopper doors in the trunk by the accepted man-handing methods. The lifting wire for the main cage was attached to the cordite cage with a separate shell cage suspended below it by a pulley system. The sketch shows that when the cordite cage rose, the shell cage followed it and, through the pulley system, gradually 'caught up' as it ascended until both cages came together at the working chamber. Here, shell and cordite were tipped out to a waiting position, whence they were rammed by a triple rammer into the gunloading cage.

The 14in/50 guns of *California*'s 'X' and 'Y' turrets dominate her quarterdeck in this August 1945 photograph. *US Navy*

HMS *Canada*, the only British capital ship to mount 14in guns until the completion of the *King George V* class of the Second World War. *By courtesy of John Roberts*

The cage comprised two distinct parts: a frame attached to the lifting wire and running on the normal trackway from working chamber to gunhouse; and a dropping section within it comprising three tiers of trays. The top and middle trays were for the pairs of quarter cordite charges and the bottom tray for the shell. On raising, the gunloading cage came to rest at the loading arm (whatever the elevation of the gun might be) in such a way that the shell was in line for ramming. Coincident with the retraction of the rammer after that event, the dropping section automatically fell to bring the first pair of quarter-charges in line, a process repeated for the second pair. By this time the dropping section was well below its initial position, but was reset upwards on the cage's arrival at working chamber level. The scheme was almost the exact opposite of that devised by the Coventry works for the Mk III series 13.5in mountings.

Automatic flash doors were fitted over the exit port from the waiting position to the working chamber, to isolate the main trunk and lower quarters, and a shutter door formed part of the entry ports into the gunloading cage to seal it as it rose, loaded, to the gunhouse. What *was* omitted, however, was a flashtight cover over the cage itself, so when it was at gunhouse level flash from action damage above had a direct path to the working chamber; but, even so, the main trunk was sealed and there was no path for flash to the magazine itself. Further sealing of that most vulnerable area was effected by the access doors in the trunk, which could only be opened if the main cage was down.

The flash doors on the gunloading cage closed immediately it started to ascend, and those at the waiting position only opened when the triple rammers advanced, closing when they retracted. It seems quite clear, therefore, that the designers of gun mountings of this period, prior to Jutland, were quite well aware of the dangers of flash and went to some lengths to combat them. The battlecruiser *Lion* undoubtedly suffered from flash effects in her 'Q' turret at Jutland (for special reasons), but although both *Queen Mary* and *Invincible* blew up in the same engagement, it seems likely that this was a straight penetration of their armour. Their destruction must remain a matter for conjecture for, when all was done, there was nothing left of the ships to analyse – any more than there was to be of *Hood* in 1941.

The control of the main cage and the working chamber rammers was centred on a single lever with 'Raise' (main cage), 'Ram', 'Withdraw' and 'Lower' (main cage) positions. A similar system was used in the gunhouse to control the opening of the breech, the raising of the gunloading cage and the ramming operation. The operating lever resembled the gear lever of a motor-car and was colloquially called a 'churn lever' because of its motion in the quadrant that housed it. The first movement opened the breech, the second brought up the cage and the third operated the rammer.

A vertical passageway in the main trunk was provided for the alternative shell supply, where the projectiles were lifted by wire to the working chamber, and an auxiliary flashtight cordite cage could be employed for charges. A second auxiliary cordite cage ran from the working chamber to the gunhouse, where radial cranes were fitted to lift shells should the gunloading cage become defective. Overhead rails with travellers were fitted to the working chamber deckhead for manoeuvring the shells, but alternative loading must have been something of a nightmare for the crew.

The gunshield was 10in thick with 3in–4in roof plates and a 3in floor. The sighting hoods were of 2in thick cast steel and the rangefinder hood of similar material 2½in thick. The total weight of the complete gunshield with all fittings was 220 tons, and the all-up weight of the complete revolving structure 720 tons. Immense though it may sound, this figure was less than half that of the British quadruple 14in of the Second World War.

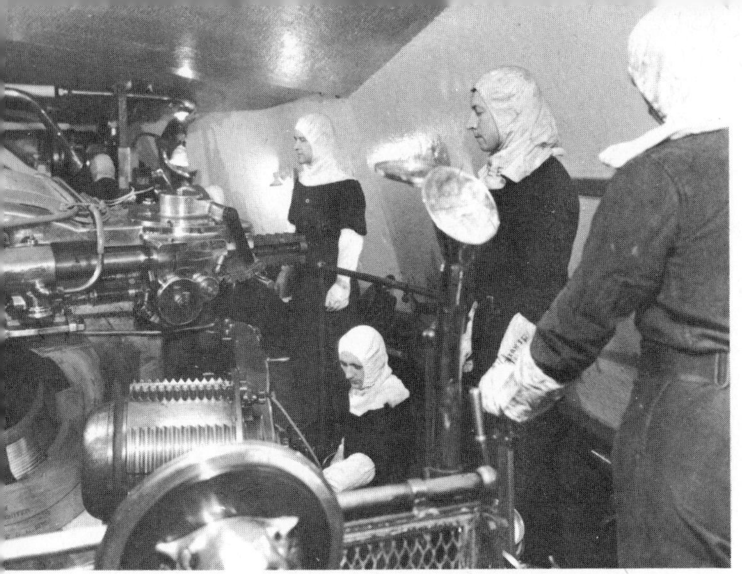

Left The interior of a 15in Mk I gunhouse showing the breech mechanism of the right gun. Note the 'stepped' interrupted screw breech with its three diameters of screwed and one diameter of plain 'lands' and the breech-operating hydraulic piston/cylinder fixed across the top of the breech-ring. *Imperial War Museum*

Below The quarterdeck of the battleship *Royal Sovereign* taken when she was returned to Britain in 1949 after five years service with the Russian Navy. Her 15in mountings remained unmodified throughout her career which spanned 23 years. *Conway Pciture Library*

Right The breech of the right gun of one of *Warspite*'s twin 15in mountings taken during the Second World War. Note the spoon tray about to enter the bottom of the breech opening as the breech block swings clear. The tray served as a guide for the shell and cordite and protected the breech threads from damage during the loading operation. *Conway Picture Library*

The post-World War I axe, honed by the Washington Treaty, despatched almost every surviving 12in and 13.5in battleship of the British Fleet. By 1924, forty-six ships had been sent to the breakers, and although *Iron Duke* and *Centurion* remained to see service in subsidiary roles in the Second World War, their sisters had been stricken – along with *Tiger* – by the early 1930s.

THE BRITISH 15in BL Mk I GUN ON THE TWIN Mk I MOUNTING[1]

The 15in twin was a logical development of the earlier British 12in and 13.5in mountings and was introduced principally to give a calibre superiority over the contemporary US and Japanese 14in weapons. The original mounting, designed for the *Queen Elizabeth* class battleships, was designated the 15in BL Mk I gun on the twin Mk I mounting. The same mounting was fitted in four of the *Royal Sovereign* class battleships but a slightly modified version, the Mk I* with different shell handling arrangements in the lower quarters, was fitted in the fifth *Royal Sovereign* (*Royal Oak*) and the battlecruisers *Renown* and *Repulse*.

The 15in BL Mk I gun and its breech mechanism weighed 100 tons and the trainable mass of the Mk I mounting complete totalled 750 tons. The barrel was built up from a number of tubes in the usual fashion of the day was was wire wound between the A tube and B tube with 170 miles of rectangular-section steel wire. The breech was of the interrupted thread pattern and normally was hydraulically operated but an alternative hand drive was also provided. The 15in 4crh shell weighed 1920lb and the standard full cordite charge 430lb. In a *Queen Elizabeth* class battleship – as a typical example – the full outfit of 15in ammunition weighed 1000 tons, and when both guns in one turret fired together at 20° elevation the shock transmitted to the ship was the equivalent of 400 tons.

The turret – to use the common if technically incorrect expression – conformed more or less to the profile of the preceding 13.5in and 12in twins. In plan, the front

[1]A detailed description of the 15in mounting is given in the Appendices.

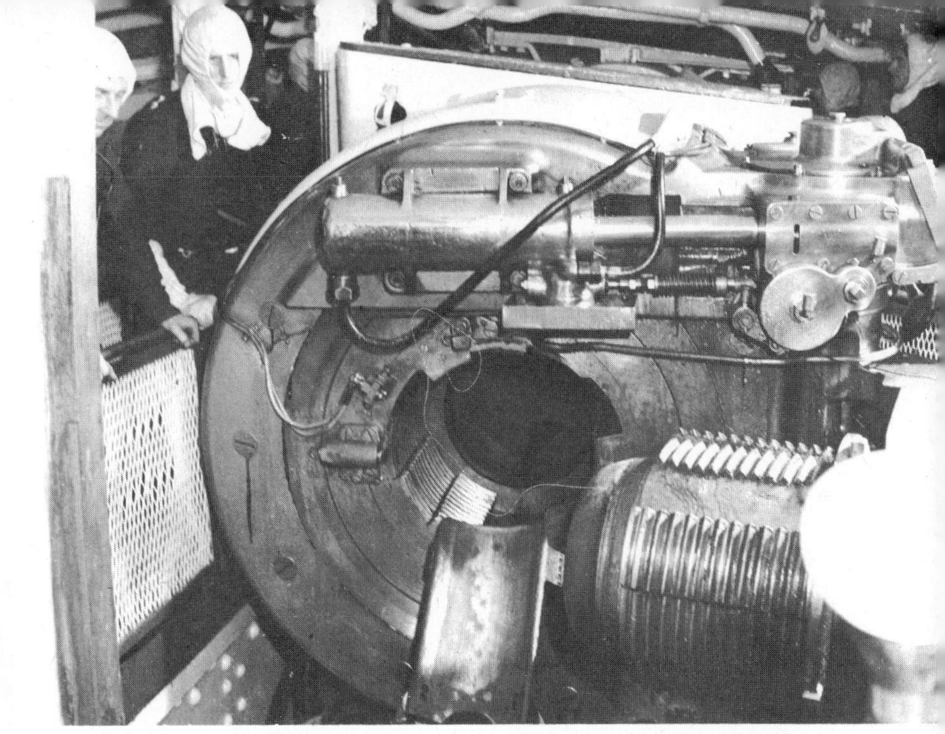

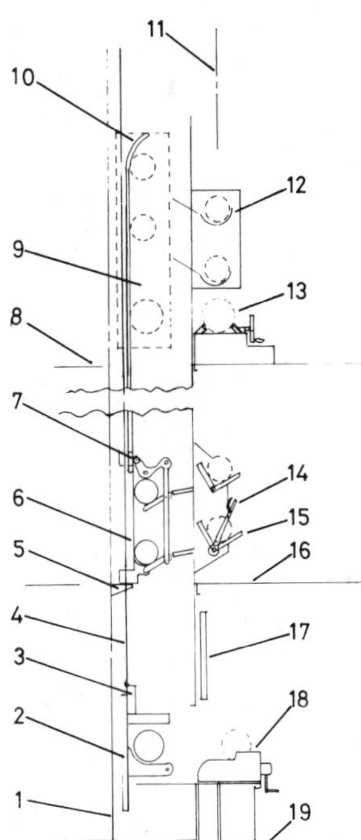

BRITISH 15in Mk I – MAIN TRUNK ARRANGEMENTS

1 Centreline of trunk
2 Shell cage
3 Buffer
4 Cage lifting wire
5 Cordite cage stop
6 Cordite cage, picked up by shell cage
7 Cam roller-follower
8 Working chamber floor
9 Envelope of combined shell and cordite cages
10 Cam rail tips out cordite charges
11 Centreline of gunloading cage and working chamber rammers
12 Cordite waiting position in flashtight compartment
13 Shell on shell carrier in 'waiting' position
14 Cordite hopper operating lever
15 Flashtight cordite hopper
16 Cordite handing room
17 Hand-operated watertight shell door
18 Shell bogie
19 Shell handing room

face was roughly circular to the diameter of the roller path and then had slightly tapering flat sides terminating in an overhang with a curved rear. The swept arc of the turret rear was 24ft from the centre of rotation but, of course, the gun muzzles moved through an arc of greater radius. In side elevation, the gunhouse roof sloped downwards in a shallow wedge shape.

Each gun was elevated by a hydraulic piston in a cylinder which was controlled either by a handwheel outboard of the barrel or by a duplicate alternative handwheel in the centre position between the guns. Training control was available at the centre position, from either of the outer positions or from a special position in the working chamber below. Two gunsights were provided for each gun – one at the outer position, and one at the centre – for use in 'quarters firing', when the guns were aimed by the sight telescopes, but the layers normally 'followed pointers' in director control. Under these conditions, the turret was in fact trained by a turret director trainer following pointers in the working chamber.

The gunhouse armour was 13in thick on the front face, 11in on the sides and rear, 4½in on the roof and 3in on the floor. Armoured domes were fitted to protect the periscopes of the gunsights, the centre sights having a noticeably larger one. These domes should not be confused with the armoured dome fitted over the the splinter plate when elevation was increased to 30° during the modernisations prior to and during the Second World War.

The next compartment below was called the working chamber and it was here that ammunition was transferred from the main cages to the gunloading cages. The four cage-lifting presses were secured to the deckhead, together with a pair of curved overhead rails arranged to run over the ready-use shell bins, the shell carrier in its outer position and a waiting tray. The tray could be served by the radial crane in the gunhouse via the access hatch already mentioned. All these units formed the auxiliary shell supply arrangements in association with a secondary shell hoist on the centreline of the working chamber floor just forward of the main cage trunk. It led directly to the shell room and was also used as the normal internal access to the lower quarters, recessed footholds being cut into one of its sides. Needless to say, it was a long, and rather wearing, climb up.

Underneath the working chambers was a non-rotating space containing the two main 'walking pipes'. The off-mounting pump was a steam-driven unit of the impeller type and distilled water mixed with a small percentage of argolene oil was used as the pressure medium. It looked rather like watered-down milk and a major leak or burst pipe quickly gave a compartment the appearance of a flooded dairy. The oil was included to give some lubrication properties to the water, in which it was soluble, and was a patent mixture of vegetable oil and soft potash soap.

The walking pipe compartment was colloquially called 'the danger space' because the amount of room therein was rather restricted and severe injury, even death, could result from becoming trapped between the closing 'legs' of the walking pipes as the turret trained. Clearly, all-round training was impossible with this arrangement (as distinct from a swivel-connection on the centre of rotation method) but in the 15in ships this was, in any case, prevented by the disposition of the mountings with respect to the superstructure and to each other.

Beneath 'the danger space', the remaining part of the rotating trunk contained only the main cages for each gun and the two auxiliary ammunition routes. It terminated in the shell room, with the magazine immediately above it.

Unlike the shell room, into which the trunk was directly led, the magazine proper was partitioned off from a space called the cordite handing room, where the charges were loaded into the cordite cages. The cordite was stowed in the magazine in cases containing two quarter-charges, each weighing about 100lb. Four such quarter-charges constituted a full charge, and these were manhandled to a

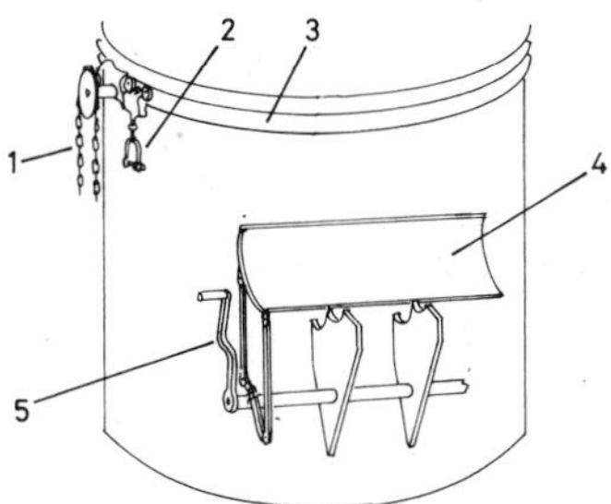

BRITISH 15in Mk I* – 'KENYON' DOOR

1 Chain traversing drive to one of four independent shell runners
2 Transfer shackle, with swivelling bottle-screw jack, connects to traverser shell grab
3 Overhead rail around trunk in shell room
4 Tipping 'Kenyon door', replacing shell bogie in Mk I mounting, rolls shell into shell cage through aperture in trunk
5 Door operating lever and linkage

flashtight hopper between the magazine and cordite handing room. A spring-loaded handle on the hopper tipped the four charges into the handing room where they were again manhandled on to similar hoppers on the revolving trunk. When these were tipped inwards, the four charges rolled into the waiting cordite cage. A mechanical telegraph lever ('cordite cage ready'), interlocked with a similar lever in the shell room, then operated a tell-tale plate in the working chamber, and the operator above was able to raise the main cage.

The shell rooms were positioned back to back, in that 'A' turret's was abaft the turret trunk and 'B' turret's forward of it; there was a similar arrangement aft. The shells were transported by overhead rails from the shell bins to two independent shell bogies which ran around the base of the trunk. The bogies could be moved round the trunk until lined up with the shell cage and then locked to the trunk so they revolved with it when the turret was trained.

Because there were two bogies, two main shell cages and duplicate traversers on the starboard side of the shell room, both guns could be served at the same time. On top of the bogies was a traversing trolley which carried the shell into the shell cage where it was held by mechanical dogs. The loading port cut in the trunk on each side was sealed by a vertically sliding watertight door and this, together with the bogie gear, was comprehensively interlocked to prevent damage. The shell cage was hauled upwards to the working chamber by a hydraulic press attached to the deckhead of the working chamber. The cordite cage was a separate unit which stopped in the trunk at cordite handing room level (above the shell room), so when the shell cage rose it picked up the cordite cage and both ascended together. The lifting gear was therefore attached to the heavier of the two cage assemblies (shell and shell cage together weighed over a ton) which carried the lighter, cordite cage (about a quarter of a ton when loaded) above it.

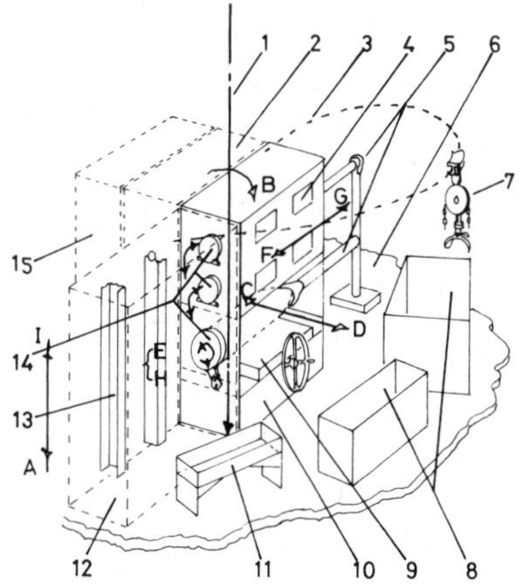

BRITISH 15in Mk I/N – WORKING CHAMBER ARRANGEMENTS

1 Plumb-line of gunhouse right-hand radial crane
2 Right gun main cage trunk
3 Track of overhead rail, plumbing outer position of shell carrier, shell bins and waiting tray.
4 Inspection windows in flashtight cordite waiting position
5 Cordite and shell hydraulic rammer cylinders
6 Working chamber floor
7 Shell grab chain purchase
8 Shell bins for emergency shell supply
9 Shell carrier
10 Moving bed
11 Shell waiting tray for emergency shell supply
12 Envelope of right gunloading cage
13 Cage guide rails
14 Cordite and shell flash doors
15 Left gun main cage trunk

Sequence
A Gunloading cage arrives from gunhouse, locked down by No 6's lever
B Main cage arrives at working chamber, cordite tips automatically to waiting position
C Traverse shell carrier in by power, pick up shell
D Withdraw shell into line with rammer
E Open flash doors. Cordite doors hinge downward and form bridge tray into cordite cage, shell door swings sideways
F Ram cordite and shell into gunloading cage
G Withdraw rammers
H Close flash doors
I Unlock gunloading cage by No 6's lever. Cage ready to be called to gunhouse by gunhouse control lever

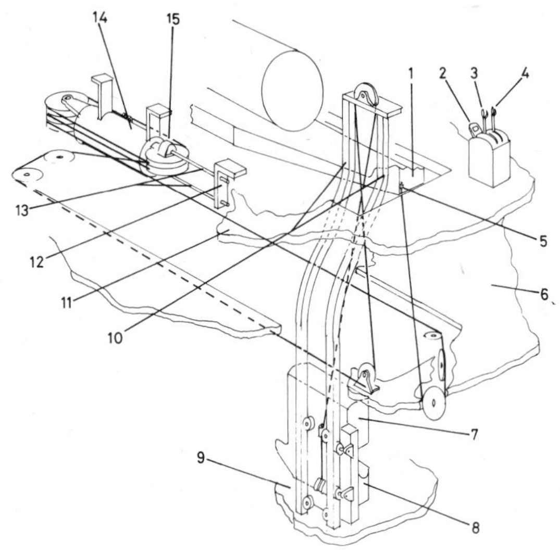

BRITISH 15in Mk I – GUNHOUSE ARRANGEMENTS

1 Rammer casing
2 'Cage Ready' indicator
3 Gunhouse radial crane control
4 Cage operating lever
5 Lifting wire anchored to loading arm, keeping cage at loading arm irrespective of elevation
6 Turntable floor
7 Cordite compartment in gunloading cage
8 Shell tray in gunloading cage
9 Working chamber floor
10 Cage guide rails, curved back to allow any-elevation loading
11 Gunhouse floor
12 Guide bracket
13 Guide rods
14 Hydraulic cage lifting press suspended below turntable floor, with opposite end of lifting wire anchorage
15 Guide block

On arrival in the working chamber the cordite was automatically tipped outwards into a flashtight waiting position, between a double-headed rammer and the gunloading cage, but the shell remained in its cage until moved to the ramming position by a power-operated traverser. The main cage was then returned and the gunloading cage sealed against flash and locked in position. The flash doors between the loading cage and the working chamber waiting position were then opened and the shell and two levels of cordite charges pushed into the cage by their single-headed and double-headed rammers respectively. The rammers were then withdrawn and the flash doors closed, totally sealing the loading cage, until, on being required in the gunhouse, it was unlocked.

The gunhouse loading arrangements centred around a loading arm attached to the rear of the elevating structure and to which the gunloading cage rose. The cage rails described a circular arc from the trunnion axis and it was thus possible to load the gun at any elevation up to 20°, although in practice the gun was brought to roughly 5° for this purpose. Nevertheless, the loading angle was not fixed, and this speeded up the rate of fire.

At the rear of each gunwell there was a console holding two control levers, the larger of the two operating the press to bring up the gunloading cage and the smaller operating the radial crane. Once the gunloading cage had been unlocked in the working chamber, a mechanical telegraph plate on the gunhouse showed 'Cage ready', and it was then brought up, coming to rest at the loading arm, with its shell position in line with the chamber. The cage control lever was locked until the breech was open and, during gun drill, the crew chanted the effect of the interlocks until they knew them by heart. The Gunnery Instructor (GI) would deliberately command 'Raise the gunloading cage' before the breech was open, whereupon the cage worker would roar 'Cannot raise the cage with the breech block closed'. An approving nod from the GI and then 'Open the breech; raise the cage', answered by 'Cannot raise the cage with the cage locked by No 6's lever'. So it went on, with roars of command and the rumble of the machinery, every member of the 70-man crew knowing his job and when to do it. At peak efficiency, a gun crew could get away two rounds per minute, which was no mean feat for a weapon of this size.

The breech operating lever and the rammer controls were on the loading arm itself, and the rammer number stepped down on to a small platform which he operated by a control lever. As the gunloading cage came up level with the loading arm, it knocked a 'spoon tray' into the breech to protect the threads from damage, and all was ready for loading. The rammer number advanced the power-operated chain rammer, pushing the shell out of the gunloading cage, over the 'spoon tray', through the chamber and into the barrel. He then withdrew the rammer and operated a cordite lever on the cage itself. This dropped the two pairs of charges one position downwards, so that the first pair of quarter-charges was in line with the chamber, in the space formerly occupied by the shell. Then he depressed a foot pedal on his platform to reduce the length of the rammer stroke, and again rammed, carrying the first half-charge into the chamber. If he forgot the foot pedal, the rammer extended fully and crushed the cordite into the base of the shell – a fearful mess. Returning the cordite lever to its normal position dropped the second half-charge, which was again rammed on reduced stroke. The second pair of charges, therefore, moved into the chamber, pushing the first before them.

Meanwhile the breech worker had inserted a new firing tube into the lock and closed its small sliding breech, but this crew member was standing beside the gun and was not on the loading arm. When the loading cycle had been completed, and the rammer finally withdrawn, the gunloading cage was sent down to the working chamber (removing the spoon tray en route), the breech was closed and the gun laid for firing.

Apart from the preliminaries to a bombardment against a land target, when one gun alone might be used as a 'ranging gun', the two forms of firing were either salvos, using alternate guns, or broadsides, when all guns fired together. Both methods had their advantages, and it was a matter of tactics which was chosen. In salvos, the overall rate of fire was more or less doubled because, as one gun was laid for firing, the other was being loaded, resulting in a steady stream of 15in projectiles – in groups of four in a four-turret ship. In broadside fire, everything went off with one tremendous bang; the rate of fire was less but eight shells arrived at a time – assuming all guns could bear on the target. Generalising on a complex tactical subject, a ship would probably employ salvo firing at long range in a running fight and broadsides as a *coup de grace* when the range closed. Among the many attributes of the twin 15in was the flexibility of fire that its design permitted.

BRITISH 15in Mk II TWIN MOUNTING

1 Officers' cabinet
2 Rangefinder
3 Gunloading cage
4 Breech (open)
5 Loading arm (attached to gun slide)
6 Breech operating hand wheel
7 Run-out cylinder
8 Chain rammer casing
9 Gun cradle and recoil cylinder
10 Trunnion
11 Splinter shield to gunport
12 Turret training locking-bolt
13 'Walking pipes' (hydraulic power to elevating structure)
14 Roller path
15 Elevating cylinder
16 Ammunition hoist lifting gear
17 Working chamber
18 Cordite rammers (hoist to cage)
19 Shell rammer (hoist to cage)
20 Electric pump
21 'Walking pipes' (hydraulic power from fixed to revolving structure)
22 Shell suspended from radial transport rail (ready-use)
23 Trunk (containing shell and cordite hoists)
24 Cordite hoppers
25 Shell traversing winches
26 Hydraulic shell lifting and traversing gear
27 Shell bins
28 Shell traversing bogie
29 Shell bin
30 Electric cables
31 Shell bogie ring
32 Revolving shell bogie
33 Shell on bogie
34 Flexible voicepipe (fixed to revolving strucure)
35 Shell waiting position
36 Shell waiting tray (ready-use)
37 Cordite waiting position
38 Training rack
39 Gunloading cage rails
40 Rammer motor

(Note: Drawing shows 'Y' turret HMS *Hood*, with 30° elevation. Shell room is reversed – ie, forward end of shell room is facing aft – for compactness on drawing.)

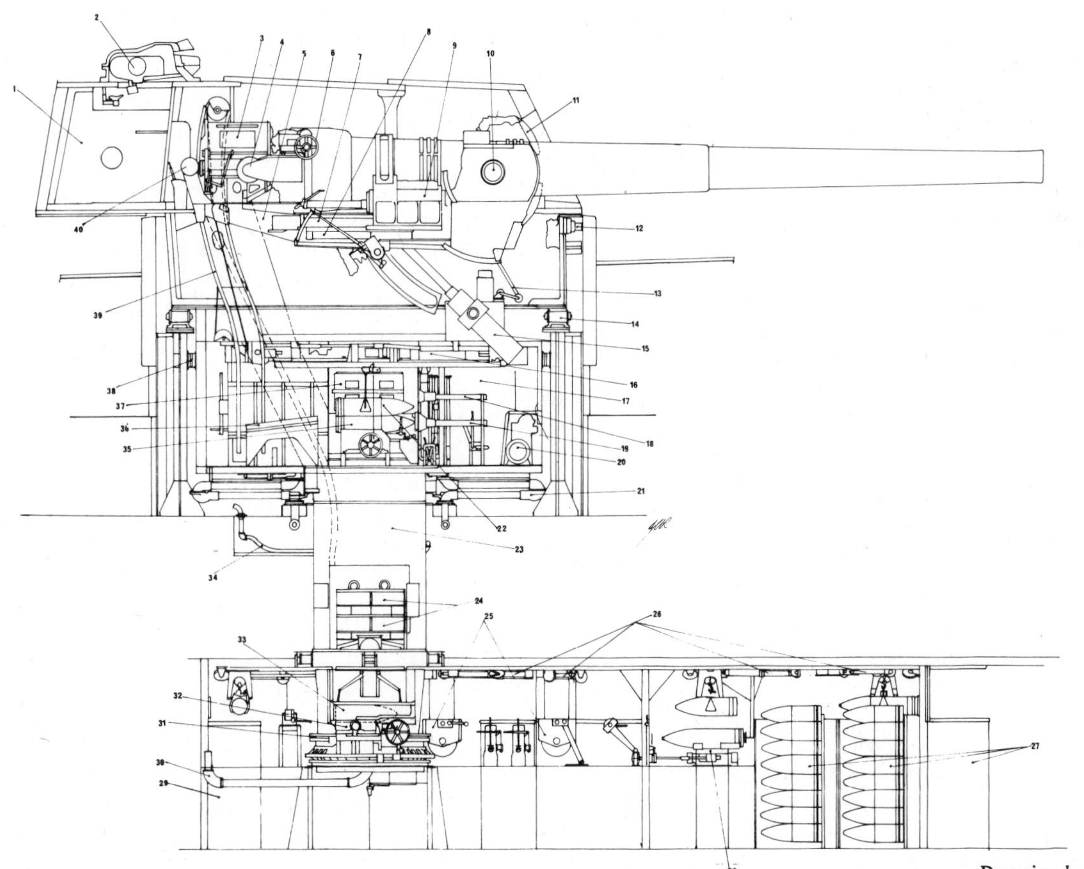

Drawing by John Roberts

The battlecruiser *Hood* on trials. *Hood* was the only vessel to carry the Mk II version of the twin 15in mounting, which provided for 30° elevation compared with 20° in the Mk I. *By courtesy of John Roberts*

THE BRITISH 15in Mk I GUN ON THE TWIN Mk II MOUNTING

The British had long pursued the goal of 'any-elevation' loading but, having in due course achieved it, found it in practice to be wanting. In the first place, it meant that the rammer number in the gunhouse crew had to remain 'riding' on the end of the loading arm and, although theoretically quite safe, he would face the somewhat daunting prospect of seeing a mass of some 100 tons recoiling directly towards him on gunfire.

Secondly, the task imposed on the rammer in thrusting a 15in shell 'uphill' at ever steepening angles was so great that shell-seating in the chamber (when the copper driving band 'bit' into the commencement of rifling) at best became erratic and at worst resulted in shell rebound. If the latter occurred, the shell slid backwards out of the breech when the rammer was withdrawn, to the natural consternation of all concerned.

The 15in Mk I mounting had been designed for 'any-elevation' loading up to 20°. Beyond this point it was, in any case, impossible because the configuration of the gunloading cage rails would not permit it.

A further inherent weakness of British gun mounting design philosophy manifested itself early in the First World War. What is more usually known as 'broadside fire' (ie, both guns in a mounting firing together) was then referred to as 'simultaneous salvos' and, under these circumstances, unacceptable demands were imposed on the hydraulic system as the British used their hydraulic 'mains' to run the guns out after recoil. In consequence, at the higher elevations, when the guns ran out 'uphill', other hydraulic machinery tended to be starved to the extent that 'stalling' might occur. Thus it was decided, early in the war, to adopt pneumatic run-out in future designs and also, where feasible, to so convert existing mountings.

Other design shortcomings had revealed themselves during this period – notably, of course, the need for much closer regard to be paid towards anti-flash precautions. In addition, problems had arisen with the shell transporting arrangements. Under heeling conditions, when the ship was responding to course alterations in action, it had been most difficult to control the geared shell bogies in the shell room, while in the hoists themselves the projectiles were prone to 'surge'. Other proposed changes were:

1 To provide telescopic gunsights sighted through the front wall armour rather than in 'hoods' on the gunhouse roof.
2 To enclose vital control equipment within armoured 'cabinets' in the gunhouse.
3 To improve armour, drenching and spraying arrangements.
4 To flash-proof all compartments as far as was possible.
5 To fit 30ft rangefinders in turrets for improved 'local control' ranging.
6 To provide isolating and spring-loaded non-return valves for hydraulic exhaust lines to prevent the escape of the hydraulic medium should such pipes be fractured by action damage.

The modifications to the 15in monitor mountings to give them 30° maximum elevation had met with such success that this facility, in addition to as much of the other improvement programme as was possible, was worked into the 15in Mk II mountings for HMS *Hood.*

The basic design remained the same but, to achieve a 30° limit, the dimensions of the elevating cylinder and of the gunhouse itself were revised. All thoughts of 'any-elevation' loading were abandoned (a decision in this

The 15in-gun battleship *Bayern*, in 1917. She and her sister *Baden* were the only World War I German dreadnoughts to mount guns larger than the 12in. *Conway Picture Library*

respect had already been made for loading the single 18in gun in HMS *Furious*) and instead the guns were laid to an arbitrary angle for reloading. One merit of the inherent design was that because any-angle had been intended in the first instance, there was no absolute loading angle and no loading angle (or 'slide locking') bolts were fitted. Thus it was merely a matter of laying the gun within a tolerable arc for reloading; and the rammer number now stepped on to the loading arm to fulfil his duties, and then vacated it before the gun elevated.

The 15in Mk II mountings were noticeably different from the Mk I and Mk I* in having higher gunhouses; the principal differences between the three were as shown in the accompanying table. The implementation of the 'improvement' ideas, outlined here, resulted in the most complex interlocked powering devices throughout the ammunition supply systems of the succeeding generations of British gun mountings, coupled with the most stringent anti-flash requirements.

15in GUN MOUNTING VARIATIONS

	Mk I	Mk I*	Mk II
Distance between centrelines of guns	7ft 6in	7ft 6in	8ft 2in
Vertical height of gunhouse rear plate	8ft 10in	8ft 10in	9ft 4in
Height of trunnion axis above working chamber floor	18ft 11in	18ft 11in	21ft 0in
Vertical height of gunhouse front plate	6ft 6in	6ft 6in	8ft 8in
Gunhouse front face shape	Polygon-faced	Circular	Polygon-faced
Shell room arrangements	Shell bogies	Overhead travellers and 'Kenyon Doors'	Shell bogies

A good deal of hydraulic powering was employed in the mounting, principally for breech mechanisms, telescopic loading rammers and transfer rammers – all of which had alternative hand drives. In addition, perhaps because of the weight of the 15in ammunition, hydraulics were used for the main hoists. These were continuous from lower quarters to gunhouse and followed British practice in having a cable to the shell cage and the charge, riding in its own cage, pick-a-back above it. The two charges lay horizontally one behind the other, with the shell similarly disposed below them. An auxiliary electric drive could be coupled to the main hoist in the event of hydraulic failure but it was very slow in operation – slower, in fact, than the auxiliary hoists proper.

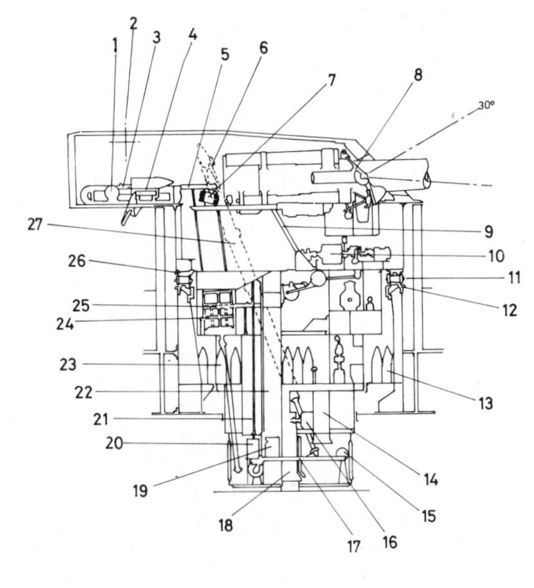

US 16in TWIN MOUNTING (*MARYLAND*)

1 Rammer drive
2 Rangefinder centres
3 Rammer casing
4 Shell bogie
5 Loading tray
6 Shell tilting bucket
7 Breech block
8 Mantlet plate
9 Elevation screw
10 Elevation motor
11 Training roller
12 Lower roller path
13 Shell stowage
14 Shell scuttle
15 Powder charge
16 Hoist motor
17 Powder trough
18 Cable conduit
19 Lower powder cage
20 Secondary powder cage
21 Secondary powder cage hoisting cable
22 Lower powder cage trunk
23 On-mounting shell stowage
24 Upper powder cage
25 Powder transfer tray
26 Upper roller path
27 Projectile hoist

THE GERMAN 15in SKL/45 IN THE DRH LC/1913 MOUNTING

The Germans completed only two 15in-gunned warships during the First World War, the battleships *Baden* and *Bayern*, although two more of the same class and three similarly armed battlecruisers were planned. The designed elevation of the 15in mounting was 16° and maximum depression 8° but the upper limit was increased to 20° in the *Bayern*, the second of the class to complete. Main training was electric and gave a maximum speed of 3° per second; auxiliary training gave about ½° per second and elevation speed was 5° per second. The all-up weight varied between 850 and 870 tonnes and the turntable was supported on a ball race of 144 steel balls each of about 6.5in diameter.

The three US battleships of the *Maryland* class in line ahead in the late 1930s. *Conway Picture Library*

The combined shell and charge cage arrived in the gunhouse on the centre of rotation of the mounting and between the guns, where an upper and lower transfer rammer thrust the load on to an ammunition 'car'. This ran on rails transversely behind the breeches but, although there was one such device for each gun, either 'car' could serve either gun, allowing flexibility in the event of the failure of one hoist. Once the 'car' had been traversed behind the breech and the shell had been rammed into the gun, the upper tray of the 'car' was unlocked and moved bodily downwards on top of the now empty shell tray, ready for the twin charges themselves to be rammed. Like the other loading arrangements, the cars were hydraulically powered and had alternative hand operation. All gunhouse ammunition movement was controlled from a central position deriving its power from on-mounting, electrically driven, hydraulic pumps. Flash doors were fitted at the top of the hoist trunk and at magazine and shell room levels but the cages themselves were of open construction.

Typical supply speeds (in main hydraulic) were: hoists 7° per second; transfer rammer (advance and retract) 7° per second; 'car' (hoist to gun) 3° per second; and loading rammer (advance /retract) 6° per second (shell) and 5° per second (charge). In main power control, the full loading cycle was accomplished in approximately 26 seconds but in hand control all motions were very much slower.

Like the British, the Germans learned to their cost of the need for better anti-flash precautions. The exposed nature of the cordite transfer systems in the gunhouses of their later 11in and their 12in mountings made the area very vulnerable but, even after the severe fires in *Seydlitz* and *Derfflinger*, the extempore additions, retrospectively fitted, were not fully effective between ship and ship or even between turret and turret.

THE US 16in/45 TWO-GUN MOUNTING

Continuing to play the international game of calibre leapfrog, the Americans next produced a 16in gun for the *Maryland* class, which was to have comprised four ships. However, the completion of *Washington* was halted by the naval treaty of the same name, leaving *Colorado*, *West Virginia* and the nameship. *Maryland* was laid down in 1917 and the class was completed between 1921 and 1922 with, of course, the exception of *Washington* which was expended as a bomb target in 1924.

The armament followed the usual pattern of development in that the calibre length dropped to 45 and the mounting was two-gunned instead of three. Both calibre length and mounting size were to be increased in later classes, again following the trend in such affairs. Shell stowage was split between fixed and moving structure, recoil length was 4ft and the mounting's all-up weight was 880–920 tons. The trunnion load on gunfire was 1,500,000lb at the maximum elevation of 30° but the two gun masses could in fact be locked together and elevated as

The twin 14in turret of one of the *Abercrombie* class monitors. These mountings were built by the Bethlehem Steel Corporation of the USA for the abortive Greek battlecruiser *Salamis*. After the outbreak of war in 1914 the guns and mountings were purchased by the British government and utilised to arm four monitors designed and built in seven months. The mounting design was of typical US pattern and resembled the contemporary USN types. *Conway Picture Library*

a pair. Flame-proof bulkheads separated the guns, and recoil and run-out was effected by a combination of six run-out spring boxes, compressed air and hydraulic buffers.

The US adoption of electric power and the absence of a hydraulic system led to a heavy reliance on run-out springs for the guns but, while these could be made to perform adequately so long as the maximum elevation remained comparatively low, once a 30° maximum had been decided upon a dual run-out pneumatic system became necessary.

Like all nations signatory to the Washington Treaty, the United States cancelled several projected capital ships in 1922. In general these vessels were to have been equipped with gun mountings providing a maximum elevation of 40° for which run-out springs would have been quite inadequate, and for which pneumatic run-out gear had, therefore, been proposed.

THE BRITISH MONITOR MOUNTINGS

In addition to the British 15in mountings already discussed, a 15in Mk I 'Special' was fitted in certain monitors and, at this point, it will be appropriate to look briefly at that rather odd type of warship and – more in context – the armament of some of the several classes.

Monitors were introduced into the Royal Navy to fulfil a need to bombard that part of the Belgian coast occupied by the Germans in the early part of the First World War. The first ships available for this suddenly created task were three river gunboats building at Vickers for the Brazilian Government. They were originally known as river monitors and, for RN service, were named *Humber, Mersey* and *Severn.* They, and several others, were grouped as 6in monitors and, like the 9.2in monitors, are not our direct concern. However, in November 1914, four much larger ships were ordered, to be armed with American twin 14in guns. Originally known as *M1, M2, M3* and *M4*, then redesignated *Admiral Farragut, Robert E Lee, Stonewall Jackson* and *General Grant* (no doubt in deference to their guns), they eventually entered service as *Abercrombie, Havelock, Raglan* and *Roberts*.

The 14in mountings were purchased from the Bethlehem Steel Company who, by an odd quirk of fate, had constructed them on the latest American pattern as subcontractors for a German firm who were themselves building a battlecruiser for the Greek Government! The complete installation, together with ammunition and armour, was shipped to the United Kingdom and re-erection was carried out by the Coventry Ordnance Works (for Belfast-built ships) and the Elswick Ordnance Company (for the one Tyne-built ship).

The mountings were electrically powered and quite unlike any British-built equipments. After the almost inevitable defects, which occurred during refit after their re-erection, they behaved very well, although the British were not very impressed with their basic design. Gun run-out was much more violent than in their own weapons and the barrels had a marked tendency to droop – so much so that they had to be changed before they had actually worn out. Power for the electrical machinery was provided by two 200kW steam driven generating sets. Ammunition stowage for 100 rounds per gun was built into each ship. *Raglan* was sunk at the mouth of the Dardenelles in 1917 but the other three survived the war. A particular point in the favour of these American mountings was that their anti-flash arrangements were superior to those of pre-Jutland British ships.

In December 1914 an order was placed for eight monitors, each to be armed with a twin 12in mounting. The 12in Mk BII mountings, from the old *Majestic* class ships *Hannibal, Magnificent, Mars* and *Victorious*, were utilised and installed complete with their loading arrangements. To increased their maximum effective range, the gun elevation was re-engineered by Elswick to permit an upper limit of 30°. On gun trials a number of defects arose, which was hardly surprising when one considers the age of the components but, nevertheless, once these were cured, the old guns performed yeoman service. Two of the ships were later fitted with single 18in guns, which are described in more detail in the next section.

A further two monitors, which were constructionally to resemble the earlier ships but were to be armed with the new 15in Mk I, were ordered in January 1915. At about this time two battleships of the *Royal Sovereign* class were cancelled and, utilising material gathered for their construction, two battlecruisers, *Renown* and *Repulse*, were ordered. As the new ships carried only three mountings, compared with four in the battleships, two mountings became available for the new monitors which became the *Marshal Soult* and *Marshal Ney*. To expedite their entry into service they were given very low horsepower diesel main engines and the latter ship could in consequence only achieve 4kts flat-out – clearly a waste of a very valuable and brand-new 15in Mk I mounting.

Therefore, when a second pair of monitors was ordered in September 1915, with more powerful steam main engines, *Marshal Ney*'s 15in mounting was removed (she received a 9.2in gun in lieu) to arm one of them. The second ship received a twin 15in originally ordered for the light battlecruiser *Furious*. The two ships, *Erebus* and *Terror*, had, like *Marshal Soult*, an even more peculiar appearance than was already inherent in the monitor type. Their outstanding feature (literally) was the very tall barbette, within which the 15in mounting was supported, a feature made necessary by the deep revolving trunk which formed an inescapable part of the 15in battleship mounting.

Modifications were worked into the mountings to suit the particular needs of the installation (giving them the 'Special' soubriquet), including a fixed loading angle of 5°; special gear to insert an elevation locking bolt at this position; and raised trunnions giving revised elevation limits of +2° to +30°.

THE BRITISH 15in B GUN IN THE COAST DEFENCE MOUNTING

The 15in B was the code given to what was, in reality, a gun of 18in bore, and both it and its mounting were originally designed for the large light battlecruiser *Furious*, a follow-on from the 15in-gunned *Glorious* and *Courageous*. The rather fortunate alphabetical progression of the initial letters of the gun and mounting led to it being referred to as the 'B C D'.

The weight of the gun, with breech mechanism, was 149 tons and it was 40 calibres long. It was, in all respects, a scaled-up version of the 15in barrel and, to obviate the need for extensive mounting design work, the existing 15in gunhouse was adapted to take a single 18in in place of its usual pair of 15in guns. The total weight of the revolving structure was 825 tons and maximum elevation was 30°, giving a range of 28,900yds at a muzzle velocity of 2270fs.

Furious was to have mounted one 18in gun forward and one aft, and three guns were constructed (one as a spare). However, during her building stage, the forward mounting was suppressed in favour of a flight deck, although she did emerge with the 15in B aft. Its installation was very short-lived, however, as this mounting was also removed when she was again taken in hand, for complete conversion into an aircraft carrier. In August 1917, the Vice-Admiral, Dover, proposed that the three 18in guns (which were now unemployable at sea) should be mounted ashore on selected sites outside Nieuwpoort, to deal with German heavy batteries in the vicinity. The scheme entailed mounting the guns in special concrete emplacements on a slide that could elevate and be traversed by 'bottle-screws' through an arc of 6° each side of centre. The front of the emplacement was to take the form of a turf-covered concrete dome, with a gunport through which the barrel projected. To enable the maximum amount of erection work to be carried out away from the firing zone, some parts were to be assembled elsewhere and transported by rail as near as possible to the site, thereafter being moved along a special broad-gauge track on wheels specially designed for the transportable sections. The all-up weight of the transportable section was 210 tons. Inspection of the site showed that the scheme was feasible. The carriage and gunslide was to have a maximum elevation of 45° with a fixed loading angle of 10°. Power was to be derived from a 'Hele-Shaw' hydraulic pump with a 105hp petrol engine as the prime mover but only ramming, elevating and ammuni-

The light battlecruiser *Furious* as completed, with her single 18in mounting aft, that forward having been replaced by an aircraft flying-off deck. Later she was fully converted to an aircraft carrier, the second mounting being removed. The 18in guns were subsequently provided with new mountings and re-employed in monitors. *Conway Picture Library*

tion handling were to be power operated. The breech was to be hand worked and the recoiling parts were to have pneumatic run-out arrangements.

The scheme was taken in hand by Elswick in September 1917 and, at the same time, an alternative proposal was made to mount the three guns in monitors should the military situation so develop as to make this more suitable. Although a ship installation would entail much more work, a mobility of the guns themselves would thus be effected. The ship-fit idea was taken up in October of the same year, although work progressed in parallel on certain parts of the shore site equipment in case this should be reverted to. No major changes were made to the carriage and elevating structure design but a lightweight box-shaped open-ended gunshield was designed for the ships. Its total weight was 350 tons and two 2pdr pompoms were mounted on the roof. Three 12in armed monitors – *Lord Clive, General Wolfe* and *Prince Eugene* – were earmarked for the new weapon and, because they already had a hydraulic installation, this was adapted for the 18in mounting. Hence the breech became a power-worked item while training was effected by means of a fixed piston and cylinder, giving a mounting slew of 10° each side of centre. A hydraulic bollard (for shell handling) was also provided.

The mounting was sited athwartships at the after end of the forecastle deck in such a way that its centre of training was at 90° to the fore and aft line which necessitated all bombardments being carried out to starboard and, because monitors were inherently shallow-draught vessels, special arrangements for the ammunition had to be made. The complete outfit of 60 shells was arranged to rest on chocks on the upper deck (ie, one deck below the mounting) and were divided into two groups of 30, one on each side of the ship. Overhead rails, with hand-worked grabs and travellers, were fitted to plumb the stowages and led to a waiting tray under the left-rear of the gunmounting. The shells were then lifted from the waiting tray by a radial crane and hydraulic bollard through a hatch in the forecastle deck and placed on the loading tray.

A normal charge for the gun was 630lb of cordite, split into one-sixth charges weighing 105lb each; in addition a special 'supercharge' of 165lb was provided. A full supercharge was made up of 5 normal charges and one heavy, giving a total cordite weight of 690lb. Stowage was for 72 full charges (including the supercharges) arranged in a group of 18 'tanks' on the forecastle deck, each 'tank' holding 4 full charges. The charges, in their cases, were placed in watertight tubes, fitted with doors, provided in the 'tank' and were then surrounded by water. A steam heating and circulatory system was designed to keep the 'tanks' – and thus the cordite – at an optimum temperature. The maximum range of the gun, at 45° elevation and using a supercharge, was 40,500yds (firing an 8crh projectile). Loading was at 10° and there was a minimum firing angle of 22°.

The charges were taken from the tanks two at a time, placed on a covered bogie running on rails on the forecastle deck and sent to the gun. The rails were arranged like a continuous railway loop with a single siding, and when emptied they were run forward again for recharging. Three bogies ran on this railway, thus providing the 6 one-sixth charges for each firing. Although the disposition of the special 165lb charges is not definitely known, it seems very likely that they were stowed in the siding.

At the beginning of October 1917, a firm decision was made to go ahead with the monitor installation and Elswick promised to have the first mounting ready for ship fitting by early March 1918 with the other two following at intervals of one month. It was thought inadvisable to introduce the weapon into service without proof testing and accordingly it was arranged that the first mounting should be erected at Silloth for a firing trial, concurrent with trials for the supercharge of cordite. The mounting, if trials were satisfactory, would then be ready for installation afloat (with an option, still open, on a shore site) and it was agreed that the other two mountings could be installed without preliminary proof.

To meet the expected delivery dates of the mountings, *Lord Clive* was ordered to Portsmouth to be taken in hand early in December 1917, followed by *Prince Eugene*. In both, the work programme was planned so that they would be ready for the mountings by the end of February 1918. The third monitor was to be started after completion of the first. Unfortunately, Elswick were unable to meet the promised dates, which caused a serious situation not only because the weapons could not enter service but also because the monitors waiting in Portsmouth could be ill-spared. Thus, early in March 1918, *Lord Clive* and *Prince Eugene* were sent back to Dover, more or less ready for the mountings, leaving *General Wolfe* in Portsmouth to be fitted out. At the same time, the option to mount the guns ashore was given up and all work on the shore side fittings ceased.

The first trial at Silloth did not take place until 17 May 1918 and that, because the rammer was found to be too weak, was abandoned. A larger rammer engine was subsequently fitted and a successful trial (apart from a few minor defects, to be rectified during ship-fitting) was carried out 26 May. The mounting was then transported to Portsmouth, where it arrived on 29 June. Then, however, *General Wolfe* was not quite ready to receive it and, because the other two ships could not be spared from the Belgian coast, further delays occurred.

Installation eventually took place in July 1918 and a trial was carried out off the Isle of Wight on 17 August. It was very successful and a rate of fire of 1 round in four minutes was achieved even though the task of shell handling proved (not surprisingly) to be extremely laborious.

General Wolfe then proceeded to Dover and carried out several useful bombardments against German positions. On 28 September a prolonged, rapid series of no fewer than 45 rounds was fired at the remarkable average rate of 1 round every 2½ minutes. On the following day another bombardment was carried out, without any breakdowns necessitating ceasing fire. All the ammunition supply arrangements functioned satisfactorily and, since the specification was for 1 round per six minutes, the complete set-up performed well above the design requirements.

The second mounting was fitted in *Lord Clive*, which carried out gun trials on 13 October before proceeding to Dover, but by the time she arrived the operations on the Belgian coast were over. Indeed, although the third mounting had already been delivered to Portsmouth, its installation in *Prince Eugene* was cancelled on 22 October 1918. Despite the disappointment caused by the delays in the project (mostly the outcome of over-optimistic forecasting) the weapons certainly proved their technical viability.

So far as the shore-site equipment is concerned, this was taken over by the Army to be put to similar use in their own Coast Defence equipments (one mounting eventually went to Dover to take a 14in Mk VII gun for firing across the Channel, and parts of a second probably went to Dover too), but work was never undertaken to prepare the actual sites at Nieuwpoort. There is a popular misconception that the three 18in guns were sent to Singapore but, although this may indeed have been mooted at some time, they did not, in fact, leave Great Britain. Between 1921 and 1926, one 18in gun and mounting was installed at the Proof and Experimental Establishment at Silloth and was used for cordite proofing tests. The remaining two mountings (ex-monitor-fitted) were similarly installed in P & E Establishments, at Shoeburyness and Yantlet on Grain Island, and again were used for proof testing. Registered Nos 2 and 3 were sold for scrap in 1933 but Reg No 1 survived until being finally sold for scrap in 1947.

The 18in was the largest calibre gun employed in the Royal Navy and no other nation, other than the Japanese, actually produced such a large calibre weapon for Fleet purposes. As an extension of the 15in mounting it was, in many ways, the end of a distinct era of development, for the next heavy gun mounting that the British designed was of totally different concept.

6 The Last of the Big Guns

After the First World War, the stage was set for a new naval race in which the principal participants were Britain, the USA and Japan. Large capital ship construction programmes were anticipated by all three and, naturally, these ships would have carried a new generation of heavy gun mountings. The Washington Conference of 1922 brought an end to these plans but one country, Britain, did gain the opportunity actually to construct the first of her immediate postwar heavy mounting designs.

The mounting concerned, the 16in Mk I triple, was intended for a class of 48,000-ton battlecruisers the construction of which had been halted by the Washington Treaty. However, as both the USA and Japan were allowed to complete a few of the 16in-gun ships which they had under construction, Britain, whose fleet possessed no capital ships with guns heavier than 15in calibre, requested and obtained the right to construct two new 16in-gun ships to maintain the balance of power. These ships, which became the *Nelson* and *Rodney*, utilised the mountings designed for the battlecruisers (which were known officially as the 'G3' design and unofficially as the super-*Hood*s) but, owing to the new Treaty limit of 35,000 tons on battleship displacements, they had to be accommodated in a much smaller hull.

The Treaty also set the upper limit for battleship guns at 16in calibre, to prevent further escalation on the lines of the recent 'calibre race' and, with the exception of the two British ships, banned the construction of capital ships for ten years, after which the replacement of over-age ships could begin. This last clause was extended to 1937 by the First London Naval Conference of 1930, but France and Italy refused to ratify the resulting Treaty thus releasing themselves for capital ship construction immediately. In 1934 Japan declared that she would not be bound by the limits agreed at the next naval disarmament conference (the Second London Naval Treaty, due to take effect in 1936) and during the last of the prewar years the remaining Treaty restrictions were steadily eroded until completely abandoned on the outbreak of the Second World War.

The Treaty restrictions, combined with the serious financial problems of the time, meant that, compared with the period prior to World War I, relatively few heavy gun mountings were produced even by the largest of the naval powers. Those that were produced were among the most sophisticated pieces of heavy engineering ever designed but, just as the Second World War was to mark the end of the battleship era, so, naturally, did it mark the end of the big naval gun.

The first of this final generation of heavy weapons – that is, weapons designed after the First World War – was, then, the British 16in. The next mounting to appear was, despite the restrictions of the Treaty of Versailles,

The two forward triple turrets of the Italian battleship *Roma*, the last ship of the *Littorio* class to be completed. The guns were 15in/50 weapons with a maximum range of 46,200yds at 35° elevation. *Conway Picture Library*

produced by Germany: this was the triple 11in mounting designed for the *Deutschland* class armoured ships (or 'pocket-battleships' as they were dubbed by journalists). Nominally of 10,000 tons, which at the time was the maximum allowed to Germany, but actually of 12,000 tons, the first of the class, *Deutschland*, was laid down in 1929 and her two sisters, *Admiral Scheer* and *Admiral Graf Spee*, in 1931 and 1932 respectively. It is believed that, at their maximum speed of 26kts, the class suffered from severe vibration, but this was not known when they emerged. However, with an endurance of 10,000 miles and a main armament of six 11in guns, it was clear that they were likely to be most dangerous commerce raiders. On a ship-to-ship basis these vessels could outgun any 8in cruiser and outrun any contemporary battleship; only Britain's three battlecruisers could better them in both respects.

The French were particularly worried by this re-emergence of German naval power and, as an answer to the *Deutschland* class, laid down the battlecruisers *Dunkerque* and *Strasbourg* in 1932 and 1934 respectively. Armed with two quadruple 13in mountings of most interesting design, they were faintly reminiscent of the British *Nelson* and *Rodney* in that they had all their main armament forward and their secondary armament aft, but the Gallic hulls were more sweetly proportioned – and, although weakly protected, they were a great deal faster.

This new construction by France initiated the second stage in the European naval race that was now developing. Italy had long maintained a strong rivalry with France for command of the Mediterranean and, feeling obliged to counter this new capital ship construction, laid down the battleships *Littorio* and *Vittorio Veneto* in 1934. They were armed with three triple mountings which carried new high-velocity 15in/50cal guns weighing 108 tons and firing a 1947lb AP projectile. Unlike earlier Italian heavy gun mountings, which were hydraulically operated, the 15in triple was powered by Ward Leonard electrics, the geared elevation drive providing 35° elevation and 5° depression. The total weight of the revolving structure of these mountings was 1570 tons.

In the same year as the Italians commenced the *Littorio*, Germany laid down the battlecruiser *Gneisenau* followed by a sister, the *Scharnhorst*, in 1935. Armed with a slightly modified version of the triple 11in mounted in the *Deutschland* class, they were seen as direct rivals to the two French battlecruisers. In 1935 France laid down *Richelieu* and *Jean Bart*, 15in-gun battleships intended to counter both Italian and German new construction, while Germany laid down the 15in-gun *Bismarck*.

The British viewed these events on the Continent with considerable concern for, although accepting that new construction must recommence after the Second London Naval Conference, they had no wish to see size of either the battleships or their guns escalate – both likely if the conference failed. In fact, Britain proposed, and actually succeeded in obtaining, a further reduction in the battleship gun calibre limitation to 14in when the conference took place in 1935–36. However, none of the European navies nor, more importantly, Japan was a signatory to this Treaty and the USA insisted on the restoration of the 16in gun calibre if Japan had failed to agree to the new limitation by April 1937. In addition, an escalator clause was added allowing the displacement limit to be raised should any non-signatory build vessels outside the Treaty limits. Unfortunately, Britain could not await the outcome of these qualifications before pressing ahead with her battleship programme and, during 1937, laid down the five 14in-gun battleships of the *King George V* class, even as the continued silence of Japan was causing a reversion to the 16in limit. The reason the British did not change immediately to a 16in gun for these new ships was simply that the delay involved would have been unacceptable – rearmament had already been dangerously delayed. Moreover, the facilities available for both ship and armament design and manufacture had been seriously eroded in the interwar years. The 14in mounting design had absorbed a considerable amount of time and effort and the construction of these weapons had already begun, the armament normally being ordered before the ship for which it was intended as it actually took longer to construct. In the event, the next group of British battleships, the *Lion* class of 40,000 tons and armed with nine 16in guns, were never built; their construction was suspended shortly after the

BRITISH 16in Mk I TRIPLE MOUNTING

1 Counterbalance weight
2 Rammer engine casing
3 'Churn' levers
4 Rangefinder
5 Telescopic rammer tube casing
6 Tilting tray
7 Position of breech at full depression (–3°)
8 Gunhouse roof support pillar
9 Rear collars
10 Recoil cylinder
11 Sliding pipes for hydraulics, air blast and 'wash-out squirt' to breech
12 Trunnion cap
13 Mantlet plate
14 Locking bolt
15 'Walking' pipes to elevating structure
16 Training base roller
17 Turret clip
18 Elevating cylinder trunnion
19 Exhaust tank
20 Steam heating pipes
21 Cable winding gear
22 Washout squirt tanks
23 Turret drenching tanks
24 Hydraulic accumulator
25 Shell room ('X' turret)
26 Watertight door
27 Shell room rammer tray
28 Pivoting tray
29 Revolving shell scuttle
30 Trunk guide roller
31 Cordite swinging tray
32 Central pivot
33 Cordite cage tilting cylinders
34 Shell bogie (in horizontal position)
35 Cordite rammer engine
36 Flash door
37 Cordite roller-conveyor
38 Triple cordite charges
39 Athwartships cordite roller conveyor
40 Cordite stowage bay
41 Shell bogie (tilted upright)
42 Shell room ('A' turret)
43 Revolving shell scuttle
44 Cordite hoist trunk
45 'Wash-out squirt' air bottles
46 Training engine and drive shaft
47 Shell striking down trunk
48 Air blast bottles
49 Training rack
50 Centre gun shell hoist trunk
51 Left gun shell hoist trunk
52 Breech in full recoil at maximum elevation (+40°)
53 Drive pinion and twin training pinion
54 Elevation buffer stop
55 Tilting engine
56 Gunhouse vents

A Upper (forecastle) deck
B Main deck
C Middle deck
D Beam line
E Lower deck
F Platform deck
G Inner bottom
H Outer bottom

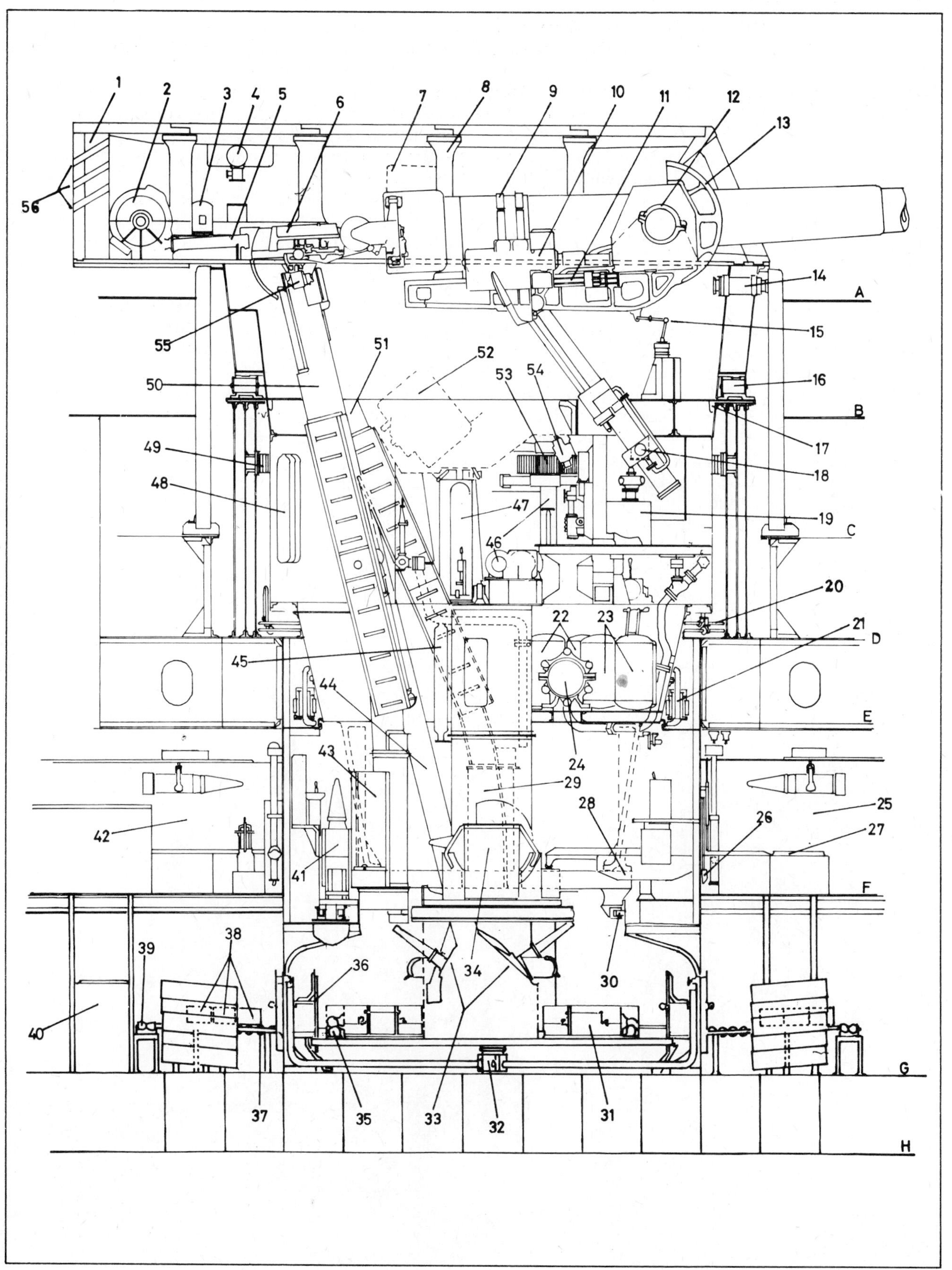
1
2
3
4
5
6
7
8
9
10
11
12
13
14
15
16
17
18
19
20
21
22
23
24
25
26
27
28
29
30
31
32
33
34
35
36
37
38
39
40
41
42
43
44
45
46
47
48
49
50
51
52
53
54
55
56
A
B
C
D
E
F
G
H

outbreak of war and, with heavy demands on material and manpower elsewhere, the capacity to complete them never became available.

The Americans, whose major concern was the Japanese, were content to await events before commencing their new construction programme, and, following the failure of the Japanese to agree to abide by the 14in limitation, modified their existing design from twelve 14in guns to nine 16in. The resultant vessels, which became *North Carolina* and *Washington*, were laid down in 1937 and 1938 respectively. They were followed in 1939–40 by the four ships of the *South Dakota* class, which had the same armament but were of modified design. In 1938, following the failure to extract any information from the Japanese as to exactly what new construction they contemplated, the USA, Britain and France invoked the escalator clause and raised the battleship displacement limit to 45,000 tons. Britain reacted immediately, altering the preparatory designs for the *Lion* class from 35,000 to 40,000 tons, a self-imposed lower limit than that now allowed, which it was hoped the European powers would respect and not exceed. The USA, however, did not take advantage of the increased limit until 1940 when the first ships of the 45,000-ton *Iowa* class were laid down; again, these ships were armed with three triple 16in mountings, but they were faster than their predecessors and carried 16in/50 rather than 16in/45 guns.

In fact, what the Japanese were doing so secretly was almost certainly beyond what anybody in the West imagined, although much concern was expressed at the possibility that they might exceed the 16in calibre. In 1937 they laid down the two largest and most heavily armed battleships ever built, the 64,000-ton *Yamato* and *Musashi*, which each mounted nine 18.1in guns. Two sister-ships were laid down in 1940 but the first, *Shinano*, was converted to an aircraft carrier while under construction and the second was cancelled.

The last years of peace saw the final acts of the European naval race. Germany laid down a sister to *Bismarck*, the *Tirpitz*, in 1936; Italy laid down two more *Littorio* class ships, the *Roma* and *Impero*, in 1938; and France a third *Richelieu*, the *Clemenceau*, in 1939. The last two were never completed, while several other battleships projected by France and Germany never progressed beyond the design stage. Other battleships were also planned by the USA, Japan and Russia but none was to see service and the prewar-designed ships proved to be the last vessels of the big gun era.

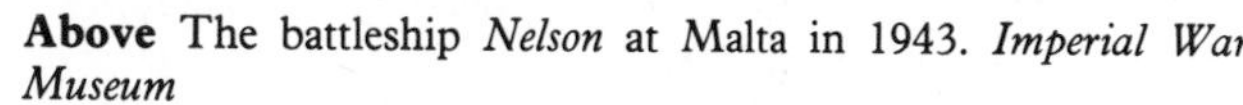

Above The battleship *Nelson* at Malta in 1943. *Imperial War Museum*
Left HMS *Rodney* carrying out a shore bombardment during the Second World War. *Conway Picture Library*

THE BRITISH 16in Mk I GUN IN THE 16in Mk I MOUNTING

Warships cannot be judged by their guns alone. The best mounting in the world, be it gun, missile or whatever, is brought to nought if it is imperfectly directed, and none can ever be truly evaluated in isolation from its control system. Before examining the detail of the British 16in triple, therefore, the reader must be introduced to some external factors that influenced its design.

For a number of reasons the early heavy calibre guns were not designed to make full use of their maximum range capabilities. In the first place there was no point in attempting to engage a target that could not be seen; in the second, no matter how high the gun director might be sited, accurate range could only be determined by optical range-finder; and thirdly, unless the gun was directed by a comprehensive computer, the greater the range, the less was the chance of an accurate fall of shot – the time of flight became progressively longer, thus making the prediction of the target's future position more and more problematical. In addition, trajectory at high elevations took a shell into the effects of upper winds, whose speeds and direction are difficult to determine.

The limited maximum elevation of the original 15in mounting allowed the designers to adopt a scheme of loading which could be carried out (on paper, at least) at any angle of elevation. In the event, it was found more practical to bring the gun to a reasonable elevation but this in no way alters the fact that it *could* be loaded at any angle within the limits of its arc of movement. However, by 1921, when the battlecruiser order was placed, many important changes had taken place. As an outcome of the deliberations of the Admiralty Fire Control Committee, convened in 1919 to interpret the lessons of the war, the somewhat scattered and rudimentary fire-control instruments were redesigned into a comprehensive calculator, called the Admiralty Fire Control Table Mk I. An inherently excellent device, it could produce a continuous and accurate prediction of target future position, far beyond the maximum ranges hitherto accepted. Its successors were the backbone of Royal Navy surface gunnery until the demise of the big ship. In addition, the benefit of a high-site director, combining its own rangefinder, had long been recognised (and indeed implemented in *Hood*), and this feature, too, was to be included in the new ships.

The natural outcome of these fire control improvements was the call for a mounting the maximum elevation of which matched the increased range capability of the system as a whole. Thus the new turret was to have three 16in guns, each able to elevate independently to 40°, for although 45° theoretically gives maximum absolute range – as we have seen – the range increase above 40° is small compared to the engineering problem of designing a 45° mounting. After all, the higher the muzzle elevates, the deeper the breech must sink into a gunwell cut in the turret platform, due allowance being made, at the same time, for the gun's considerable setback in full recoil.

It goes without saying that the best gun in the world, directed by the best fire control system in the world, will yet be rendered useless if it cannot be efficiently supplied with ammunition. The gunloading cage of the 15in, moving as it did on a radial arc behind the breech, was an ideal solution (so long as the maximum elevation was low), but this principle could not be implemented on a gun with a maximum of 40° and a complete re-think on shell and cordite supply had to take place. How the designers met the requirements will be seen when the ammunition routes are described in detail.

Some of the foregoing might seem at first sight to be a divergence from the subject, but taken in context, each point has relevance when considering the British 16in triple. It will be equally relevant to look briefly at the overall design of the only two ships to mount this, the largest calibre gun in service with the Royal Navy in the Second World War.

To the reader who is not conversant with the warships built for the Royal Navy between 1919 and 1939, the expression 'Cherry Tree class' will probably be meaningless. This epithet, in fact, was given to *Nelson* and *Rodney* because they were 'cut down by Washington' and referred, of course, to the mutilation of the original battlecruiser design caused by the limitations of the Washington Naval Treaty. Getting the triple turrets of the 48,000-ton battlecruiser design into a well-balanced 35,000-ton battleship design presented substantial problems. With the benefit of hindsight, it may well have been more practical to reduce the main armament to six 16in, disposed in triple turrets forward and aft. However, the designers were obviously anxious to retain the intended number of major guns and juggled with their disposition and protection within the tonnage confines of the Treaty. The staff solution resulted in all three triple turrets being mounted forward of the superstructure on a disproportionately long forecastle in order that the magazines could be grouped together within the main armoured citadel. The vastness of the forecastle was further accentuated by the diminutive quarterdeck, giving the ships a cut short appearance that reflected the design transition from the intended battlecruisers.

Like the First World War British capital ships, the new vessels were given an armoured control position immediately forward of the bridge. A popular misconception was that this tower was the nerve centre of the gunnery system when, in fact, it was the tertiary director for the 16in armament. The primary DCT stood on the main superstructure tower – otherwise known as 'Queen Anne's Mansions' – with a second, duplicate, DCT aft. The latter was not, however, particularly well sited.

Despite the controversy that followed the ships throughout their careers, that they were massively strong is undeniable. Both survived considerable action damage during the war and it was *Rodney*'s 16in guns that wrought such fearsome havoc on the already crippled German battleship *Bismarck*.

The total weight of the rotating mass of one 16in turret was about 1100 tons, a further 320 tons being added by the three gun barrels. Much of this weight was taken up by the gunhouse armour which was 16in thick on the vulnerable front face, with lesser (but still considerable) thicknesses on the sides, roof and rear. A gun, complete with its breech mechanism, weighed 108 tons, the outer barrels were 16ft apart, and all three were independently elevated by their own hydraulic piston, working in a trunnioned cylinder. It is emphasised that the weight quoted does not take into account either the off-mounting equipment or the 16in thick armoured barbette that surrounded the turret trunk. The maximum training speed was 3° per second, but this was reduced (by gun drill) to 2° per second when the ship's maximum roll exceeded 5°. To achieve infinitely variable training speeds between zero and maximum, one of a pair of 400hp hydraulic engines drove, through reduction gears, to two sets of double pinions, set almost diametrically opposite each other. The second engine was automatically de-clutched from the power drive so that one alone was in engagement, with the other as a reserve.

Unlike the comparatively simple (and very successful) twin 15in, the ammunition supply arrangements in the big triples were extremely complex. They shared several features with the contemporary and similarly over-complicated 8in twin, clearly indicating the design philosophies of the day. Bedevilled by the Staff Requirement for a high maximum elevation, the 'gungineers' had to

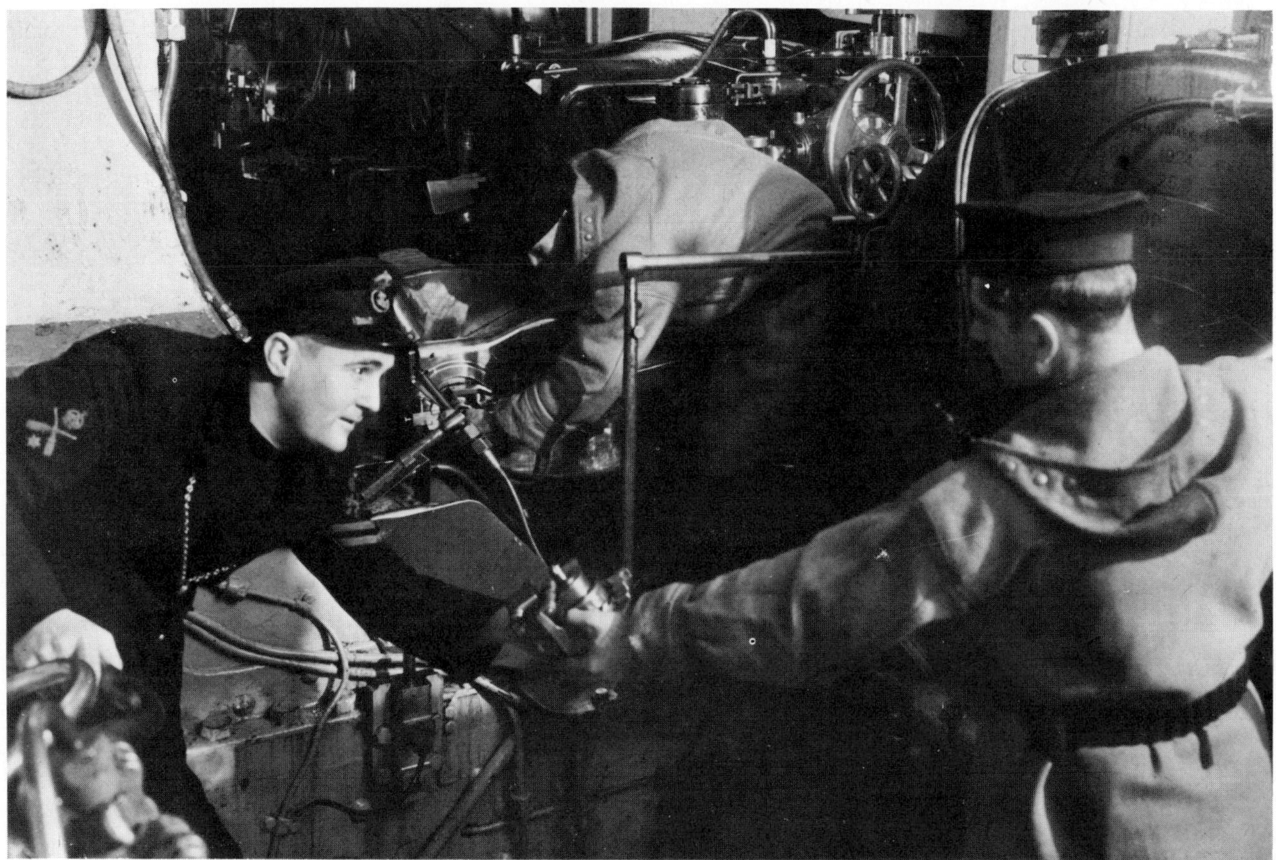

The interior of the gunhouse of a triple 16in Mk I mounting. The breeches of all three guns are visible. *Imperial War Museum.*

revert to the earlier practice of loading at a fixed angle, to which the gun was returned as soon as it had fired.

This system of supply was quite different from earlier British practice, being based on US mounting design with both shell and cordite transported direct from handing rooms to gunhouse. There were separate shell and cordite hoists for each gun, both hoisting their loads in a vertical instead of a horizontal position as in earlier mountings. The shell hoists were of the pusher type with a maximum capacity of four shells, while the cordite was raised by wire rope. The system involved tipping both shell and cordite through 90° at the top and bottom of each hoist. In the gunhouse the ammunition arrived to one side of each breech from whence it was transferred sideways, in sequence, to the rear of the gun and rammed into the chamber[1].

In the preliminary design stage, it was intended to provide cordite supply system similar to that for the shell, but when Britain was forced to abandon the battlecruiser programme these arrangements were completely revised. The outcome was a disadvantageous compromise, for, while a column of shells would always be available (once the hoists had been loaded), the cordite charge had to be brought, in one load, direct from the magazine to the gunhouse.

Because of the vulnerability of cordite, it was usual for the magazine to be afforded maximum protection by being the lowest of the compartments and therefore almost always immediately below the shell room – although the twin 15in (other than those in *Vanguard*) was one exception. The Royal Navy learned bitter lessons during the First World War about the lethality of cordite flash, following enemy shells exploding inboard, and elaborate precautions were taken thereafter, while a number of emergency modifications were hurriedly carried out to existing gun mountings. As has been mentioned, the cordite was, for ease of handling, made up into bags each weighing approximately 100lb, and six were required to make up a full charge for the 16in. The bags were made from silk, because this material was totally consumed when the cordite exploded in the chamber and therefore left no dangerous, smouldering residue. Within the magazine, the charges were kept in flashtight cases and were only removed from them immediately before being loaded into the magazine exit point. Once exposed from their protective cases, the charges were highly vulnerable and were quickly placed into a flashtight hopper. This worked on an airlock principle such that there could never be a free path for flash

[1] A detailed description of the loading arrangements is given in the Appendices.

from the hoist trunking to the handing room: the hopper was either open to the handing room and closed to the trunk or vice versa.

Quite apart from the inherent complications of the gear there were nearly 50 mechanical interlocks associated with the loading arrangements of each gun – and, of course, everthing was in triplicate, so to speak. Even a cursory glance at the formidable list of mechanical interlocks given in the Appendices should be sufficient to make the reader aware of the vast complications of this mounting. Looking back, it may well be that the designers were subjected to the demands of a non-technical naval staff and found the interlocking problems nothing more than an interesting exercise in technical ingenuity.

Naturally enough, the three guns themselves loomed very large in the confines of the gunhouse. Their trunnions, working in bearings, were carried in heavy trunnion supports bolted to the gunhouse floor. The supports for the centre gun were particularly large, extending almost to the gunhouse rear, because they also supported the inner trunnion pins of the left and right guns.

The barrels were carried on two cradles, which moved to the rear on the slide when the gun recoiled. The slide could be regarded as a platform, pivoted at the trunnions and elevated by a hydraulic piston. Side by side, underneath the rear cradle, were two recoil buffer cylinders with pistons whose rods were fixed to the non-recoiling structure. Thus, when the gun fired and 'sat back', the cylinders were drawn over the pistons giving the necessary buffering action. At the same time a ram, attached to a lug underneath the front cradle, moved backwards into a slide-mounted air cylinder, increasing its already high air pressure, so when the recoil had been arrested by the recoil buffers the air pressure, acting on the ram, forced it forward and thrust the gun back to its 'run out' position. The static air pressure in the recuperator, as it was called, was sufficiently high to keep the gun forward, even at maximum elevation. It is worth remembering that when the gun was fired at 40° elevation the recuperator had the uphill task of pushing 106 tons outwards to return the gun from its recoiled position.

Triple sliding pipes, like telescopes, carried hydraulic pressure to, and exhaust from, the power-operated breech, the third pipe being used for high-pressure air to the air blast gear. The breech itself was of conventional design, with an interrupted thread. Its lock-and-box slide opened automatically with the main breech block, but was closed manually (by No 2) when the tube had been inserted.

Beneath the gun, in the rear of the trunnions, was the gunwell, which accommodated the breech end at high elevations, the elevating cylinder occupying the forward part. Immediately behind the arc swept by the breech as it descended were the twin trunkings of the shell and cordite hoists, and bolted to the 3in thick gunhouse floor, behind the gunwell, was the rammer casing. The rammer itself consisted of seven telescopic sections, covering a heavy chain. The chain was wound around a drum and when the appropriate control lever was put to 'Ram' a hydraulic engine revolved the drum, unwinding the chain and extending the telescopic sections. The rammer casing was angled upwards at 3° to the deck and thus matched the fixed loading angle of the gun. Close to the rammer casings were the loading control levers, mentioned earlier, and a seat was provided for the captain of the turret, who was able to oversee all operations. A rangefinder, whose ends projected beyond the gunhouse sides, straddled all.

On the left-hand side there was a stowage position for three 6pdr sub-calibre guns. Each weighed about half a ton and it was quite a task to insert them into their parent gun barrels when a sub-calibre shoot was ordered. This type of practice firing was really only for the benefit of the fire control teams, for none of the normal loading arrangements was used and the 16in barrels were simply employed as carriers. The 6pdrs had their own small QF type breech which was loaded by hand with a combined shell and cartridge case. Another form of practice was reduced charge firing, which employed the normal calibre ammunition but less cordite. This saved expenditure of cordite while exercising the whole gunnery department and also lessened barrel wear as the muzzle velocity went down *pro rata*. In both cases, suitable changeover arrangements were provided on the fire control instruments to correct the gun elevation and training for the non-standard conditions.

On the right-hand side of the gunhouse there was an enclosed compartment, called 'the silent cabinet', manned by control personnel. These included the officer of the quarters, communication ratings and the crew of the local director sight (LDS). The sight projected through an aperture in the side of the turret armour and included a prism system so that the operators' line of sight was parallel to the bores of the guns. The local director sight-setter received range from the turret rangefinder and RE ('Range to Elevation') gear and converted it to gun elevation, which was transmitted to the three elevation receivers via a changeover switch. Datum elevation was provided by the LDS layer but the LDS trainer had an auxiliary training control and actually trained the turret in quarters firing. There were also range and rate officers and all the personnel had seats.

The rotating mass of the turret rested on a circle of steel rollers, running between machined paths, one on the underside of the moving structure and one on a heavy ring bulkhead within the main armoured barbette. It was to this ring bulkhead that the toothed training rack, with which the training pinions engaged, was fixed. The training pinions were set fairly high above the deck of a compartment divided diametrically by the training power drives. The rear half was occupied by the six ammunition hoists and the two striking-down trunks, together with nine large high-pressure air bottles (for the air blast gear and as a reserve supply for the recuperators). The other half held the twin training engines, the hydro-dynamos (for firing circuit and fire control supplies in emergency conditions), the gunhouse exhaust trunking and the control positions for the layers and turret trainer.

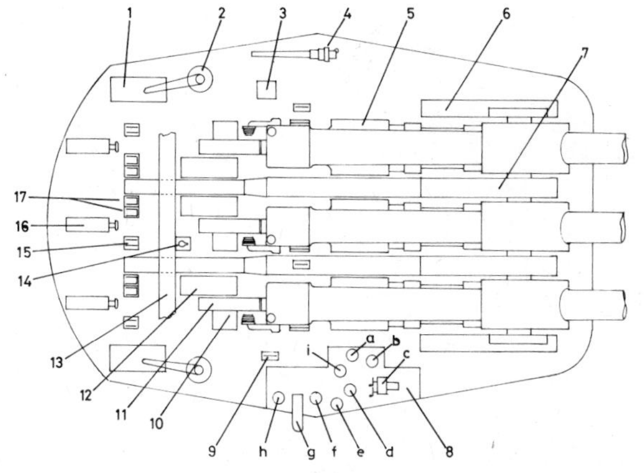

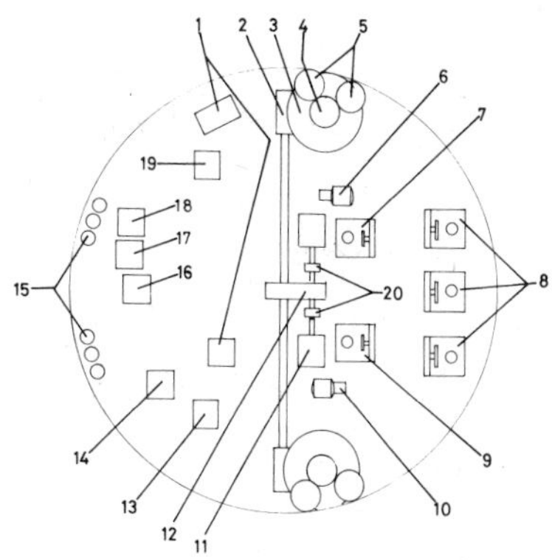

BRITISH 16in Mk I MOUNTING – SCHEMATIC GUNHOUSE ARRANGEMENTS

1 Ready-use shell bin
2 Radial crane
3 Striking-down hatch to return ammunition
4 Triple stack of sub-calibre (practice) barrels
5 Left-hand recoil cylinder
6 Outer trunnion support
7 Inner trunnion support
8 Control compartment:
a Telephone operator
b Range officer
c Sight-setter
d Rate officer
e Dumeresq operator
f Layer
g Local director sight (LDS)
h Trainer
i Officer of the quarters (OOQ)
9 Firing circuit interceptor (circuit breaker)
10 Tilting platform (tilted down)
11 Shell tilting bucket
12 Cordite tilting bucket
13 Support beam for rangefinder
14 Captain of the turret's position
15 Hoist control levers
16 Telescopic rammer casing
17 Loading control 'churn levers'

BRITISH 16in Mk I – TRAINING ENGINE SPACE

1 Striking-down trunks for returning ammunition
2 Training worm
3 Training wormwheel
4 Drive pinion
5 Twin training pinions
6 Hydro-generator (firing circuits)
7 Trainers' position
8 Layers' positions
9 Range followers' position
10 Hydro-generator (local fire-control circuits)
11 400hp hydraulic training engine
12 Transfer gearbox
13 Right gun shell hoist trunk
14 Right gun cordite hoist trunk
15 High-pressure air storage cylinders
16 Centre gun shell hoist trunk
17 Centre gun cordite hoist trunk
18 Left gun cordite hoist trunk
19 Left gun shell hoist trunk
20 Interlocked training engine drive selector clutches

The turret trunk tapered away, in a more or less conical fashion, as it descended towards the lower quarters. Beneath the training engine space was a smaller compartment containing the turret ventilation fans but thereafter it was fully occupied by the ammunition trunkings. Under all, on the centre of rotation, was a heavy swivel connection that received hydraulic pressure from, and returned exhaust to, an off-mounting steam-driven pump unit. As will have been observed, all the machinery was hydraulic – even to the emergency generators.

Although the elevating gear was fairly straightforward in 'A' and 'B' turrets and had the usual style of automatic cut-off at the limits of elevation and depression, the third turret (called 'X' incidentally and not 'Q' or 'C') needed most complex safety arrangements. When trained fore and aft, its muzzles lay beneath the overhang of 'B' turret so its elevating gear had to include the means of preventing it elevating under the overhang of 'B', depressing into the overhang of 'B', and training into the overhang of 'B' at the critical elevation.

EARLY PROBLEMS

When a mounting of this size was built, it was usual to carry out what was called a 'pit trial'. The complete assembly, from magazine level to gunhouse, was erected in a deep pit containing a mock-up of the internal arrangements which were to surround the weapon itself in its parent ship. It was fully tested in all functional respects and then, amazingly, broken down into components and reassembled in the building vessel. The pit trial was always important but never more so than with a new design, for it was then that many faults revealed themselves which could be rectified by incorporating modifications of one kind or another.

However, in the case of the triple 16in, no complete pit trial was conducted, besides which three radical changes were made to the design:

1 The hydraulic pressure medium was changed from water to oil because, it having become obvious that much of the shell hoist mechanism would be inaccessible, it was thought that the natural leakage of oil into the trunks would provide a 'bonus' lubrication effect

2 Independent shell bogies were abandoned, resulting in the guns only being capable of being loaded more or less simultaneously

HMS *Rodney* in 1944. *Ministry of Defence (Navy).*

3 The original cordite bogies were replaced by a skip-cage

The mountings were installed in *Nelson* and *Rodney* during 1926 and 1927 and the gear immediately began to give considerable trouble. In July 1927 *Rodney*'s roller paths showed that the inner edge of the lower paths were cutting into the flanges of the turret rollers so, for safety's sake, the maximum training speed was reduced. An immediate inspection of *Nelson*'s revealed the same fault. Both ships continued to operate their turrets, but at reduced training speeds, while a set of vertical rollers were manufactured to take the considerable side thrust of the rotating mass. The work commenced in 1928 but was not finally completed until October 1929. It was, however, successful and the training speed restrictions were lifted.

Other major modifications were made to the mountings:

1932 The shell handling room pivoting tray rammers in *Nelson*'s 'B' turret were changed from wire operation to hydraulic ram, and 'signal box' interlocks were introduced for all pivoting tray operations

1931 – 32 Arrangements for leading electric power on to the rotating structure were changed from cable winding gear to cable platform gear

1933 – 34 All turrets in both ships were modified as above

1933 – 34 The original automatic tray traverse mechanism in the gunhouse was changed as an outcome of a modification suggested by Chief Ordnance Artificer (COA) Waterson (thereafter known as 'Waterson's Mod')

May 1934 For the first time, *Nelson*'s mountings were simultaneously subjected to a test of prolonged firing of 16 rounds per gun

Dec 1934 A conference, attended by representatives of the Home Fleet, Admiralty and the gunnery experts from HMS *Excellent*, was held in *Nelson* to discuss material breakdowns

July 1935 The gun slide on the right of 'A' mounting in *Nelson* was found to be cracked, and similar cracks were found in the centre gun slide of 'B' mounting in *Rodney*

May – June 1936 Persistent shearing of the drives made it necessary to disconnect the shell scuttle drives from the shell hoist gear; thereafter they were rotated by hand and three extra men added to the mounting crew to operate them

A summary of the modifications in hand in 1938 can be found in the Appendices.

Fortunately, the bulk of the problems had been resolved, one way or another, by the outbreak of war in 1939, when the mounting had become as near a going concern as could be expected. The fact that it was only fitted in two ships inevitably meant that, while there were any number of 'fifteen-inch men' – at all levels of skill and rank – the sixteen-inch expertise was much thinner on the ground.

What the outcome of a straight ship-to-ship fight between *Rodney* and *Bismarck* would have been is a matter of conjecture, although one cannot help but think that the great German ship would have won, with her vastly superior speed and better main armament layout. Be that as it may, it was *Rodney*'s 16in that opened fire first in *Bismarck*'s last and fatal engagement at 0847 on 27 May 1941. By 1000, the British battleship was firing nine-gun broadsides at virtually point-blank range with horrifying results to *Bismarck*'s already shattered hull. Meanwhile, defects in the 14in mountings of *King George V* had reduced her main armament firepower to 20 per cent of maximum. Following so closely on the failure of the same mountings in *Prince of Wales* one can only feel grateful for the persistence of the design teams who struggled with the difficulties of the triple 16in between the wars – and not least to men like COA Waterson who, with many like him, knew the great weapons from centre pivot to gunhouse roof.

A matter of conjecture, too, is the form that the triple 16in for the *Lion* class battleships would have taken. Neither of the major gun mountings produced after the classic 15in came anywhere near matching its efficiency, and perhaps the stillborn successor to the 16in Mk 1 would have reverted to the First World War design.

For all the headaches, heartache and grief they undoubtedly caused all who came across them (and they could scarcely be overlooked) the 16in were regarded with grudging affection in the Service and with great pride by the British people.

THE GERMAN 11in SKC/34 IN THE DRH LC/34 MOUNTING AND THE 11in SKC/28 IN THE DRH LC/28 MOUNTING

Germany had lost a decade of continuity in heavy mounting design and, when she began to rearm seriously, she had neither the time nor, perhaps, the inclination to adventure into new concepts. However, the Germans lost little in leaning heavily on their dreadnought period experience when they produced their new mountings. Neither did they make any basic design changes between their two 11in triples and their 15in twin. In fact, the two triple 11in mountings were virtually identical and differed only in that the earlier version had thinner armour and guns of lighter construction.

Germany had been permitted by the contemporary naval treaties to commission up to six ships within the 10,000-ton displacement limit, and her original intention seems to have been to build six instead of what were in the event three 'pocket-battleships'. For her own reasons, these ideas were revised and the second group of six 11in triples formed the main armament of her two three-turreted battle-cruisers *Scharnhorst* and *Gneisenau* instead.

The general principles of the mountings' layout were similar to those of the 15in twin, described next, but there were, of course, differences created by the three-gun configuration and the lighter (and thus more easily handled) ammunition. Remote power control (RPC) was provided for elevation between the limits of 40° elevation and about 10° depression at a maximum speed of 8° per second. Auxiliary elevation speed was 2° and training speed, provided by an electric motor, 6° per second. The total revolving weight was in the order of 750 tonnes in the battlecruiser version (Drh LC/34) and about 630 tonnes in the other (Drh LC/28). The rate of fire was 7 rounds in 2 minutes.

Because the charges were comparatively light, no circumferential rings, as found in the 15in, were fitted around the trunk in the magazine. The main charges were conveyed along sliding channels by tongs and the fore charges were simply transported by hand.

The main hoists were electric and carried a two-layer charge cage, with the main charge above its partner. The hoists were direct from lower quarters to gunhouse, the left arriving between the left and centre guns and both centre and right between the right and centre guns. An electric auxiliary hoist was also fitted for each gun, that for the centre arriving immediately behind the breech, where its charges could be loaded by the normal rammer. However, the auxiliary hoists for the outer guns emerged behind and to one side of the breeches, from which position the ammunition was transported by overhead rails and tongs. Loading in both modes was at 2° elevation.

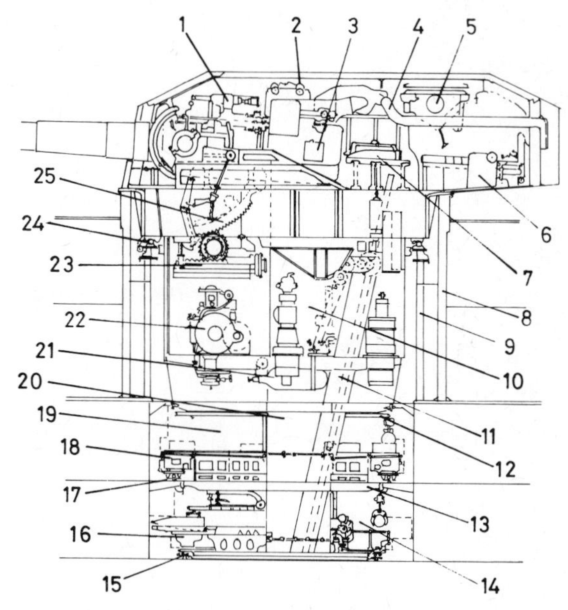

GERMAN 15in TWIN MOUNTING (*BISMARCK*)

1 Local gunsight telescope
2 Main cage cable sheaves
3 Breech mortice
4 Exhaust fean trunking
5 Rangefinder
6 Rammer
7 Shell on shell tray
8 Armoured barbette
9 Training base support trunk
10 Machinery compartment
11 Auxiliary ammunition hoist trunk
12 Overhead cordite rail
13 Overhead shell rail
14 Shell handing room
15 Shell ring rollers
16 Revolving shell ring
17 Cordite ring rollers
18 Revolving cordite ring
19 Cordite handing room
20 Main ammunition trunk
21 High pressure air cylinder
22 Hydraulic pump unit
23 Elevating gear
24 Training base ball bearing
25 Toothed elevating arc

THE GERMAN 15in SKL/34 IN THE DRH LC/34 MOUNTING

This mounting, fitted in the *Bismarck* and *Tirpitz*, was hydraulic in all main movements with the exception of training which was electric. Run-out was, of course, pneumatic in the usual German fashion. The elevation drive was by rack and pinion and the guns were normally coupled together as a pair and fired simultaneously. Hydraulic power was derived from two on-mounting pumps driven by electric motors, and working pressure was approximately 1000psi.

A machinery compartment below the gunhouse contained the hydraulic pump units, electric-motor starters, switch boards and so on, and also two hydraulic accumulators. The last were of the piston-cylinder type, with system pressure led to one side of a piston head and high-pressure air led to the other. They acted as reservoirs to meet any sudden demands on the hydraulic medium. In German mountings, this medium was always an approximately 50/50 mixture of distilled water and glycerine, with a small additive of castor oil (which acted as a lubricant). The British used water in their heavy mountings, with the exception of the 16in triple, but a medium grade mineral oil was the normal medium in all their contemporary light hydraulic mountings. The Germans disliked oil, believing it to hold a higher fire risk, and perhaps they were sensitive about its availability in wartime.

The elevation limits were 30° elevation to 5½° depression with a loading angle of 2½°; run-out was pneumatic; the breeches were hydraulic; maximum recoil was about 40in; and maximum elevation speed 6° per second. There was an auxiliary electric elevation drive, geared to the elevation arc under the gun cradle. The training drive was by conventional twin worm and worm-wheel geared to the training pinions. An alternative training drive was provided, maximum speeds being 5° and 1½° per second respectively. In addition, there was an emergency rig which could be coupled by a chain drive to the worm shaft. RPC was planned for the training motion but in the event was not fitted; however, elevation could be controlled by this automatic means. The revolving structure ran on the usual ball race and its total weight was 1064 tonnes.

The ammunition trunks ran directly from the lower quarters to the gunhouse and, like the British designs, the cages were lifted by hydraulic machinery and wire ropes and descended by their own weight. Cordite cars ran on a circumferential ring around the trunk at magazine level. The shells had similar shell rings and cars, from which they were transferred by rammers with magnetically operated claws.

The main hoist cage had a single tray for the main and fore charges and arrived in the gunhouse between the guns in the familiar German fashion. Transfer rammers thrust the ammunition rearwards into a waiting tray which then moved sideways into the loading position. These transfer rammers were hydraulic (with an auxiliary electric drive) and there was a separate rammer for each tray of the cage. The shell was brought into the ramming position by a pivoted loading tray, which moved through the arc of a circle the centre of which lay parallel to the gun bore. Above it was the charge tray, from which the forecharges were rolled into the pivoted loading tray down a bridging ramp, while the main charges had their own pivoted cartridge tray. These transfer movements were all hydraulic but, again, had an auxiliary electric drive. Ramming was carried out by a hydraulic, telescopic chain rammer whose casing was set in the side of the gunhouse, provision being made for hand ramming in the event of power failure. However, it took about a dozen men to operate the emergency device.

There was also a secondary supply system, routed to the rear of the guns. Shells and charges were raised vertically in the same trunk (and in the correct sequence for loading) by electric power and were delivered into a tilting tray directly in line with the breech and main rammer. Under normal loading conditions, a rate of fire of slightly better than 2 rounds per minute could be achieved.

The 15in twin of the *Bismarck* class was the final German heavy naval gun mounting to see active service, for history repeated itself. In the same way that many of her shipbuilding and weapon projects had been abandoned after Jutland, so were they in the 1940s. The loss of *Graf Spee* in 1939, *Bismarck* in 1941, the débâcle (from the German point of view) of the Battle of the Barents Sea and finally the destruction of *Scharnhorst* caused them once again to turn, almost exclusively, to undersea warfare. Nevertheless, the menace of *Tirpitz*, lying in a Norwegian fiord, was such that the Russian convoys needed distant heavy support; thus *Bismarck*'s sister effectively tied down a pair of Allied capital ships and often an aircraft carrier (together with their destroyer screens) simply by remaining where she was. After the *Bismarck* action, the British were not to be caught out a second time.

The Allied Mission which visited Germany in 1945 soon after hostilities had ceased seems to have been more interested than impressed by German mounting design and felt that anti-flash arrangements were, in general, much poorer than in the Royal Navy. The advantages of the wedge breech have already been discussed, but, from the writer's point of view, one of the strangest features of the normal mounting layout was the route of the main ammunition hoists, which complicated the transfers in the gunhouse, where, as it has been noted, anti-flash arrangements were probably at their weakest. Paradoxically, the auxiliary hoists, often arriving directly behind the breeches, appear to have been better directed than their main counterparts, and the transposition of their functions might have been of benefit. Having said that, however, overall loading cycle times were quite impressive.

Viewed from forward, the bridge and forward triple 11in Drh LC/28 mounting of the German armoured ship *Deutschland* (later renamed *Lützow*). *Conway Picture Library*

THE FRENCH 13in/50 GUN IN THE QUADRUPLE 13in MOUNTING

This mounting, fitted in the battlecruisers *Dunkerque* and *Strasbourg*, was designed by St Chamond and had elevation limits of 35° elevation to 5° depression and an intended rate of fire of about 3 rounds per gun per minute. The guns were grouped in pairs, in two separate cradles, and could be loaded at any angle. The revolving structure was supported on a ball race and weighed 1500 tonnes. Maximum training speed was 6° per second and elevation speed 5° per second; both motions had Ward Leonard style electrics and remote power control. One 75hp elevation motor drove each twin-gun cradle and there were two 100hp training motors. The gunhouse was divided into equal parts by a longitudinal bulkhead extending downwards into the gas-tight working chamber. Run-out was pneumatic.

The hoists and chain gunloading rammers were all electrically powered but the shell supply arrangements in the shell rooms proved to be inadequate and the designed rate of fire was not met – in fact it was virtually halved.

Some reports state that the two guns of each common cradle had limited elevation motion relative to each other, but how this movement was achieved is not known. Perhaps one gun had some form of manual elevation 'adjustment' merely to allow the guns to be matched for range.

THE FRENCH 15in/45 GUN IN THE QUADRUPLE 15in MOUNTING

This was a very large mounting indeed, with a total revolving weight of 2476 tonnes. It was, in many ways, a scaled-up development of the quadruple 13in, having the same style of powering for elevation and training and a similar performance. In the lower quarters, ammunition was stowed on two deck levels, each level serving a pair of jointly cradled guns. The firing interval of 25 seconds was apparently achieved, no doubt aided by the fact that not only did the hydro-pneumatic breech open upwards automatically on gun run-out but also that the breech itself had an automatic lock holding 10 firing tubes.

Unfortunately, the two ships in which these mountings were eventually fitted, *Richelieu* and *Jean Bart*, were not complete at the time France surrendered and they never had the opportunity to show how effective they or their guns would have been in a surface action. *Richelieu* was damaged by the British bombardment of Dakar in 1940 but eventually joined the Free French forces. She was refitted in the United States, and served in the East Indies towards the end of the war. *Jean Bart* escaped, in partly fitted-out condition, to Vichy-controlled Casablanca and was not completed until after the war.

THE BRITISH 14in Mk VIII GUN IN THE 14in Mk II (TWIN) AND 14in Mk III (QUADRUPLE) MOUNTINGS

Whether the British were influenced by the appearance of the French quadruple 13in or were still measuring a battleship's potential by weight of broadside is difficult to say, but, for whatever reasons, the sketch designs for their new capital ships allowed for twelve 14in guns in three quadruple turrets. In the event, the requirement to work in improved protection made it necessary to reduce the main armament by two barrels, resulting in a twin at 'B', and quads at 'A' and 'Y' positions. The twin became the Mk II (following the Mk I in *Canada*) and the quadruple the Mk III. It was a rare example in the Royal Navy of the main armament turrets having dissimilar numbers of barrels in the same ship.

From their introduction in the late 1920s, both the 16in triple and the 8in twin had been a source of trouble – almost entirely centred on the complications of their loading arrangements; on the other hand, the much earlier 15in twin was still giving excellent service and the (then) new 6in twins and triples, of a similarly simple design concept, were equally reliable. The mounting designers very wisely moved away from the intricacies of the *Nelson* and *Rodney* turrets when they tackled their new task, but it was literally a monumental one. In electing for a twelve-gun battleship in the first instance, the Naval Staff sought to give the new ships half as many guns again as the *Queen Elizabeth*s and

The bridge and main armament of the French battleship *Jean Bart* viewed from the forecastle. Note that the four guns in each turret are grouped in pairs; each pair elevated as a unit although there was means of relative adjustment for calibration purposes. *Conway Picture Library*

BRITISH 14in Mk III QUADRUPLE MOUNTING

1 Navigating compartment ('A' mounting only)
2 Navigator's periscope
3 Rangefinder
4 Flash door linkage
5 Gunloading cage
6 Breech-screw (open)
7 Upper balance weight
8 Manual breech-operating hand wheel
9 Power breech-operating cylinder
10 Automatic recuperator gland pressure intensifier
11 Recuperator cylinder
12 Right-hand recuperator tie-rod
13 Power elevation control wheel
14 Recuperator ram
15 Recuperator ram crosshead
16 Look-out periscope
17 Mantlet plate
18 Telescopic air-blast and hydraulic supply sliding pipes to breech mechanism
19 Hydraulic 'walking pipes' to elevating mass
20 Elevation cut-off cam
21 High-pressure air cylinders
22 Elevation buffer
23 Training roller
24 Training clip
25 Safety firing cam rail
26 Cut-off linkage from safety firing cams
27 Elevation cylinder
28 Rammer and traverser control console
29 Rammer, 'traverser to gunloading cage'
30 Retracted chain-rammer casing
31 Traverser
32 Training gear
33 'On-mounting' shell-ring hydraulic motor
34 Shell-ring power drive
35 Revolving shell-ring
36 Cordite rammers
37 Cordite hopper flash doors
38 Rammer/flash door linkages
39 On-mounting pressure supply
40 Centre-pivot swivel connection
41 High-pressure air supply
42 Off-mounting pressure connection
43 Off-mounting exhaust connection
44 On-mounting exhaust line
45 Cordite cage
46 Trunk guide rollers
47 Spring-loaded shell cage stops
48 Shell cage
49 On-mounting rammer, shell-ring traverse and locking-bolt control console
50 Retracted chain rammer casing
51 Cage lifting cables
52 Ammunition lift rails
53 Electric cables to 'winding' platforms
54 Retracted chain rammer casing
55 Rammer, 'ammunition cage to traverser'
56 Bridge trays
57 Ammunition cage winches
58 Vertical guide roller
59 Gunloading cage rails
60 Training buffer
61 Gunloading rammer casing
62 Gunloading cage lifting press
63 Link rod from elevation control hand wheel
64 Breech thread protection tray operating linkage
65 Gunloading rammer

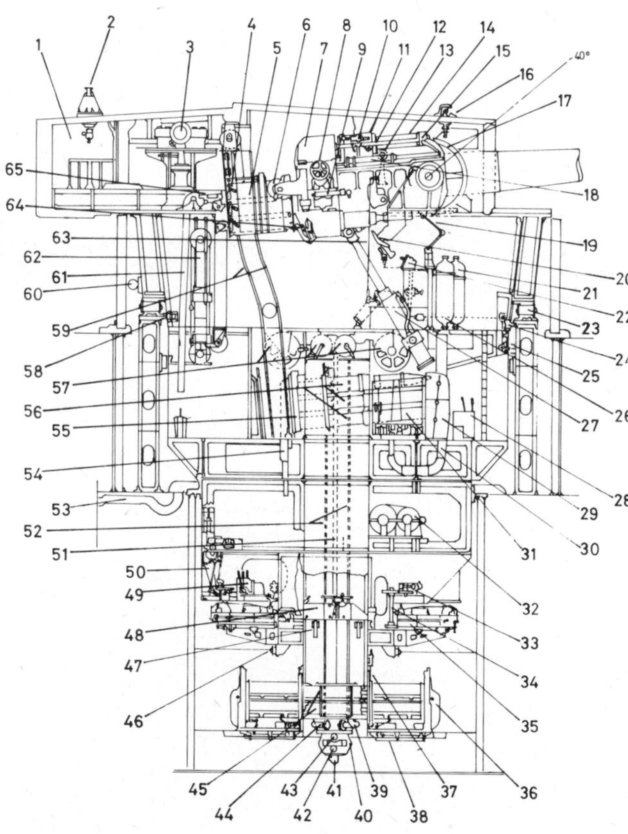

Above: A quadruple 14 in Mk III mounting assembled by the manufacturers before breaking down for transfer to one of the *King George V* class battleships. One gun is being either lowered into position or removed.

Below: The third ship of the *King George V* class to complete: HMS *Duke of York* on 3 November 1941. *National Maritime Museum.*

Royal Sovereigns while, at the same time, saving the longitudinal deck space of a complete mounting. However, although the general loading arrangements were to be simpler than before, in a turret having four guns with independent elevation, all the gear was in quadruplicate. What the designers gained on the swings of simplicity, they lost on the roundabouts of multiplicity.

A very important aspect of the 14in gun itself was the method of its construction. The wire-wound system had long been accepted as the ideal method for most ordnance up to and including the 16in calibre. However, it had several disadvantages: the total manufacturing time was extensive; the process was delicate and expensive; and it did nothing to improve the tendency of a long barrel to droop. After World War I, further developments took place. By using high quality steels and subjecting them to a series of heat treatments and very high internal pressures, sufficient strength was achieved without the need for the miles of wire previously used so, after the 16in and 8in, wire-wound guns were no longer manufactured. Several mountings, originally designed with them, were re-gunned with modern barrels, and the 14in was the largest built by the new method to see active service afloat. Described as an 'all-steel' gun, it was assembled as a rifled inner A tube, an A tube and a jacket, and weighed 79 tons with its breech mechanism.

If a gun barrel is trunnioned about its natural centre of gravity the space required behind and beneath it may become intolerable due to the overall effect on the practical dimensions of the gunhouse, or, at best, it may present considerable design difficulties. Such problems were, indeed, revealed in the 16in triple, whose gunwells took up a great deal of space, but they were largely overcome in the 14in by adopting the Elswick principle of gun balancing. In this, the breech was pushed forward, towards the trunnion axis, making the gun muzzle-heavy but for the addition of massive counter-balance weight blocks, positioned above and below the breech-ring. Hence the arc described by the breech-end as it descended was shortened and the guns were able to reach 40° elevation within the confines of a fairly compact gunhouse.

The benefits of the Elswick system of balancing are clearly revealed when one compares the twin 15in Mk I gunhouse with that of the twin 14in Mk II. They were both of roughly similar dimensions but the former, with guns balanced at the centre of gravity, was designed for 20° elevation while the latter achieved 40°. In some ways, indeed, the 14in Mk II could be regarded as a modernised version of the 15in Mk I, but its emergence so close to the outbreak of the Second World War kept even outline details of its performance from the popular naval journals and books of the day. The one point heavily stressed was that its range was greater than that of the 15in, but there was no magic in this. It was achieved by the extra elevation – a feature common in contemporary foreign weapons anyway – and a better shaped shell (6/12crh instead of 5/10crh of the 15in).

Apart from the increased height of the ammunition hoists, the difference between the twin and the quadruple mountings lay only in the number of barrels carried. So far as the loading arrangements are concerned, the left and right inner guns of a quadruple turret exactly corresponded to those of the two guns in a twin. The detailed routes of the ammunition supply, which were similar to those of the 15in Mk I, are covered later in the book and the following description of the quadruple turret will, therefore, serve to cover the twin.

The total training mass of this, the biggest gun mounting of British naval service, was 1500 tons (the Mk II was not, of course, simply half as big and came out at 900 tons – somewhat heavier than the modernised 15in). The gunhouse was rather box-shaped (but with sloping sides), very wide in proportion to its length and had a squared-off, flat front face. In this respect the profile differed sharply from German naval gun turrets, which were built of similar shape irrespective of the calibre of gun and sloped upwards from all sides at a shallow angle to the flat gunhouse roof. Quite apart from the weight of the guns and the gunhouse armour, the rotating trunk was packed with heavy equipment, making it easier to understand how the total weights were reached.

The turret trainer sat right forward, between the inner guns, while an auxiliary training position was similarly sited between the right guns. It was balanced by a local director sight (LDS, for use in quarters firing) between the left guns. The gunlayer's seats and controls were set alongside the trunnion supports of their respective guns, all these positions being approached by narrow walkways running between the gun wells and flanked by guard rails.

In the rear of each well, a trackway for the gun-loading cage ran from the working chamber to a sheave mounted on a stanchion rising from the gunhouse deck plate. The gun rammer engine casings were positioned at the same level, in alignment with the gun bores, at the fixed loading angle of 5°. Above the quartet of rammers and their adjacent control lever consoles, a rangefinder was mounted on supports for quarters-firing ranging. A geared drive allowed it to be independently traversed with respect to the centreline of the turret, so it could remain aligned to the bearing of a target when the mounting was itself aimed-off in deflection.

In the extreme gunhouse rear there was an armoured roof-mounted access hatch behind the left outer gun; a gun wash-out tank and the captain of the turret's position behind the left inner; a periscope behind the right inner; and the sub-calibre gun stowage on the extreme right. Centrally in this area, in 'A' gunhouse only, there was a navigational compartment which broadly corresponded to the armoured conning-tower of earlier capital ships.

Instead of having the old-fashioned gun slide, each gun was mounted in a jacket which moved in recoil through a tubular cradle from which the trunnion pins projected. The front of the cradle terminated in a curved, armoured mantlet plate that sealed the slot cut in the gunhouse front face. On top of the cradle was a fixed recuperator cylinder filled with high-pressure air and, on the underside, two heavy lugs projected downwards, each holding the tail rod of a recoil buffer piston. A cut-off cam, close to one of the lugs, stopped the hydraulic elevating gear at the upper and lower limits of elevation. Another, centrally positioned lug received the cross-head pin of the elevating piston.

The breech-ring was cube-shaped with the balance weights bolted to its top and bottom faces, the lower weight containing twin recoil buffer cylinders. As the gun recoiled, therefore, the oil-filled cylinders moved over the pistons fixed to the cradle to absorb the recoil shock. From the upper balance weight, two tie-rods projected forward, ending in a cross-head that lay above the trunnion axis when the gun was in its normal position. The cross-head ran on a slide-way on the top of the cradle and held the ram of the recuperator. As the gun recoiled, the tie-bars pulled the cross-head backwards, in turn, forcing the ram into its cylinder and increasing the air pressure so, when the gun has been arrested in its rearward movement, the recuperator forced it outwards again.

The recuperator and recoil cylinders worked in conjunction with each other: the former absorbed about 30 per cent of the recoil shock and provided the power to push the gun back to its run-out position; the latter, by their internal design, controlled the speed of the recoil movement, and in reverse, the speed of run-out. A large recess was cut into the upper balance weight to accommodate the end of the recuperator cylinder.

The breech was of the usual interrupted thread pattern and was almost identical in design to that of the 8in. It was in normal circumstances operated remotely, by admitting pressure to a piston-and-cylinder gear, but it also had a hand/power changeover clutch allowing it to be operated by hand, through a geared drive, from a large handwheel.

Hydraulic pressure and exhaust arrived at the elevating cradle through a pair of 'walking pipes' positioned under the trunnions, and was transferred from non-recoiling cradle to the recoiling breech gear by telescopic pipes. A second pair of similar pipes carried air-blast and water-squirt supplies – the first from high-pressure air bottles and the second from the gun wash-out tank.

A lever mechanism operating a trough was suspended below the breech. When the breech was open, the gunloading cage could be raised and, as it came up to gunhouse level, it struck the levers, so swinging the trough upwards and inwards, through an arc, to cover the threads of the breech-ring. This protected them from damage by the shell and rammer as they moved into the chamber. When the loading cage descended, it tripped the lever mechanism in the opposite direction, removed the trough, and allowed the breech to be swung to and locked with a part-turn. The guns were 'handed', the two left-hand breech mechanisms pivoting on the left side of the breech-ring and the two right-hand mechanisms opening outwards in the opposite direction.

The space below the gunhouse through which the gunwells passed was called the turntable compartment. Here were heavy brackets holding the trunnioned elevating cylinder for each gun, the elevation limit buffers and the lower portion of the hydraulic 'walking pipes'. Close to them was a pair of powerful hydraulic jacks, capable of supporting the total weight of the gun and cradle while maintenance was being carried out on the trunnion bearings. Again, there were walkways past each gunwell, and the massive, double-flanged turret rollers ran around the periphery of the trunk at walkway level. This part of the rotating structure was surrounded by the barbette and was not itself armoured. On the right-hand side, a turntable securing bolt could be extended, by a handwheel in the gunhouse above, to lock the rotating mass to the barbette in the fore-and-aft position.

Under the forward end of the left inner gun was an enclosed compartment – 'the silent cabinet' – containing a calculator called the Admiralty fire control box. This was a simplified version of the larger calculating tables and clocks but was quite comprehensive and could produce an accurate fire control solution within certain limits. It could be used in quarters firing, in conjunction with the local director sight (the latter providing datum gun pointing), and the turret rangefinder. A large rotary changeover switch, operated by a tram-car style handle, transferred the fire control circuits.

The next compartment below was the working chamber, where ammunition was transferred from the main cages to the gunloading cages and beneath that were, in succession, the training gear space and the training engine space. Training power was derived from one of two hydraulic engines, driving a common gearbox through a clutch gear. Only one engine could be engaged at a time, leaving the other automatically disconnected. The twin-engine scheme was a popular device, providing as it did an alternative engine in case of material failure or damage, as well as allowing maintenance on one unit while the other was working. Shafting drove outwards from the gearbox to the training worm and wormwheels and thence upwards, through reduction gears, to the double training pinions in engagement with the fixed training rack set inside the ring bulkhead supporting the turret rollers.

Lower down, the trunk tapered away in a conical fashion until it was of sufficient size to hold only the four ammunition cage trackways, side by side. The dimensions hereabouts varied considerably, of course, between the tall slim twin and the squatter quadruple mountings. The lower portion of the trunking was surrounded by double bulkheads but, although it was below the barbette protection, it was within that of the ship's side armour. On the centre of rotation, at the lowest point of the trunk and above the double-bottom, there was a massive swivel connection, leading to and from the hydraulic pump unit. The swivel also received an incoming high-pressure air supply from the ship's compressors so that the several on-mounting air bottles could be charged up.

The forward turrets of *Duke of York*: in 'A' position the quadruple Mk III mounting, and in 'B' position the twin Mk II. *Imperial War Museum*

The shell hoists, of the pusher type adopted in the 16in and 8in mountings, proved to be a source of trouble for a number of years, although the principle was excellent and was successfully implemented in a number of later, but smaller, gun mountings. For the 14in mountings, therefore, the designers reverted to the well-proven double cage system. This comprised an ammunition cage running upwards from the lower quarters to the working chamber, where the ammunition was transferred to a gunloading cage for its final journey to the gunhouse. As has already been related, this arrangement speeded up the loading cycle but, in any case, the quadruple turret was so wide that the alternatives would have been either to extend the trunking vertically downwards at the full width or to twist the trackways of the cages through a tortuous path. Neither was acceptable, the first because it would be too space-consuming and the second because it would be very difficult to engineer.

The ammunition cage was actually two separate containers, each hauled towards the working chamber by a wire rope leading upwards to a sheave and thence downwards to a pair of power-driven winch drums on a common shaft. The upper of the two containers, called the shell cage, accepted one shell; the cordite cage, consisting of two tubes, one above the other, took the four charges. In the quadruple turret, the shell cage rose about 20ft, in its journey from shell room to working chamber, but the cordite cage had to travel further, the magazine deck being some 8ft lower. This was rather cleverly taken care of by the two winch drums, which had different diameters but revolved together: the smaller drum hauled the shell cage wire and the larger the cordite cage. In consequence, as they rose, the lower cage 'caught up' with the upper and both arrived at the working chamber together, the cordite cage then being immediately below the shell. When the cages were sent down, they gradually parted company en route, again ending up displaced by 8ft.

The service somewhat resignedly accepted that an installation of this complexity would go through a series of teething troubles following its introduction. The troubles indeed occurred, as they had with the 16in and 8in, but whereas these mountings had been built and modified in time of peace, the Second World War had run fifteen months of its course before *King George V* was accepted into service. She was quickly followed by the ill-fated *Prince of Wales* but the last of the class, *Howe*, was not completed until August 1942.

A defect in the shell handing room of *Prince of Wales* occurred while she was in action with the *Bismarck* in May 1941 and this, combined with damage already sustained, caused her to break off the engagement. Later, when *Bismarck* was engaged by *Rodney* and *King George V*, the latter's 14in armament was reduced to 20 per cent output by the close of action – which sounds remarkably like the state of affairs where only the twin was still functioning. The British public knew nothing of the shortcomings so nakedly revealed by the *Bismarck* action; and the German battleship's eventual destruction did little to deaden the shock of *Hood*'s loss. Within the Royal Navy, a good deal of understandably bitter criticism was levelled at the new heavy gun mountings. In what was a critical year of the war, the hard pressed Senior Service lost *Hood*, *Barham*, *Repulse*, *Prince of Wales*, the 15in monitor *Terror*, *Ark Royal*, nine cruisers and many smaller but no less vital ships. With the modernised battleships *Queen Elizabeth* and *Valiant* lying severely damaged and immobilised in Alexandria, the Royal Navy had problems enough in 1941 without being saddled with a new gun mounting of questionable efficiency. The expectation of teething troubles was in itself an indictment of the design philosophy of the day; and statements to the effect that more was learned of the mountings' weaknesses in the few days of *Bismarck*'s sortie than would have been revealed by years of peace time trials were hardly even mitigating, let alone a reasonable defence. However, by 1943 the 14in teeth seem to have begun finally to break through the reddened gums of the earlier years. They performed fairly well in *Duke of York* in the last major surface action of the Royal Navy in the Second World War (when she sent the battlecruiser *Scharnhorst* to the bottom in December of that year) but even then the 14in output was only 68 per cent and only one gun in the twin was trouble-free throughout.

The 14in was conceived and introduced at a time when the battleship was already in decline and consequently had a shorter working life than either of the other RN heavy calibre capital ship guns of the period. Within the Service, it was less well known than the 15in twin but was, very properly, preferred to the 16in triple. On reflection, perhaps, the *King George V* class would have been better served by four twins in the accepted positions. Merely to state that the only battleship built for the Royal Navy after the *King George V* class reverted to 15in twins would be greatly to oversimplify the case. Nevertheless, in contemplating the heavy calibre guns of British capital ships, it is interesting to observe that with *Vanguard* – the last of the line – the Royal Navy accepted a main armament that dated from the *Queen Elizabeth*s laid down before the commencement of World War I.

Finally, and more directly related to the subject of the 14in, it was usual for the Royal Navy to order scale models of the larger mountings. They were used in the gunnery schools for instructional purposes and were often loaded for public viewing on such occasions as Navy Days in the Royal Dockyards. Mostly constructed from wood (but nonetheless highly detailed), and with working

ammunition hoists and loading arrangements, they provided an excellent overall visual aid to the installation as a whole. One such model, of the quadruple 14in mounting, is in the Imperial War Museum in London and long may it be preserved as a testimony to the ingenuity of the engineers who designed it under the considerable pressures of a deteriorating international situation.

THE US 16in/45 Mk 6 GUN IN THE 16in THREE-GUN MOUNTING

This was the penultimate American battleship mounting and closely resembled its successor, except in such areas as hoist motor horsepower and trunnion load on gunfire. The maximum elevation was 45° and the all-up training weight was approximately 1430 tons. The mounting was fitted in the *North Carolina* and *South Dakota* class battleships, which were the outcome of the rearmament programme of the later 1930s and, although the two classes were quite different from each other in appearance, set a pattern of main armament disposition which thereafter remained constant in the battleships of the US Navy. The three 16in mountings were set in 'A', 'B' and 'X' positions, separated by the main superstructure which was itself flanked by a heavy concentration of the ubiquitous 5in/38 twin DP mounting.

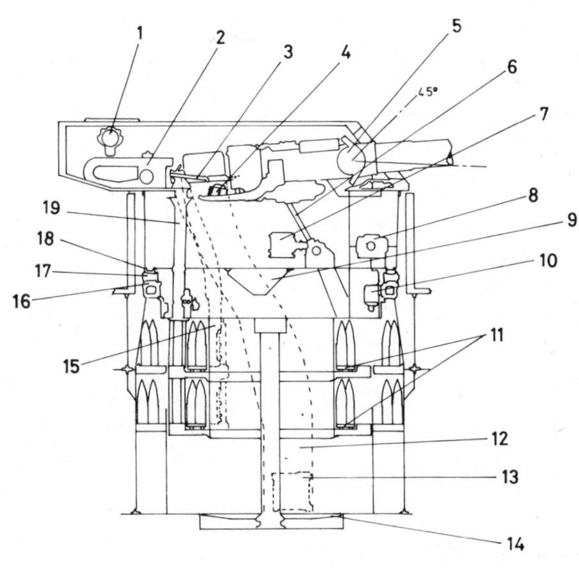

US 16in TRIPLE MOUNTING (*NORTH CAROLINA*)

1 Rangefinder
2 Rammer casing
3 Tilting shell bucket
4 Breech block
5 Armoured mantlet plate
6 Elevation screw
7 Elevation motor
8 Training motor
9 Gunwell
10 Training drive
11 On-mounting shell-rings
12 Powder cage trunk
13 Powder cage
14 Powder loading platform
15 Route of left and right gun projectile hoists
16 Lower roller path
17 Training roller
18 Upper roller path
19 Centre gun projectile hoist

USS *Washington* as completed, 29 May 1941. She carried nine 16in/45 Mk 6 guns in 3 three-gun mountings. *US Navy*

The US 16in-gun fast battleship *New Jersey* as she appeared when reactivated from reserve to operate as a bombardment vessel in the Vietnam War. *US Navy*

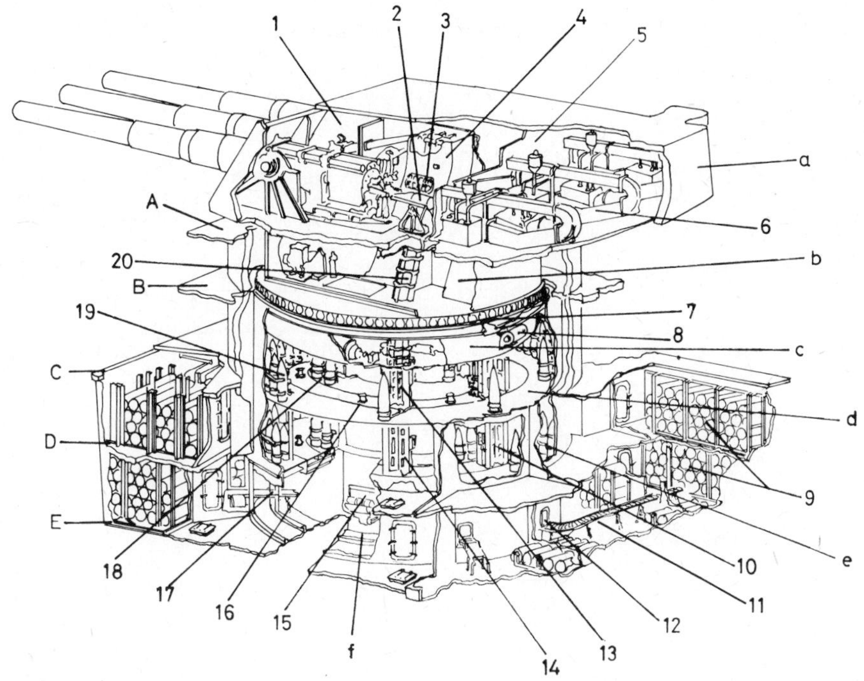

THE US 16in/50 Mk 7 GUN IN THE 16in THREE-GUN MOUNTING

Having already built and evaluated a 16in 3-gun mounting, the Americans now, predictably, stretched the gun design to 50 calibres length for this, the final visual evidence of their heavy mounting design. The magnificent *Iowa* class battleships, for which the mountings were designed, were worthy vehicles for this superb example of weapon engineering but were themselves planned to be followed by the *Montana* class with a displacement of 60,500 tons. These ships would have had four (instead of three) 16in turrets but the class of five was cancelled in mid-1943 before the keels were laid.

US 16in/50 (*IOWA*)

1 Longitudinal flashtight bulkhead
2 Shell cradle
3 Powder charge door
4 Powder trunk
5 Lateral flashtight bulkhead
6 Rammer casing
7 Turret rollers
8 Training buffer
9 Upper and lower powder stowages
10 Centre gun lower shell hoist shutter casing
11 Roller conveyor
12 Powder scuttle
13 Left gun upper shell hoist shutter casing
14 Left gun lower shell hoist shutter casing
15 Powder hopper
16 Shell transfer capstan
17 Powder transfer tray
18 Upper revolving shell-ring
19 Upper fixed shell stowages
20 Shell hoist trunking
A Main deck
B Second deck
C Third deck
D First platform
E Second platform
a Gunhouse
b Pan floor
c Machinery floor
d Upper projectile handling floor
e Lower projectile handling floor
f Powder handling floor

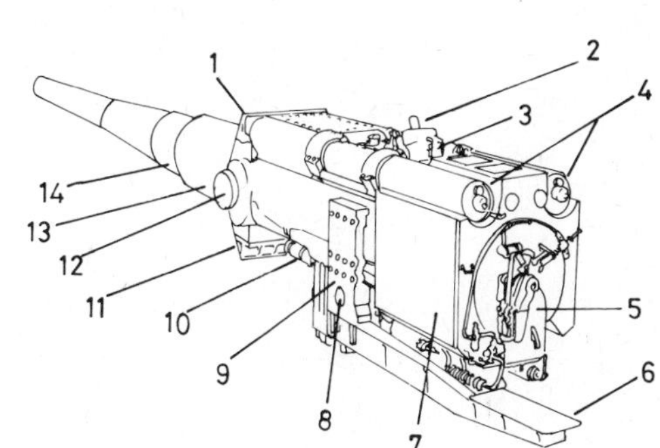

US 16in/50 GUN (*IOWA*)

1 Upper shield plate
2 Depression buffer
3 Yoke locking link
4 Counter-recoil (run-out) cylinders
5 Downward opening breech
6 Loader's platform
7 Yoke
8 Slide locking pin
9 Rear end bracket
10 Recoil system expansion tank
11 Lower shield plate
12 Slide trunnion
13 Neoprene gun cover
14 Gun slide cylinder

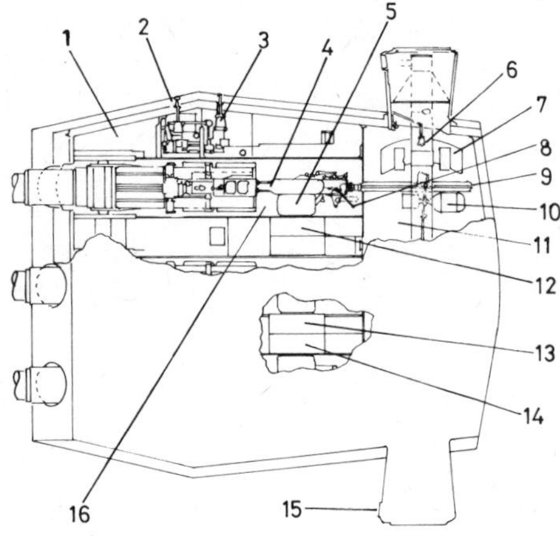

US 16in/50 THREE-GUN TURRET (*IOWA*) – GUNHOUSE PART-PLAN

1 Sight-setters compartment
2 Trainer's telescope
3 Pointer's telescope
4 Spanning tray
5 Right gun powder hoist door
6 Rangefinder
7 Rangefinder traversing support platform
8 Right gun projectile cradle
9 Chain rammer casing
10 Rammer 'A' end electric drive motor
11 Flashtight rammer compartment
12 Right gun powder trunk
13 Centre gun powder trunk
14 Left gun powder trunk
15 Rangefinder hood shutter
16 Flashtight gun compartment

Note: Apart from powder trunks, turret is symmetrical about the centreline

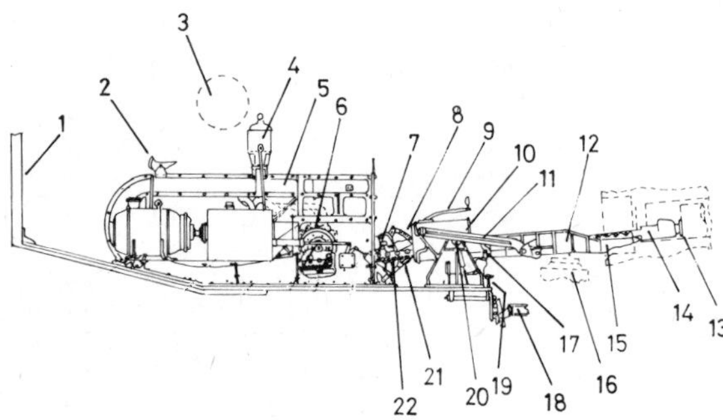

US 16in/50 (*IOWA*) – GUNLOADING ARRANGEMENTS

1 Rear bulkhead
2 Rangefinder operator's seat
3 Rangefinder
4 Header tank
5 Chain rammer casing
6 'B' end
7 Rammer withdraw buffer
8 Control lever bracket
9 Projectile latch release lever
10 Projectile cradle
11 Control link
12 Spanning tray
13 Rammer head buffer
14 Rammer head link
15 Folding breech protection tray
16 Breech, opening downwards
17 Cradle opening buffer
18 Loading platform
19 Cradle release foot-pedal
20 Cradle axis
21 Control lever
22 Rammer tray

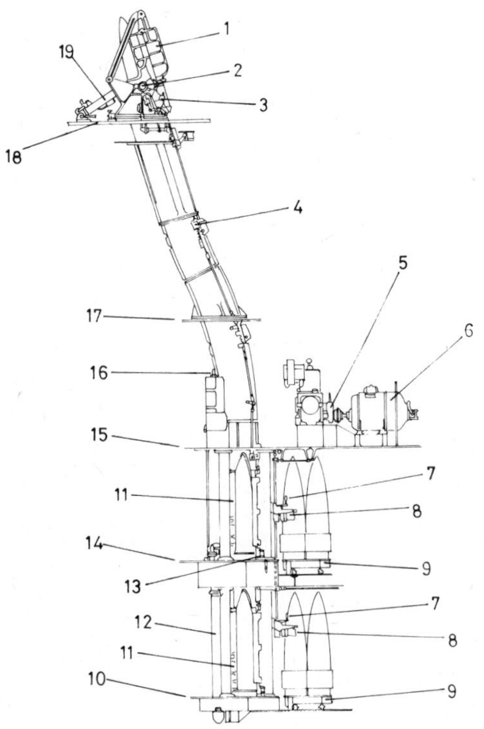

US 16in/50 (*IOWA*) – OUTER GUN PROJECTILE HOIST

1 Spanning tray
2 Cradle axis
3 Cradle buffer
4 Hoist pawl operating cylinder
5 Solenoid brake
6 Hoist 'A' end electric drive motor
7 Hoist control handle
8 Hoist/projectile ring interlock solenoid
9 Projectile ring
10 Lower projectile handling floor
11 Hoist shutters
12 Shutter operating cylinder
13 'Parbuckling' roller
14 Upper projectile handling floor
15 Machinery floor
16 Shutter cylinder indicator
17 Pan floor
18 Gunhouse floor
19 Cradle operating cylinder

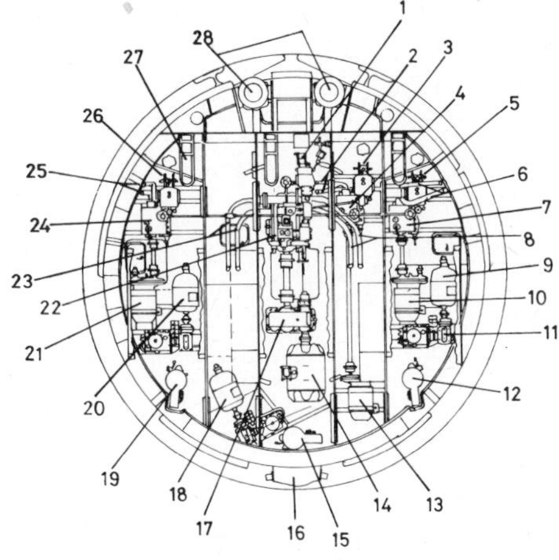

US 16in/50 (*IOWA*) – MACHINERY FLOOR

1 Trainer's handwheels
2 Pipework up to centre gun elevating 'B' end
3 Centre gunlayer's handwheels
4 Centre gun elevation 'A' end
5 Right gunlayer's handwheels
6 Pipework up to right gun elevating 'B' end
7 Right gun elevating 'A' end
8 Pipework up to training 'B' end
9 Right gun projectile hoist electric motor
10 Right gun elevating 'A' end electric drive motor
11 Reduction gear box
12 Right gun projectile hoist
13 Centre gun elevating 'A' end electric drive motor
14 Training 'A' end electric drive motor
15 Centre gun projectile hoist
16 Training limit buffer
17 Training gear reduction gearbox
18 Centre gun projectile hoist electric motor
19 Left gun projectile hoist
20 Left gun projectile hoist electric motor
21 Left gun elevating 'A' end electric drive motor
22 Training gear 'A' end
23 Pipework up to training 'B' end
24 Left gun elevating 'A' end
25 Pipework up to left gun elevating 'B' end
26 Left gunlayer's handwheels
27 Pocket for elevating screw
28 Training pinions

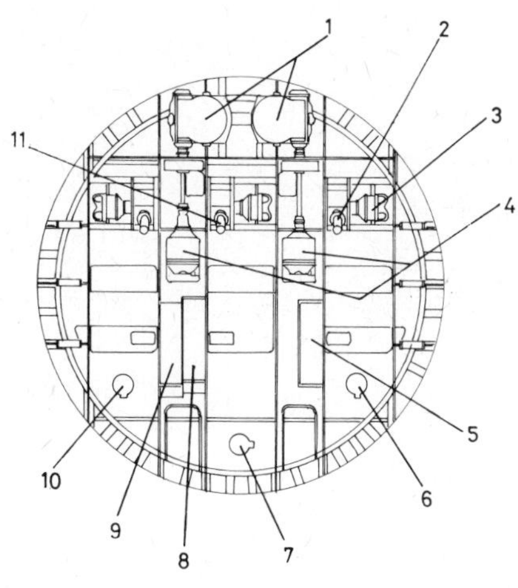

US 16in/50 (*IOWA*) – PAN FLOOR

1 Training gear worm and wormwheel gear boxes
2 Right gun elevating screw
3 Right gun elevating 'B' end
4 Training gear 'B' ends
5 Right gun powder trunk
6 Right gun projectile hoist
7 Centre gun projectile hoist
8 Centre powder trunk
9 Left gun powder trunk
10 Left gun projectile hoist
11 Centre gun elevating screw (offset to the left)

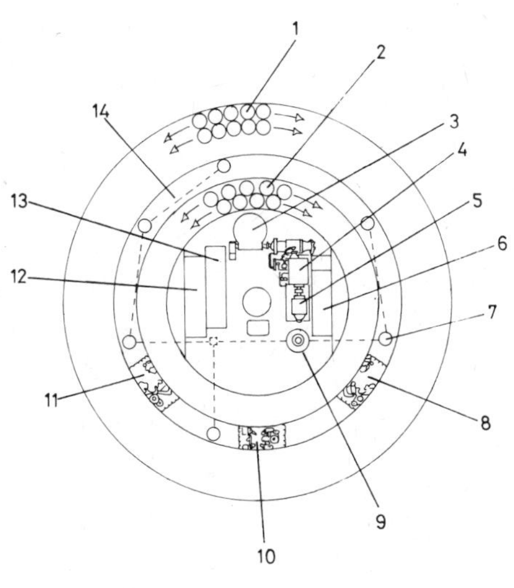

US 16in/50 (*IOWA*) – UPPER AND LOWER PROJECTILE STOWAGE AND HANDLING ROOM

1 Fixed circumferential projectile stowages
2 Rotating circumferential projectile stowages on powered projectile ring
3 Projectile ring drive gearbox
4 Hydraulic unit
5 Projectile ring electric motor
6 Right gun powder cage trunk
7 Projectile capstan, used to transfer projectiles by 'parbuckle' cables from fixed to moving stowages
8 Right gun projectile hoist
9 Electric capstan motor
10 Centre gun projectile hoist
11 Left gun projectile hoist
12 Left gun powder cage trunk
13 Centre gun powder cage trunk
14 Shaft drive to transfer capstans

The Japanese battleship *Yamato* running trials in December 1941. She carried the largest guns and the heaviest mountings ever fitted in a battleship, the total revolving weight of each triple 18.1in mounting being about 2500 tons. *Imperial War Museum*

Despite its formidable porportions (the all-up weight was 1700 tons) electro-hydraulic powering gave 12° per second in elevation and 4° per second in training, the latter from a 300hp motor. With three 60hp elevation motors, three 60hp rammers, two 40hp shell-rings, three 75hp shell hoists and three 100hp powder hoists per mounting, the power consumption must have been enormous. Shells were stowed both on- and off-mounting, at two levels, and the powder hoists ran direct to the gunhouse. The centre gun shell hoist ran vertically at the rear of the mounting and the wing shell hoists started forward of the trunk centreline and then curved to bring them to the same relative gunhouse position. The maximum elevation was 45° giving the 2700lb AP shell a range of 42,345yds – much in excess of the previous model of 16in gun which had a lighter propellant charge and a lower muzzle velocity (see Appendices).

THE US 12in/50 Mk 8 GUN IN THE 12in THREE-GUN MOUNTING

To counter Japanese heavy cruisers, the United States designed what was officially classified as a large cruiser but which was, in fact, a battlecruiser type. Large it certainly was, with a displacement of 27,500 tons and 150,000shp for a designed speed of 33kts. Only two of the intended six ships were completed, *Alaska* and *Guam*, their building programme being held in abeyance to make way for more urgently needed warships.

Weapon layout followed the established cruiser pattern and a 12in/50 gun was reintroduced for the main armament. Maximum elevation was 45° and modern electric powering gave high speeds of nearly 12° per second in elevation and 5° per second in training. Powered shell-rings fed the (by then) conventional American ammunition supply arrangements and the all-up weight of the mounting was approximately 930 tons.

The *Alaska* class ships were splendid vessels and the 38,500yd range of their nine 12in guns made them more than a match for any cruiser afloat – and a good deal else, nominally more powerful – but they emerged too late for other than the closing stages of the Pacific war.

THE JAPANESE 18.1in TYPE 1934 GUN IN THE TRIPLE 18.1in MOUNTING

Like many other emergent maritime nations, the Japanese originally relied largely on British equipment for their expanding fleet. The name ship of their first class of dreadnoughts, *Kongo*, was British-built and British-equipped and, although the Japanese thereafter undertook their own construction, the mountings of subsequent vessels were all copied from the British pattern. Thus, while the pagoda-like forward superstructure was distinctive in its own right, the gun mountings of the *Kongo* and following classes unmistakably showed their origins. Indeed, there seems little doubt that British and Japanese gun crews could have found their way about each other's equipment with equal ease. The principal powering for Japanese gun mountings was hydraulic following the original British practice, but many had an auxiliary electric drive, as well as the emergency hand-worked drives. However, movement by electric power was very slow and was probably intended more for maintenance purposes than as a viable action alternative to the main system.

Shortly after World War I, work commenced in Kure Dockyard, and at the Kamegabuki proving ground, on a 19in gun. The first model split during testing but a second performed satisfactorily and survived, albeit unused, until it was discovered by Allied forces in December 1945. During their period of observance of the Washington Treaty, the Japanese ceased further work on this project but, in the mid-1930s, when *Yamato* and her sisters were being planned, it was decided that they would be equipped to outgun the contemporary British and American 16in. In consequence, because they considered the 19in calibre too large (!), the Japanese began work on a 46cm triple mounting, which in Imperial terms gave the guns an actual bore diameter of 18.11in. By now paying lip service to the Naval Treaties (as, to be truthful, was everybody else) the Japanese announced their intention of building only 40cm (16in) guns. Official British Naval recognition handbooks of foreign warships, issued and updated by the Naval Intelligence Department, still credited the *Yamato* class as having 16in guns as late as April 1945; it was not until the war was over that the Allied Military Missions which arrived on the mainland of Japan discovered the truth of the matter.

Both *Yamato* and *Musashi* were sunk in action, whilst all documentation ashore was destroyed before the arrival of the victorious Allied forces. However, a partially completed trial mounting still existed ashore, as did some turret spares, and from these the inspecting teams were able to establish a good deal. Giving the lie to the belief that the Japanese were mere copyists, the massive equipments were totally different in concept from anything elsewhere. The basic dimensions were quite staggering, as the accompanying table shows.

Yamato in October 1941. *Marius Bar*

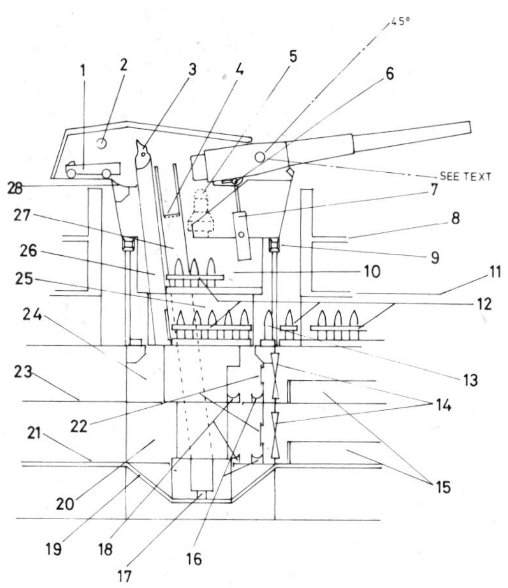

JAPANESE 18in TRIPLE MOUNTING (*YAMATO*)

1 Combined shell bogie and rammer
2 Rangefinder
3 Tilting shell bucket
4 Flash door
5 Training engine
6 Variable-geometry elevation cross-head
7 Elevation cylinder
8 56mm armour
9 Training roller
10 Upper shell handing room
11 200mm armour
12 Shell conveyor gear
13 Shell transfer bogie
14 Ring bulkhead doors
15 Cordite stowages
16 Cordite receiving trays
17 Centre pivot
18 Cordite transfer bogie
19 80mm armour
20 Lower cordite handing room
21 Lower magazine
22 Flashtight scuttle
23 Upper magazine
24 Upper cordite handing room
25 Lower shell handing room
26 Shell hoist
27 Cordite cage trunk
28 Shell bogie rails

PARTICULARS OF JAPANESE 18.1in GUN MOUNTING

Guns	Length overall	69ft 1½in
	Weight with breech mechanism	162 tons
	Weight of shell (AP)	3220lb
	Weight of shell (common)	3000lb
	Weight of full charge	7281lb
	Life of gun before relining	200–250 equivalent full charges
	Range at 45° elevation	45,960yds
Rate of fire	At maximum elevation	3 rounds/2min
	At loading angle	2 rounds/min
Mounting	Total revolving weight of triple turret	*c*2500 tons
	External diameter of roller path	42.8ft
	Length of recoil	4.69ft
	Training speed	2°/sec
	Elevating speed	6°/sec(designed) 8°/sec (actual)
Shell stowage	In revolving structure	60 rounds per gun
	In shell room	40 rounds per gun
	Total	100 rounds per gun
Gunhouse armour	Front	25.6in
	Side	9.85in
	Back	7.94in
	Roof	10.63in

Gun elevation was by conventional hydraulic piston and cylinder, with absolute limits of 45° elevation to 5° depression. The anchor point of the piston rod under the cradle was not the usual heavy fixed lug, however, but took the form of a sliding cross-head. The cross-head could be moved into two distinct positions by an auxiliary hydraulic piston which changed the geometry of the arrangements and thus the total elevation arc available. In one position the arc was +45° to −5°, and in the other +41° to +3°.

This scheme was introduced to obviate the need for any gun-locking arrangement during loading for, as 3° elevation was the loading angle, all the gunlayer had to do was keep his controls at 'depress' and leave the mounting's hydraulic cut-offs to ensure that the gun remained stationary. An indicator showed him when loading was complete. The mounting was normally operated in this elevation mode (for ease of reloading) but maximum elevation to 45° was quickly arranged if required.

Only one of the two sets of training gear was engaged at a time, each consisting of a vertically mounted 500hp hydraulic engine driving through a gear train to its own training pinion. Because no self-locking worm-and-wormwheel drive was employed, gunfire caused the turret to 'throw-off', and this was absorbed in a 'free-wheel' arrangement within the gear train.

In the ammunition supply system, only one 'layer' of six cordite charges was accommodated within the cordite cage instead of the more usual two, and consequently its flashtight trunk was comparatively large at approximately 3ft wide by 9ft 6in long. The charges could be loaded into the hoist at either 'lower' or 'upper' magazine levels and the cage ran directly, on a straight trackway, to the gunhouse, hauled by the piston-rack/winch-drum method.

JAPANESE 18in TRIPLE – SHELL CONVEYOR GEAR

1 Fixed gate (in inactive stowed position)
2 Moving gate (at centre of gravity of shell)
3 Shell trackway

Sequence

A Moving gate moves from vertical (inactive) stowed position
B Fixed gate releases shell noses
C Moving gate shifts laterally, moving shells one pitch
D Fixed gate relocates over shell noses
E Moving gate moves clear of shells
F Moving gate shifts back laterally. Sequence repeats

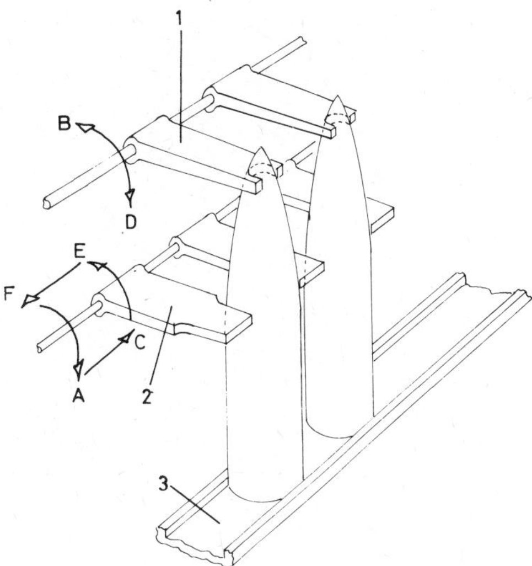

The forward turrets and bridge of USS *Idaho* on 3 January 1941. During the early 1930s her 14in mountings were modified to provide 30° elevation, increasing the maximum range to 36,800yds.

Above USS *Tennessee*, and her sister-ship *California*, were the last of America's 14in-gun ships. Their four 3-gun 14in mountings were designed to give 30° elevation. *Conway Picture Library*

Below The hulk of the Japanese battleship *Haruna*, of the *Kongo* class, at Kure in 1945. Her 14in/45 guns were of the type fitted in all Japanese 14in-gun ships and fired a 1485lb AP shell. The mountings were eventually modified to give 43° elevation, providing a maximum range of 38,800yds. *Conway Picture Library*

Of the total outfit of 300 shells per turret, 120 were carried on the revolving structure at two levels and the remainder in a shell room above the upper magazine. The transfer of projectiles from shell room to revolving structure was only intended between actions and normally they were supplied in the first instance from the lower shell handing room on the revolving structure. This was 'topped up' from the shell room during lulls, but if none occurred supply was provided by the smaller, upper shell handing room. A shell bogie running on circular rails around the trunk was used to transfer shells from the shell room.

The massive projectiles were stowed on their bases throughout (as was the American practice) and there were entries into conventional pusher hoists at the two shell handing room levels. The method by which the shells were moved was unique. They rested on twin rails alongside a long horizontal shaft, fitted with projections terminating in twin 'fingers'. These projections corresponded with the spacing of the shells and when the shaft was revolved through 90° the fingers swung down and held each shell by its nose. Below this shaft was a second shaft also fitted with projections, but this time they were designed with flat surfaces which would rest against the side of the shells. The lower shaft was set at the centre of gravity level of the shells and could not only revolve, but also move in a linear direction. The two shafts worked in conjunction with, but in opposite motion to, each other. When the upper shaft had revolved to engage its fingers with the shells, the lower shaft was in a position where its projections were vertical and clear of the projectiles. This was the inactive 'stowed' position, the fingers preventing toppling in a seaway.

The upper of these two shafts was known as the fixed gate and the lower as the moving gate. To supply shells, the moving gate shaft revolved, placing its projections in a horizontal attitude. The fixed gate then revolved, swinging its fingers clear, whereupon the moving gate moved laterally, taking the complete column of shells along one pitch. The fixed gate then revolved back to engage with the shells while the moving gate first lifted, then slid back to its original position; and so the process was repeated.

The on-mounting shells were stowed in athwartships bays leading to a fore-and-aft bay and thus to the shell hoist. All were fitted with the gate-gear which could be worked in reverse to ammunition ship. Hook-shaped projections were fitted at each end of the moving gates. One pulled a shell from an athwartships bay into a fore-and-aft bay, and the other pushed the shell into the shell hoist.

The 16-in battleship *Nagato* in the late 1920s. She was extensively modernised in 1934–36 which included modifying her main armament from 30° to 43° maximum elevation. *Conway Picture Library*

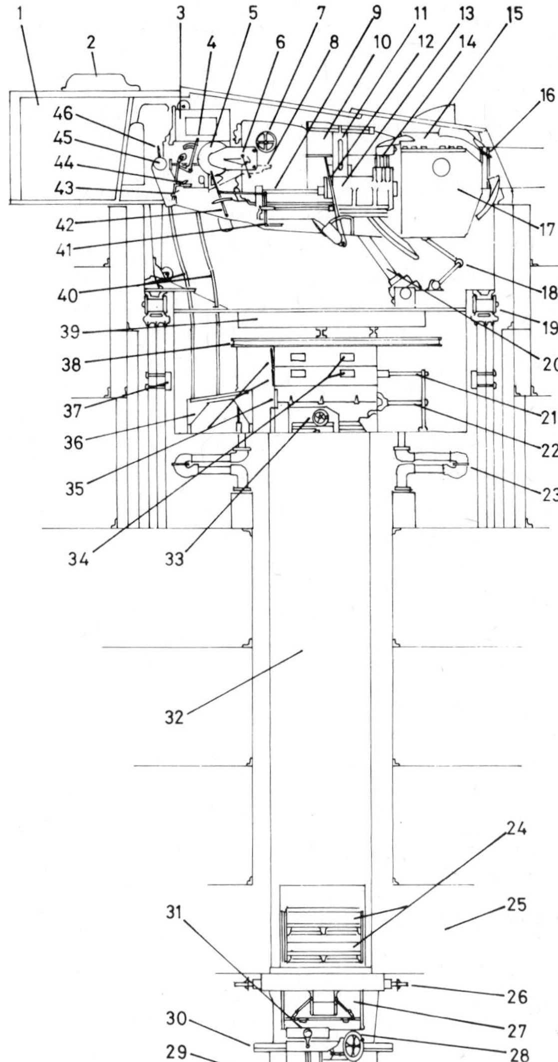

The battleship *Queen Elizabeth* under reconstruction in 1937–40. Note the modified front plates on the 15in gunhouses to accommodate the new 30° maximum elevation of the guns. *Conway Picture Library*

BRITISH 15in Mk I/N MOUNTING

1 Cabinet
2 Rangefinder hood
3 Cordite compartment of gunloading cage
4 Cordite dropping lever
5 Breech-screw
6 Lever actuating lock, on carrier
7 Alternative breech hand-drive
8 'Spoon tray' in position over breech threads
9 Recoil piston tail-rod
10 Balance weight
11 'Kicking strap'
12 Locking-bolt lever
13 Recoil cylinder
14 Rear collars on gun
15 Saddle cap
16 Front collars
17 Trunnion arm
18 Elevation 'walking pipes'
19 Training roller
20 Elevation cylinder
21 Cordite rammer
22 Shell rammer
23 Training 'walking pipes'
24 Cordite hoppers
25 Cordite handing room
26 Trunk guide rollers
27 Shell door
28 Shell bogie training hand wheel
29 'Fixed' rack on shell room deck
30 'Moving' rack on trunk
31 Shell traversing handle
32 Main ammunition trunk
33 Shell carrier
34 Inspection windows in flashtight cordite 'waiting' position
35 Automatic flash doors
36 Shell waiting tray
37 Training rack (training gear not visible in this section)
38 Overhead rail in working chamber for secondary shell supply
39 Envelope of cage lifting press
40 Gunloading cage rail
41 Interlocking linkage to breech lever
42 Breech worker's lever
43 Rammer lever
44 Rammer foot-pedal
45 Chain rammer engine
46 Gun 'wash-out squirt' lever

The shell hoist terminated in a tilting 'bucket' which moved down to an angle of 8° elevation. The shell rolled sideways on to a waiting tray and then rolled again on to a combined four-wheeled shell bogie and rammer, running on rails in the gunhouse rear. A downward inclination of the bogie rails caused it to tip to the 3° loading angle, whereupon the rammer rammed the shell into the breech. When the shell loading gear had retracted, an internal flashtight container, within the open-framework of the cordite cage, swung out sideways so that the six cordite charges were in line with the chamber. The container then moved forward to cover the breech threads. The cordite rammer assembly, pivoting on its base on the opposite side, similarly swung across into line and all six charges were rammed in one stroke. The shell bogie and what was in effect a retracting rammer assembly (since the latter was built into the bogie itself) was incorporated to leave space for the cordite loading arrangements.

Despite its enormous proportions and its novel design, the mounting gave less trouble than even the designers expected and they were justifiably pleased with it. Although never called upon in a surface action in the Pacific war, it was used with success in the bombardment role and also in barrage fire against aircraft formations. Reliance was placed on good drill rather than on the complex interlocking of control and, like German mountings, the anti-flash arrangements were less comprehensive than those of the Royal Navy. Nevertheless, the mounting was a remarkable example of weapon engineering for which the Japanese deserve great credit.

MOUNTING MODERNISATIONS

As has been mentioned, the improvements which took place in fire-control during and shortly after the First World War made it possible for battleships to engage each other at much greater ranges than previously considered feasible.

Britain's last battleship HMS *Vanguard*, during gunnery practice off Malta; the last such was carried out in 1954. *Imperial War Museum*

However, to utilise this new technology, the guns themselves required mountings giving high elevations, in order that they might realise their full range potential, and the majority of existing heavy guns could not elevate beyond 15°. Under normal circumstances this would have been taken care of by new ships, carrying new gun mountings – as indeed it was by a few ships such as the US and British 16in gun battleships with 30° and 40° elevation respectively – but the Washington Conference resulted in the major naval powers having to rely on their older ships to provide a substantial part of the strength of their battlefleets during the 1920s and 1930s.

However, the Washington Treaty did allow for the modernisation of the older battleships and although this clause was originally intended only for improvements in defence (bulges, deck armour and AA weapons) it was ultimately utilised to provide increased elevation for the heavy gun mountings as well. The improvements carried out by individual countries are given below.

USA From 1927 to 1931, when the 14in-gun battleships of the *Nevada, Pennsylvania* and *New Mexico* classes were modernised, their mountings were modified to increase maximum elevation from 15° to 30°. The 12in-gun vessels remained unaltered until 1940–41 when similar modifications were carried out in *Arkansas, New York* and *Texas*. The 16in-gun ships and the 14in-gun *California* class were built with 30° mountings and were not, therefore, modified.

France Between 1926 and 1929 the modernisations of *Courbet* and *Océan* included increased elevation for the main armament, raising the range of their 12in guns from 14,500 to 23,000yds. The newer *Bretagne* class had the elevation of their 13.4in guns increased from 18° to 23° in 1921–23 and later, during reconstruction in the early 1930s, they were re-gunned with new 13.4in weapons (originally built for the cancelled *Normandie* class) while *Lorraine* also had her centre turret removed to provide space for an aircraft catapult.

Italy Both the *Cavour* and *Duilio* classes were reconstructed between the wars in a most imaginative manner. The triple 12in was lifted from 'Q' position, the hull lengthened by some 40ft, and the engine power increased to give a speed of 27kts (compared with the original 22kts). The remaining turrets had their guns relined to 32cm (12.6in) calibre and power drives changed to Ward Leonard electrics for both training and elevation, with the natural result that elevation became geared with arc and pinion. Maximum elevation was increased to 27° in *Cavour* and *Cesare* and to 30° in *Duilio* and *Doria*.

Japan The maximum elevation of the 14in/45 mountings in the *Fuso, Ise* and *Kongo* classes was successively raised from the 'as built' 25°, through an interim 33°, to a final 43° (although in the *Ise* class both 'X' and 'Y' mountings remained unmodified at 25° maximum for want of sufficient space). The 16in/45 *Nagato* class twins were designed for 30° but were also increased to the 43° maximum by the interesting expedient of lowering the gunhouse floor and making similar adjustments to the lower deck levels within the rotating structure.

Britain In the 1930s those 15in-gun ships which were able to undergo a full modernisation had their mountings considerably modified to bring this elevation up to 30° maximum. These ships were *Warspite, Queen Elizabeth, Valiant* and *Renown*, and their mountings were then known as the Mk I/N or, in the case of the battlecruiser, Mk I*/N. The monitors *Erebus, Terror* and *Roberts* had special mountings, with 30° elevation but a lower limit of 2° elevation instead of 5° depression, whilst *Abercrombie* had the modernised Mk I/N. The final version, fitted in *Vanguard*, was given remote power control (in training only) and was known as the Mk I/N RP 12. The Mk I to Mk I/N modifications are dealt with in more detail in the Appendices, as is the special 'wangle' by which the unmodified 20° mountings managed to reach 28,700yds.

A gunnery practice target being straddled by a 15in salvo from *Vanguard*. *Imperial War Museum*

The bridge structure and 'A' and 'B' turrets of *Vanguard* viewed from the forecastle in 1953. *Conway Picture Library*

Inset, left The two muzzles of one of *Vanguard*'s twin 15in Mk I/N mountings. *Conway Picture Library*

Inset, right The after mountings of HMS *Vanguard* at the end of her career in 1960. The 15in twin remained in continuous service with the Royal Navy for a total of 45 years. *Conway Picture Library*

Because it was necessary to remove the gunhouse roof to expose the guns themselves for modification, the opportunity was taken to improve the roof armour, which was increased to a thickness of 5in. This, together with additional equipment and a 12-ton balance weight on each gun, pushed the all-up training structure mass to 815 tons. With the 15in twins mounted in *Vanguard* the pendulum of design swung back thirty years. A nucleus of 15in know-how still existed in the fleet and their thunder was occasionally heard in the postwar years. In 1954 *Vanguard* carried out the last 15in shoot – filmed for posterity from an attendant destroyer – but although she survived until 1960, her great guns remained silent. Some wished to preserve a twin 15in mounting in its entirety as a symbol of – even a memorial to – the extinct creature that was the British battleship: a laudible sentiment, unhappily not shared by those who held tight the parsimonious peacetime purse strings.

The hope lingered on until 1968 for, while the monitor *Roberts* survived, albeit as an accommodation ship, so did her 15in twin. But when all was done, this too was broken up, and all that remains of an era is the pair of 15in barrels mounted on a concrete plinth outside the Imperial War Museum in London. The breech mechanism on the right-hand gun is of particular interest because it was once used for instructional purposes at Woolwich Arsenal, and many ordnance specialists – the author included – stripped and re-assembled it as part of their technical training.

Appendices

APPENDIX 1: GUN CHARACTERISTICS

GREAT BRITAIN									
Parent mounting	**Gun**	**Max elevation (degrees)**	**Length (calibres)**	**Weight (tons)**	**Charge weight (lb)**	**Projectile weight (lb)**	**Muzzle velocity (fs)**	**Approx maximum effective range(yds)**	**Approx mounting weight (tons)**
BII, BIII BIV, BV	12in Mk VII	13½	35½	61	258	850	2350	14,860	184
BVI, BVII BVII(S)	12in Mk IX	13½[1]	40	50	254[2]	850	2525	16,650	200
BVIII, BVIII* BIX, BX	12in Mk X	13½	45	58	258	850	2700	18,630	450-500
BXI	12in Mk XI, 12in Mk XII	15	50	67	307	850	2825	20,960	510-540
Agincourt 'Special'	12in Mk XIII	16[3]	45	65	260	850	2700	20,435	460
13.5in Mk II II*, II** III, III*, III**	13.5in Mk V	20	45	76	293 297	1250(L) 1400(H)	2550 2450	23,405 23,181	600
Erin 13.5in 'Special'	13.5in Mk VI	20	45	77	265	1400	2400	22,505	600
14in Mk I	14in Mk I	20	45	84¾	344	1586	2475	23,950	720
15in Mk I, 15in Mk I*	15in Mk I	20	42	100	428(MD) 432(SC) 490 (super- charge)	1920 (4crh) 1938 (6crh)	2400 2400 2575	23,387 23,624 28,732 (super- charge)	768 (battle- cruisers) 804 (battle- ships)
15in 'B' Mk I (18in)	15in 'B' Mk I (18in)	30	40	149	630	3320	2270	28,886	825
15in Mk II	15in Mk I	30	42	100	428	1920	2400	29,182	889
15in Mk I/N	15in Mk I	30	42	100	428	1920 (4crh) 1938 (6crh)	2400	28,972 32,218	815
16in Mk I	16in Mk I	40	45	108	495	2048	2525(AP) 2550(HE)	37,689 39,884	1100
14in Mk II, 14in Mk III	14in Mk VII	40	45	79	338¼	1590	2400	36,322	900 1500

[1]The 12in Mk IX guns in the B VII(S) mountings in *Commonwealth* and *Zealandia* were later altered to 30°, giving 25,230yds range.
[2]*King Edward* class only; others 246.
[3]Originally 13½° giving 18,630yds range.

USA

Gun	Weight inc BM (to nearest ton)	Bore length (calibres)	AP shell (lb)	Propellant charge (lb)	Muzzle velocity (fs)	Range (yds)	Remarks
16in Mk 7	107 (less BM)	50	2700	660	2500	42,345 at 45°	*Iowa* class
16in Mk 6	86 (less BM)	45	2700	540	2300	36,900 at 45°	*North Carolina* and *South Dakota* classes
16in Mks 1, 5, 8	105	45	2240	540	2520	35,000 at 30°	*Maryland* class. Originally 2100lb shell 2600fs
14in Mks 4, 6, 7, 11	80	50	1500	420	2700	36,800 at 30°	*New Mexico* and *California* classes. Originally 1400lb shell 2800fs
14in Mks 8, 9, 10, 12	63	45	1500	420	2600	34,300 at 30°	*Texas*, *Oklahoma* and *Pennsylvania* classes
14in Mks 1, 2, 3, 5	63	45	1400	360	2600	21,000 at 15°	Above classes originally
12in Mk 8	49 (less BM)	50	1140	270	2500	38,573 at 45°	*Alaska* class
12in Mk 7	55	50	870	337	2900	23,500 at 15°	*Arkansas* class (probably similar in *Rivadavia* class)
12in Mk 6	54	45	870	340	2850	23,000 at 15°	*Utah* class – MV later reduced to 2750fs
12in Mk 5	53	45	870	305	2700	21,600 at 15°	*Louisiana*, *Kansas*, *Idaho*, *South Carolina* and *Delaware* classes
12in Mks 3, 4	52	40	870	240	2400	19,000 at 15½°	*Ozark*, *Maine* and *Virginia* classes. Originally intended 2600fs

JAPAN

Gun	Weight inc BM (to nearest ton)	Bore length (calibres)	AP shell (lb)	Propellant charge (lb)	Muzzle velocity (fs)	Range (yds)	Remarks
18.1in Type 1934	162	45	3230	728	2559	45,960 at 45°	*Yamato* class. Shell also given as 3219lb, range as 45,276yds at 45°
16in Type 1914	100	45	2249	483	2559	42,000 at 43°	*Nagato* class
14in Type 1908 and VSM	84	45	1485	318	2526	38,800 at 43°	*Kongo, Fuso* and *Ise* classes
12in EOC, VSM	67	50	850	300	?2850	?27,600 at 25°	*Kawachi* class (centreline turrets)
12in various	57 – 59	45	850	255	2706	23,100 at 20°	*Kashima, Tsukuba* and *Kurama* classes; *Satsuma, Aki* and *Kawachi* class wing turrets
12in EOC	49	40.4	850	155	2400	?	*Fuji* and *Shikishima* classes; *Mikasa*

GERMANY

Gun	Weight inc BM (to nearest ton)	Bore length (calibres)	AP shell (lb)	Propellant charge (lb)[1]	Muzzle velocity (fs)	Range (yds)	Remarks
15in SKC/34	109	48.4	1764	232 + 220	2690	38,880 at 30°	*Bismarck* class
15in SKL/45	76	42.4	1653	192 + 211	2625	22,200 at 16°	*Baden* class
12in SKL/50	51	47.4	893	201 + 76	2805	22,900 at 16°	All battleships and battlecruisers with 12in guns
11in SKC/34	52	51.3	728	170 + 91	2920	45,820 at 40°	*Scharnhorst* class
11in SKC/28	48	49.2	661	157 + 80	2985	40,500 at 40°	*Lützow* (ex-*Deutschland*) class
11in SKL/50	41	47.4	666	174 + 57	2887	21,300 at 16°	*Moltke* class and *Seydlitz*
11in SKL/45	39	42.4	666	174 + 57	2805	22,800 at 20°	*Nassau* class and *Von der Tann*
11in SKL/40	46	36.8	529	146	2690	20,600 at 30°	*Braunschweig* and *Deutschland* classes

[1]The two figures in this column refer to individual weights of main and fore charges respectively.

FRANCE

Gun	Weight inc BM (to nearest ton)	Bore length (calibres)	AP shell (lb)	Propellant charge (lb)	Muzzle velocity (fs)	Range (yds)	Remarks
15in M1935	93	45.4	1949	564	2575	41,065 at 35°	*Richelieu* and *Jean Bart.* MV originally 2723fs
13.4in M1912	65	45	1268	333	2559	26,600 at 23°	*Bretagne* class (earlier 1221lb shell 2605fs)
13in M1931	69	50.4	1235	423	2854	45,600 at 35°	*Dunkerque* and *Strasbourg*
12in M1906 – 10	53	45	950	274	2569	?	*Courbet* class
12in M1906	54	45	960	282	2559	?	*Danton* class
12in M1893 – 96	47	40	770	284	2839	?	*République* and *Liberté* classes
12in M1893 – 96	47	40	770	245	2674	?	*Gaulois* class, *Iéna* and *Suffren*
12in M1893	{45 43	45 40}	770	{196 217}	2559	?	{*Bouvet* *Massèna*
10.8in M1893 – 96	35	40	579	187	2674	?	*Henri IV* and rearmed *Caïman, Indomptable* and *Requin*
10.8in M1893	35	45	579	149	2559	?	*Bouvet, Massèna*

ITALY

Gun	Weight inc BM (to nearest ton)	Bore length (calibres)	AP shell (lb)	Propellant charge (lb)	Muzzle velocity (fs)	Range (yds)	Remarks
15in M1934	108	50	1951	599	2789	46,216 at 35°	*Littorio* class
12.6in M1934[1]	63	43.8	1157	359	2625		Reconstructed *Cesare* and *Duilio* classes. Guns were relined 12in/46
12in EOC, VSM	63	46	997	346	2756	?	*Dante*; *Cesare* and *Duilio* classes
12in EOC	51	40	943	194	2347	?	*Brin* and *Vittorio Emanuele* classes (EOC records show same gun in these ships). Original shell 850lb

[1]German figures give 42,760yds range at 45° for the 12.6in, with a 1157lb shell, indicating a very good aerodynamic form. If correct this would give 34,800yds at 27° and 36,820yds at 30°.

Gun	Weight inc BM (to nearest ton)	Bore length (calibres)	AP shell (lb)	Propellant charge (lb)	Muzzle velocity (fs)	Range (yds)	Remarks
RUSSIA							
12in M1910	48	50	1038	346	2500	26,350 at 25°	*Gangut* and *Imperatrice Maria* classes
12in/40	43	38.3	729	234	2600	?	12in ships from *Trisvititelia* to *Imperator Pavel*
AUSTRIA-HUNGARY							
12in/45	53	42.4	992	304	2625	?21,870 at 20°	*Radetzky* and *Viribus Unitis* classes
SPAIN							
12in VSM	65	50	850	287	2933	?	*España* class (quite different from other VSM and EOC 12in)
BRAZIL							
12in EOC	61	45	850	285	2800	?	*Minas Gerais* class

MISCELLANEOUS GUNS AND MOUNTINGS (BRITISH)

Mounting	Ship	Gun	Length (calibres)	Weight (tons)	Weight of charge powder (lb)	Weight of projectile (lb)
Vavasseur Centre Pivot	*Sans Pareil, Victoria*	10in Mks II, III, IV	32	29	252	500
Turret Mk I	*Thunderer*					
Turret Mk II	*Devastation*					
Barbette Mk III	*Barfleur, Centurion, Renown*					
Early Breech Loaders		12in Mks III, IV, V	25	45	295	714
Royal Sovereign class barbette		13.5in Mks I, II, III, IV	30	67	630	1250
Benbow barbette and *Victoria* class turret		16.25in Mk I	30	110	960	1800
Swiftsure turret		10in Mk VI	45	39	147 (cordite)	500
Triumph turret		10in Mk VII	45	31	147 (cordite)	500

APPENDIX 2: BRITISH GUN MOUNTING ALLOCATIONS

Mounting	Ship	Period
12in BII	*Majestic* *Magnificent* *Hannibal* *Prince George* *Victorious* *Jupiter* *Mars*	1894 – 96
12in BIII	*Caesar* *Illustrious*	
12in BIII	*Canopus* *Goliath* *Ocean*	1897 – 1902
12in BIV	*Albion* *Glory*	
12in BV	*Vengeance*	
12in BVI	*Formidable* *Implacable*	1902 – 03
12in BVII	*Irresistible*	
12in BVI	*London* *Bulwark*	1902
12in BVII	*Venerable*	
12in BVI	*Duncan* *Montagu* *Russell* *Cornwallis*	1903 – 04
12in BVII	*Exmouth* *Albemarle*	
12in BVI	*Queen*	1904
12in BVI	*Prince of Wales*	
12in BVII(S)	*King Edward* *Commonwealth* *Dominion* *Hindustan* *Zealandia* (ex-*New Zealand*) *Hibernia* *Africa* *Britannia*	1905 – 06
12in BVIII	*Lord Nelson* *Agamemnon*	1907 – 08
12in BVIII	*Dreadnought*	1906
12in BIX BIX and BX	*Invincible* *Inflexible* *Indomitable*	1906 – 08
12in BVIII*	*Bellerophon* *Temeraire* *Superb*	1909
12in BXI	*St Vincent* *Collingwood* *Vanguard*	1910
12in BXI	*Neptune*	1911
12in BXI	*Colossus* *Hercules*	1911
12in BVIII*	*Indefatigable* *New Zealand* *Australia*	1911 – 12
13.5in Mk II	*Orion* *Thunderer* *Monarch*	1912
13.5in Mk III	*Conqueror*	
13.5in Mk II	*Lion* *Princess Royal*	1912 – 14
13.5in Mk II*	*Queen Mary*	
13.5in Mk II*	*King George V* *Centurion* *Audacious*	1911 – 13
13.5in Mk III*	*Ajax*	
13.5in Mk II**	*Iron Duke* *Marlborough* *Emperor of India*	1914
13.5in Mk III**	*Benbow*	
13.5in Mk II**	*Tiger*	1914
12in 'Special'	*Agincourt*	1914
13.5in 'Special'	*Erin*	1914
14in Mk I	*Canada*	1915
15in Mk I	*Queen Elizabeth* *Warspite* *Barham* *Valiant* *Malaya*	1915 – 16
US 14in	*Abercrombie* *Havelock* *Raglan* *Roberts*	1915
Modified 12in BII (ex-Majestic class)	*Lord Clive*[1] *Earl of Peterborough* *General Craufurd* *General Wolfe*[1] *Prince Eugene* *Sir John Moore* *Sir Thomas Picton*	1915
15in	*Marshal Ney* *Marshal Soult*	1915
15in Mk I 'Special' (ex-*Marshal Ney* and *Furious* spare)	*Erebus* *Terror*	1916
15in Mk I*	*Renown* *Repulse*	1916
15in Mk I*	*Glorious* *Courageous*	1916
15in Mk I	*Royal Sovereign* *Revenge* *Ramillies* *Resolution*	1916 – 17
15in Mk I*	*Royal Oak*	
15in 'B' (18in)	*Furious*	1917
15in Mk II	*Hood*	1920
16in Mk I	*Nelson* *Rodney*	1926
15in Mk I/N	*Queen Elizabeth* *Valiant* *Warspite*	Modernisation 1937 – 40
15in Mk I*/N	*Renown*	Modernisation 1937 – 39
14in Mk II and Mk III	*King George V* *Prince of Wales* *Duke of York* *Anson Howe*	1939 – 41
15in Mk I 'Special' (ex-*Marshal Soult*)	*Roberts*	1941 – 42
15in Mk I/N 'Special'	*Abercrombie*	
15in Mk I/N RP12 (ex-*Glorious* and *Courageous*)	*Vanguard*	1946

[1] 15in BCD aft

APPENDIX 3: THE BRITISH 15in Mk I MOUNTING

GUN AND CRADLE

The 15in Mk I was of standard wire-wound construction with inner 'A' tube, an A tube, wire winding and a B tube. The jacket was shrunk over all, and had two sets of collars machined on it which located in grooves cut into the front and rear cradle, so that when the gun recoiled the barrel and cradles slid backwards on the sliding faces. The slide, on which the cradles moved in recoil, was bushed at each side to receive the trunnion pins, and the whole assembly was elevated or depressed by a piston working in a cylinder. Above the front cradle, a saddle piece, attached to the top of the jacket, slid under a non-recoiling saddle-cap to prevent the forward part jumping upwards when the gun fired, and a similar device called the kicking-strap secured the breech end to the rear cradle.

BREECH MECHANISM

In power operation, hydraulic pressure was admitted to the breech operating cylinder, whose piston had a double rack machined on its tail rod. The first movement of the main rack revolved a pinion and shaft, drove through internal gears and revolved the breech block to unlock it. The rotational drive then turned the complete carrier on its hinge, while an auxiliary rack, working through a gear-chain, operated a cut-off valve to close pressure to the cylinder, coincidentally with the fully open position. In hand operation the pinion shaft was declutched from the pinion and clutched to a wormwheel driven through gears from the handwheel.

RECOIL AND RUN-OUT

Two recoil cylinders were machined into the rear cradle, each with a piston carried between the trunnion arm and a tail rod bracket. Normal working recoil was 46in and metal-to-metal 47¼in. ('Metal-to-metal' describes the absolute maximum movement when recoiling and non-recoiling components would strike. This only occurred as a malfunction and usually brought considerable damage in its wake.) A hydraulic run-out gear was positioned centrally below the barrel and was rather cumbersome in operation. An air 'recuperator' (later introduced into new weapons in the 1920s) had not been perfected and, although run-out springs could be used on guns of up to 6in calibre, none could be made powerful enough to return a 100-ton gun to its run-out position. The gear consisted of two cylinders built into the (non-recoiling) slide body with a large hollow ram linking the two. The ram was attached to the recoiling cradles and so moved backwards into the run-out cylinder on gunfire. Its forward end was open (like a drainpipe) but its rear end contained a spring-loaded bypass valve, set to lift just above 1000psi.

A take-off line of system hydraulic pressure at 1000psi from the main turret pump led to a stop valve (normally locked open), an automatic cut-off valve, and thence to a valve block with an operating lever marked 'Run Out' and 'Run In'. It, too, was lockable, and was normally set at run-out. In this position the valve directed system pressure into the run-out cylinder and, since the bypass valve would only lift *above* 1000psi the pressure acting against the sensibly solid end of the ram held the gun in the run-out position, even at maximum elevation.

When the gun recoiled the ram was forced backwards into the run-out cylinder, and immediately created an over-pressure which lifted the bypass valve off its seating, allowing the hydraulic

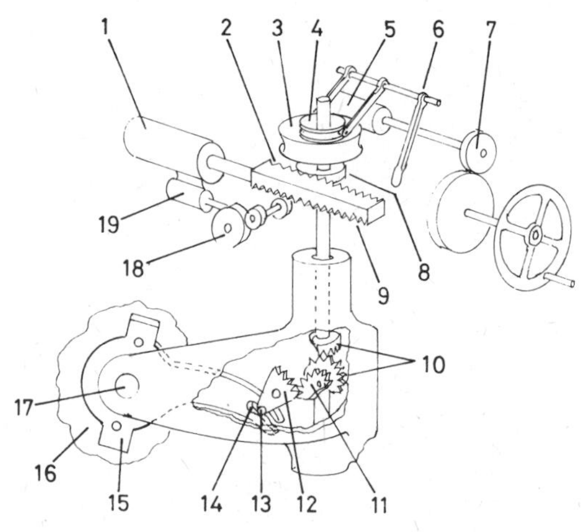

BRITISH 15in BL Mk I – BREECH MECHANISM

1 Hydraulic cylinder
2 Power-drive rack
3 Hand-drive wormwheel
4 Hand-power dog-clutch
5 Hand-drive worm
6 Clutch lever
7 Reduction gears
8 Power-drive pinion
9 Cut-off gear rack
10 Skew gears
11 Intermediate pinion
12 Crank pinion
13 Crank pin
14 Cam slot in crank
15 Breech-screw lever
16 Breech-screw
17 Firing lock
18 Cut-off gears
19 Cut-off valve cylinder

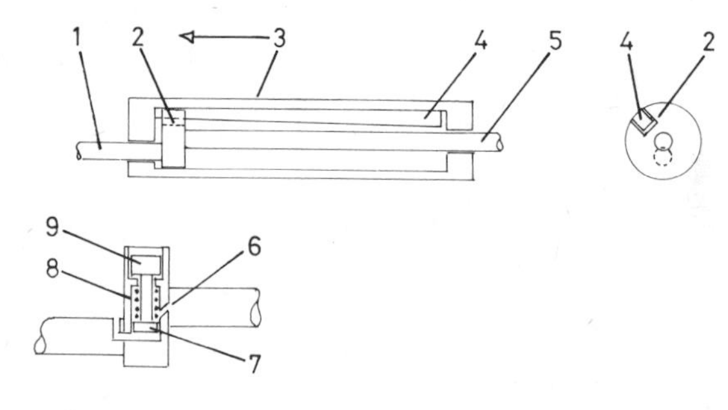

BRITISH 15in Mk I – RECOIL CYLINDER

1 Fixed tail-rod
2 Slot in piston head
3 Recoiling cylinder
4 Tapered key
5 Fixed piston-rod

Inset
Modified piston head for Mk I/N mounting

During recoil, fluid on right side of piston head flows through port 6, holding piston valve (7) down. Recoil controlled by tapered key (4) working in piston head slot (2).

During run-out (powered by air recuperator) liquid on left side of piston head lifts piston head (7) against spring (8), block 9 lifts to close slot against tapered key. Liquid can then only flow through hole 6. Because controlled run-out speed was impossible with this extemporary modification, run-out buffers were additionally fitted to absorb the final shock of run-out movement.

BRITISH 15in Mk I – RUN-OUT ARRANGEMENTS

1 Run-out cylinder
2 Spring-loaded bypass valve
3 Hollow run-out ram attached to rear cradle lug
4 Lug on rear cradle
5 Tappet
6 Run-in cylinder
7 Actuating lever
8 Combined throttle and exhaust valve
9 Directional control valve lever, normally locked at 'Run-out'
10 Directional control valve
11 Intercepting valve

Sequence

A Gun recoils on firing
B Spring-loaded valve (2), set to render above system pressure only, allows liquid to transfer into hollow ram. Gun arrested by (separate) recoil buffers. Over-pressure in 1 closes spring-loaded valve in 11
C At full recoil, 2 closes, 11 opens (under system pressure)
D System pressure re-opened to run-out cylinder
E Gun runs out
F Exhaust liquid flows through 8
G Exhaust discharged to exhaust line. At extremity of run-out, 5 strikes 7 and throttles exhaust flow to bring gun to rest
H Pressure diverted by valve at 'Run-in'
I Pressure opens 11, now linked to exhaust via 10
J Pressure opens independent internal poppet valve in 8
K Pressure enters run-in cylinder, gun runs in discreetly controlled by 9
L Exhaust from 1 directed by 10, runs to G

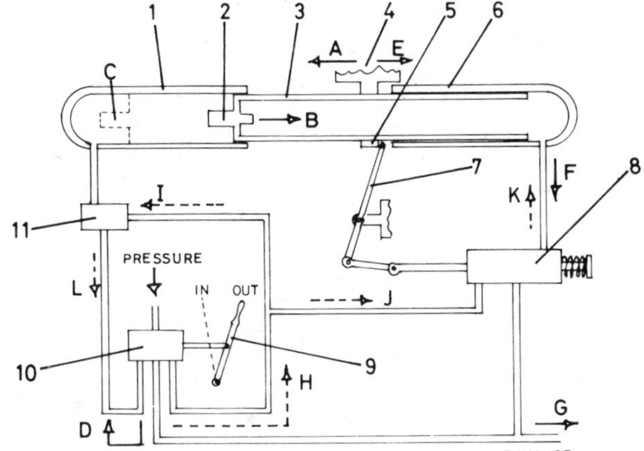

BRITISH 15in Mk I/N – MODIFIED RUN-OUT ARRANGEMENTS

1 Original run-out cylinder, converted for high-pressure air
2 Twin 'U'-section flexible gland-rings
3 Pneumatic ram
4 Lug on rear cradle
5 Redundant run-in cylinder retained as guide
6 Existing pipework retained as vent to atmosphere
7 Ratchet handpump to charge intensifier with liquid
8 Intensifier
9 Liquid lead from intensifier to 'U' glands
10 Full/empty indicator
11 Air charging stop-valve

Sequence

A Gun recoils, carrying ram into run-out cylinder
B Air pressure, normally at 1100psi, rises in proportion to recoil
C Air pressure acts on larger surface area of piston head of intensifier
D Liquid on smaller surface area of piston head, led to gland to expand 'U' seals
E Gun arrested in recoil by recoil buffer, increased air pressure runs gun out

Intensifier principles

Assume intensifier piston head to have a surface area of 3 sq in and tail-rod to have a cross sectional area of 1 sq in. Then, normal air pressure at 1100psi acts on 3 sq in and, therefore, applies a force of 3000lb on piston, which cannot move because liquid is virtually incompressible. Effective area of piston head on 'liquid' side is 3 sq in less the tail-rod, ie 2 sq in. For equilibrium, therefore, liquid pressure must be 1650psi and will always be higher than air pressure

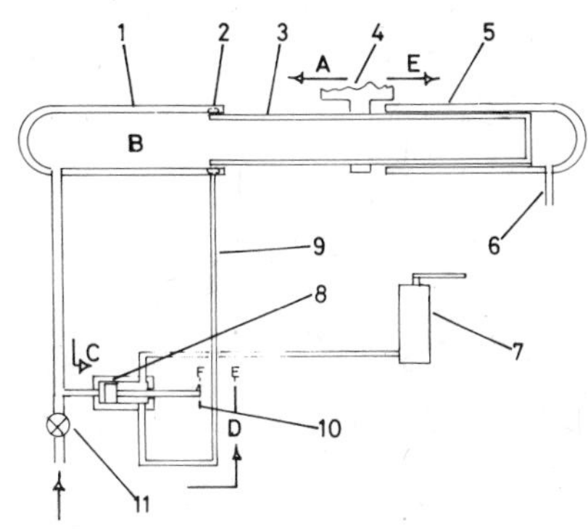

fluid to escape through the ram into the run-in cylinder. Because the internal volume of the assembly was constant, the fluid simply transferred from one cylinder to the other. As soon as the recoil shock had been absorbed by the twin recoil buffers, the bypass valve reseated itself and system pressure pushed the gun back outwards.

For inspections, maintenance or repairs the gun could be run-in by changing over the control lever. This transferred the pressure supply to the run-in cylinder. The hydraulic liquid then flowed through the ram but could not escape past the relief valve, while the line from the run-out cylinder was now connected to exhaust. Thus the complete gun (locked at zero elevation for this procedure incidentally) ran backwards as though in recoil; by closing the stop valve it could be discreetly moved any amount within its limits of travel. To return the gun to normal was simply a case of resetting the control lever to 'Run Out'. When the main turret pump was shut down, the cut-off valve closed in the run-out position, locked the pressure in the run-out cylinder and prevented the gun from accidentally moving to the rear.

The run-in facilities had obvious advantages but, on the whole, the system was inefficient (although, of course, common to all large guns of the day). One of the major changes during the conversion of the mounting to Mk I/N was the replacement of this gear by a pneumatic recuperator. The inefficiency of the hydraulic run-out gear centred on the fact that a liquid is virtually incompressible, whereas a gas is not. In the 15in Mk I, the gun depended on 1000psi to run it out but, with a completely sealed air 'recuperator', the air pressure rose (because air is compressible) in direct relationship to the introduction of the ram into the cylinder as the gun recoiled. In the 15in Mk I/N, for example, the standing air pressure was 1100psi but it rose to 2170psi in full recoil and it was this energy which pushed the gun back to the run-out position. An air recuperator also assisted the recoil buffers – a function not performed by the hydraulic equivalent – while the heavy demand on system hydraulic pressure was considerably reduced. In the modified arrangement the ram was closed at its outer end and the redundant run-in cylinder was retained solely as a guide.

To retain the high pressure air in the system, a gland was fitted to the cylinder. It was charged with a thick soapy liquid by a small charging pump, and worked in association with a device called an intensifier. This arrangement was cleverly designed in

BRITISH 15in Mk I – SHELL ROOM ARRANGEMENTS

1 Traverse press on shell room deckhead extending under hydraulic pressure
2 Trolley on overhead rail
3 Traverse press at 'exhaust', controlled in parallel with 1 above, retracting by movement of trolley
4 Lifting press at 'exhaust', retracting by weight of shell. At pressure, extends to lift shell grab
5 Anchor point of lifting wire
6 Lead of opposite end of lifting wire to auxiliary (locked) hand-drive. With 4 stationary, trolley can traverse without shell moving in vertical plane
7 Shell-steady, to prevent shell swinging
8 Shell descending by own weight (see 4 above)
9 Quick-release shell grab
10 Drive from auxiliary hand-traverse winch
11 Auxiliary hand-traverse wire (normally disconnected from trolley)

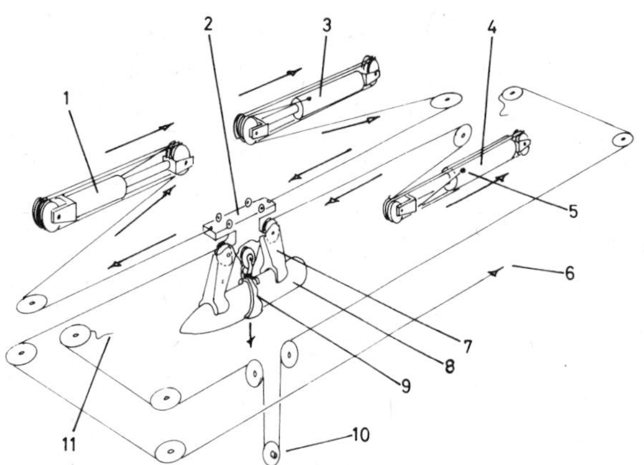

BRITISH 15in Mk I – SHELL BOGIE GEARS

1 Training handwheel drive to worm and wormwheel
2 Rack on revolving trunk
3 3-position clutch
4 Rack on fixed structure

In upper position of clutch (as shown), upper pinion is locked by wormwheel. Thus, as trunk revolves, bogie is carried around with it. In mid-position, both gear wheels are free to rotate, and empty bogie may be pushed around trunk. In lower position, hand-drive is connected to lower pinion and loaded bogie may be driven around trunk.

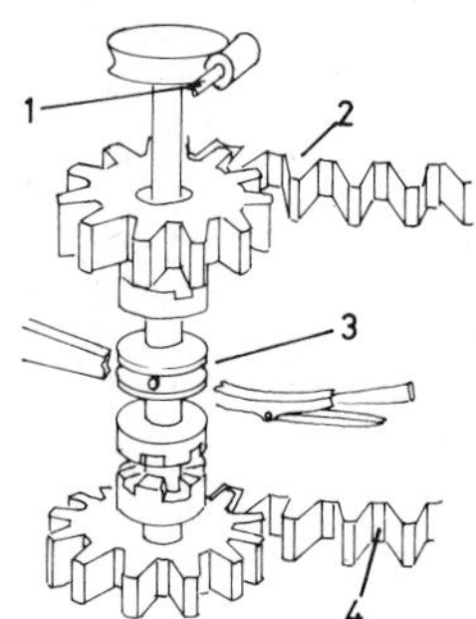

such a way that the pressure of liquid in the gland was always higher than that of the air. The system was, in fact, common to all modern gun mountings.

In the case of the recoil buffers, the cylinder moved in relation to the piston but, of course, it was immaterial which component actually did the moving. The system used a mixture of distilled water and glycerine as a hydraulic medium and, when the gun recoiled, the liquid trapped behind the piston-head could only escape through a port cut in it working over a tapered valve key. This progressively restricted the size of the port so the flow of liquid was gradually throttled, until at full recoil it was blocked completely. This too, was slightly modified on modernisation to Mk I/N standards.

GUNHOUSE LAYOUT

Power control levers were positioned in rear of the gun wells for each gunloading cage and each hydraulic radial crane. The latter could serve shell bins in the gunhouse with stowage for 3 rounds per gun, and there was further stowage for another 6 rounds per gun in the working chamber below. In an emergency, a hand-loading tray could be fitted in rear of the gun which its radial crane could also serve. Centrally, and behind the gun wells, there was a trunk for an auxiliary cordite hoist which ran directly to the cordite handing room – again for use in emergencies if the normal cages were defective. It had its own lifting machinery, controlled by a lever close to the top of the trunking. There were stowages for the two sub-calibre guns on the rear sides of the gunhouse, access hatches leading downwards abreast each gun, and another (armoured) hatch on the gunhouse roof just to the left of the centreline. The rear of the turret – called 'the cabinet' – housed a rangefinder, but its presence was not always obvious.

In 'B' and 'X' turrets, in the ten battleships fitted with the 15in twin, there was a 30ft MG14 rangefinder whose arms projected well beyond the gunhouse sides. Most ships had small platforms projecting outwards under these rangefinders to provide access to their extremities. In 'A' and 'Y' turrets the rangefinder was a 15ft MG8 contained completely within the gunhouse and thus not externally visible.[1] Small sighting ports were cut in the gunhouse armour in line with the lenses at the ends of the shorter rangefinder. *Renown* and *Repulse* conformed to the usual arrangement in having a 30ft rangefinder in 'B' turret only and 15ft units in 'A' and 'Y' but *Hood* had 30-footers in all four turrets. *Vanguard* was a special case: she had a 24ft 6in FX stabilised rangefinder in 'B', 'X' and 'Y' turrets but no instrument was fitted in 'A'. Instead the space was used as a secondary conning position, as was the case in the forward quadruple 14in Mk III.

TRAINING ENGINE SPACE

The area below the gunhouse floor was called the training engine space and held two indpendent hydraulic engines. Each drove a worm and wormwheel, the latter being engaged with or disengaged from the training pinion shaft by a handwheel-operated clutch. The handwheels were close to the layers' position, but only one engine was used at a time. It was a matter of gunhouse drill to ensure that one was de-clutched because the slightest 'mismatch' in engine speeds, if they were driving at the same time, resulted in serious strain to the training gear. The training engine space formed the gun wells behind each breech-end and also carried the trunnions of the elevating cylinders and the elevation 'walking pipes'. Under the trunnion axis of each gun, and secured to the engine space deck, were two hydraulic jacks which were extended to support the weight of the gun when maintenance on the trunnion bearings was undertaken.

[1] The 30ft rangefinders were not original equipment, being fitted after the ships had entered service. As built all the mountings carried 15ft rangefinders.

SHELL ROOM MACHINERY

Each shell room had large bin stowages in which the shells were laid horizontally, every bin having three overhead rails with power-operated conveyors above the sub-division of the stowage. The innermost rail, called the loading rail, ran from the inboard section of the shell bin to a point adjacent to the turret trunk, but the centre and outer rails had merely transfer conveyors. Once the shells in the bin beneath the loading rail had been expended, the transfer conveyors picked up their own ammunition and carried it to a sloping ramp called a Vaughan chute. Here it was rolled down to a point beneath the loading rail and again conveyed to the turret trunk.

The conveyors were moved along their respective rails by wires, hauled by the extension of a hydraulic press. This consisted of a ram with sheaves mounted on it, working in a cylinder having its own sheaves. One end of the wire was anchored to the cylinder, ran around the sheaves in succession rather like a large pulley-block system and then passed around jockey wheels, terminating at the conveyor. When pressure was admitted to the cylinder by a control valve, the ram extended, drawing the conveyor along its rail. The traversing presses were mounted in pairs to enable the conveyor to be moved in each direction. They worked together but in opposite directions so, when one extended, the other retracted to 'pay out' cable. An auxiliary hand traversing winch was also provided in case of power failure but its wires were disconnected when not in use.

Exactly the same principle was used to raise and lower the shells. In this case, one end of the wire was secured to a choke valve on the lifting cylinder which restricted the flow of pressure when the shell grab was rising unloaded, and the other end went to a hand lifting winch. This had a self-locking worm and worm-wheel drive and formed an anchor point for the opposite end of the lifting wire. If power failed, the shell could be raised or lowered by the hand winch. The lead of the lifting wires on the conveyors worked in a way similar to those on a hammerhead crane. Horseshoe-style steadies prevented the shell from spinning, while the hand-operated grabs – like a pair of massive steel pincers – held it around its centre of gravity.

The revolving trunking in the shell room was circular in cross section and had a continuous toothed rack secured to it. A second rack, fixed to the shell room deck, surrounded it. The two independent shell bogies ran around this rack system on guide rollers and each had a 3-position clutch. With the clutch lever in the lower position, a training handwheel on the bogie was connected, through shafting, to a pinion in engagement with the fixed rack so that a loaded bogie could be 'wound' around the trunking. In the upper position, the bogie was locked to the trunking and revolved with it when the turret trained. In the mid-position all gears were disconnected and the bogie could then be pushed around on its guide rails. The sequence of operation was:
1 Bogie freed and pushed around trunk until beneath the loading rail
2 Bogie clutched to fixed rack, and shell lowered on to it
3 Bogie moved around trunk by bogie training handwheel until opposite shell cage door in trunk
4 Bogie locked to trunk

MAIN CAGE CONTROL IN THE WORKING CHAMBER

The main cage was controlled by a very complicated lever system in the working chamber, the left and right main cages each having a control console with two levers, named after the crew members who operated them. The accompanying schematic diagram shows the two levers, 'No 5's' and 'No 6's', drawn in their normal position. The former had a right-angled handgrip and, when pulled vertically upwards to the hatched position, opened the appropriate control valve for the main cage hydraulic press which then extended and drew the combined shell and cordite cages upwards.

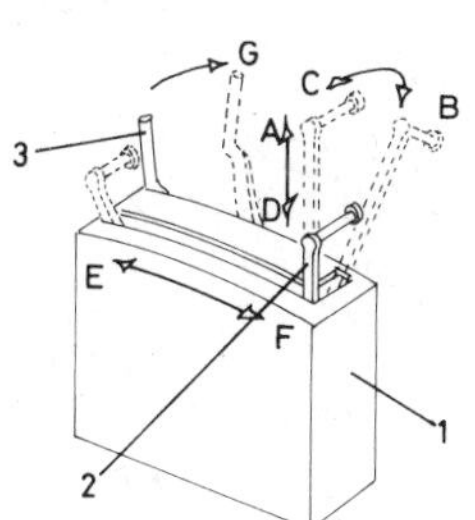

BRITISH 15in Mk I – WORKING CHAMBER CONTROLS

1 Console
2 No 5's lever in normal position with main cage down and rammers withdrawn
3 No 6's lever in normal position with gunloading cage down and locked, and flash doors over cage closed

Sequence
A Raise main cage
B Traverse shell carrier into trunk, pick up shell
C Withdraw shell carrier from trunk and into line with rammers and gunloading cage
D Lower main cage
E Ram shell and cordite into gunloading cage
F Withdraw rammers
G Unlock gunloading cage, open flash doors, 'cage ready' indicator shows 'ready' in gunhouse.

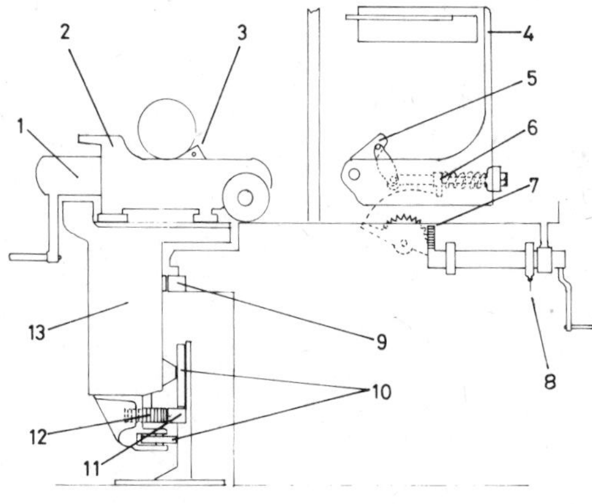

BRITISH 15in Mk I – SHELL HANDING ROOM ARRANGEMENTS

1 Traversing drive
2 Shell traversing trolley
3 Spring-loaded shell stop
4 Shell cage
5 Spring-loaded shell-dog
6 Tappet
7 Gear drive to withdrawal gear, depresses 5 when unloading
8 Spring-loading of unloading shaft
9 Rack on revolving structure
10 Thrust and guide rollers
11 Rack on fixed structure
12 Training pinion (training hand wheel not shown in this section)
13 Shell bogie

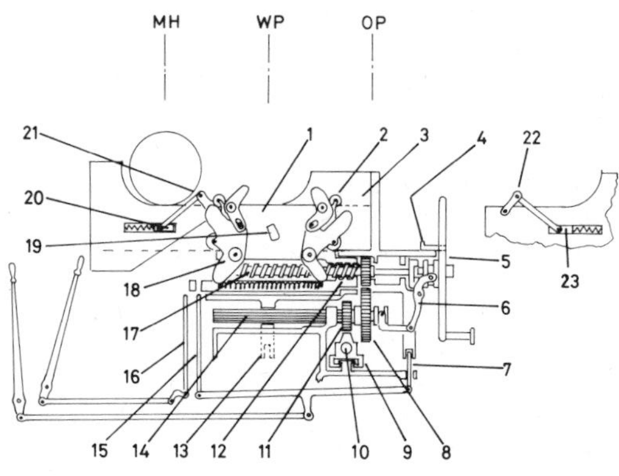

BRITISH 15in Mk I – WORKING CHAMBER SHELL CARRIER

1 Shell carrier
2 Carrier roller
3 Moving bed
4 Hand wheel locking plate
5 Alternative hand-drive
6 Hand/power clutch linkage
7 Moving bed locking-bolt
8 Gear drive
9 Moving hydraulic cylinder (with integral toothed rack) operated by No 5's lever
10 Fixed piston
11 Rack pinion
12 Internal thread on carrier
13 Slot for 7 in outer position
14 Splined shaft
15 Carrier locking-bolt
16 Carrier stop-bolt
17 Drive shaft
18 Spring-loaded carrier dog
19 Stop plate
20 Spring-loaded tappet
21 Shell cage dog
22 Moving bed dog
23 Spring-loaded tappet
MH Centreline of main hoist
WP Centreline of waiting position, working chamber rammers and gunloading cage
OP Centreline of outer position, plumbed by working chamber overhead rail and radial crane

Shell carrier is drawn in normal condition, clutched to 'power'. 'Traverse' movement of No 5's lever operates rack cylinder (9) and drives through gears 11 and 8 to revolve shaft (17). Carrier (1) is screwed into shell cage. Stop (19) strikes tappet (20), depressing dog (21) and freeing shell; at same time dog on carrier (18) passes under shell and spring-loading lifts dog beyond shell. Reversing No 5's lever withdraws shell to waiting position.

To move carrier to outer position, bolt 7 is withdrawn and, at the same time, bolt 15 is inserted into carrier. Carrier is now locked and moving bed unlocked.

Operating No 5's lever causes moving bed to move outwards to outer position, leaving carrier as drawn (11) sliding on splines (14). Moving bed is then locked into outer position by bolt 7 engaging in slot (13). Shell lowered on to moving bed and held by moving bed dog (22). Operating No 5's lever moves carrier outwards, outer carrier dogs function as inner dogs, stop (19) strikes tappet (23) and frees shell from moving bed. Carrier then free to take shell from outer position directly to shell cage. Reverse procedure restores moving bed to waiting position.

Hand operation identical except that stop bolt (16) is raised to locate carrier in waiting position when hand-traversing from outer position.

To move the shell outwards from its cage and into line with its rammer, for transfer into the gunloading cage, a power-operated traverser was run into the top of the trunk – the reverse of the loading process in the shell room. The 'traverse in' movement was initiated by No 5's lever being angled sideways, whereupon the traverser dogs slipped under the shell as it rested in the shell cage. Returning No 5's lever to the upright position withdrew the traverser and shell together, so that the two tiers of cordite charges (automatically tipped into a waiting position on arrival of their cage) were again above the shell, but now outboard of the main cage and in line with the working chamber rammers. No 5 now returned this lever to its initial 'down' position, sending the main cage back to the magazine and shell room. Assuming that the gunloading cage had now arrived at working chamber level, No 6 worked his lever: this closed a hinged flashtight 'box' sealing the whole gunloading cage from any flash coming down the gun well from the gunhouse above and, at the same time, locked the cage to the working chamber floor. No 5 pushed his lever forwards, along the slot in the console, and in so doing first operated flashtight doors between the working chamber waiting position and the gunloading cage. As soon as they were open, double-headed and single-headed rammers advanced, thrusting the two levels of cordite charges and the shell into the gunloading cage. The shell rammer head was cup-shaped to take over the nose cap. Finally, moving No 5's lever back to its start point withdrew the rammers and closed the flash doors, so that the gunloading cage was loaded but totally sealed. When the gunhouse was ready to receive the next charge of ammunition, No 6 worked his lever, unlocking the cage from the working chamber floor, and opening the hinged 'box' around it. Every movement of the two levers opened (or closed) hydraulic control valves – all sequentially interlocked – so that the internal complications of the console can well be imagined.

MAJOR CHANGES ON MODERNISATION TO Mk I/N

Very extensive re-engineering of the elevation arrangements was necessary to produce the 30° elevation sought by the Naval Staff. The gunhouse roof was removed completely to provide access to the guns, which were taken out of the turrets for the work to be carried out. The trunnion axis on the front cradle was shifted backwards towards the breech so that when the guns were replaced in the mounting, they were set further towards its front face; the resulting 'muzzle-heaviness' was compensated for by a balance weight fitted over the 'kicking strap'. This scheme gave the extra clearance necessary in the gun wells but the gunloading cage rails had to be reset to conform to the new position of the breech. The elevation cylinder and elevation walking pipes also required re-engineering and extra interlocking was added to the loading gear. Interlock No 21, for example prevented the breech from being opened in power above 20° and its counterpart, No 31, prevented the gun from being elevated above 20° if the breech was already open.

Externally, the gunhouse roof had to be modified in way of each gun at the new maximum elevation, where an armoured hood extended the arc of the slot cut in the front face armour. The extent of this hood is revealed by the shape of the blast bag over the mantlet plate of Mk I/N mountings and was their principal recognition feature.

MODIFICATIONS TO HMS *VANGUARD*'S MOUNTINGS

The two major changes in the four 15in mountings fitted in *Vanguard* made for the light battlecruisers *Glorious* and *Courageous* and retained as spares on their conversion to aircraft carriers) were not visible. The original training power-drive had been simply a worm on the training engine shaft engaged with a wormwheel whose own shaft drove the training pinion, giving an overall gear ratio of approximately 800:1. When it was decided to provide a remote power control facility to *Vanguard*'s mountings, the power drives were redesigned.

Worm and wormwheel drives have the advantage of giving a very high gear reduction ratio while, at the same time, turning the direction of drive through 90°. However, worms themselves can be subject to considerable wear, leading to backlash which must be avoided at all costs in remote power follow. An alternative is to use 90° bevel wheels (which were adopted in *Vanguard*) but these, like plain spur gear wheels, cannot provide the high reduction ratios possible with a worm and wormwheel arrangement. Thus when they were introduced into the final version of the 15in mounting, a compound reduction gear chain had to be added to achieve an acceptable overall ratio, which eventually worked out at 676:1

After several decades of accepting the disposition of the magazines and shell rooms in the original 15in form, the designers of the new battleship decided to reposition the magazine below the shell room. The full implementation of this would have entailed a very major change to all the loading arrangements because the shell would then be above the cordite in the main cage instead of below it. As a compromise, the relative positions of the shell room and cordite handing rooms remained the same, but separate off-mounting cordite hoists were provided to shift the charges from magazine level, past the shell room and up to a new cordite handing room above it.

Equally unusual was the decision to mount a twin 40mm (STAAG) Bofors on the roof of 'B' gunhouse. Perhaps direct close-range fire coverage dead ahead was deemed necessary but, unlike the other close-range mountings which were frequently carried on the roof of the gunhouses, the STAAG was a very delicate unit and one feels that it would not have suffered too many 15in firings without becoming defective.

No other British heavy gun mounting ever quite matched the 15in twin – a point of view which the reader may share when comparing its design with that of its successors, the 16in triple and the 14in quadruple and twin.

15in Mk I – INTERLOCKS (by designated numbers)

Working chamber

1 Cannot put No 5's lever to raise main cage until shell doors and cordite hoppers are closed
2 Cannot lower main cage until shell carrier is withdrawn from trunk
3 Cannot traverse shell carrier to trunk until No 5's lever is fully up
4 Cannot traverse shell carrier to trunk until main cage is up
5 Cannot put No 5's lever to open waiting position flash doors or to ram until lever has been put to 'Lower Main Cage'
6 Cannot open waiting position flash doors until gunloading cage is locked
7 Cannot open waiting position flash doors until cordite rammers have been withdrawn clear of flash doors
8 Cannot ram until waiting position flash doors are open
9 Cannot free gunloading cage until waiting position flash doors are closed
10 Cannot open flash doors over gunloading cage unless gun is at less than 20° elevation (Mk I/N only)

Shell room

11 Cannot put main hoist telegraph to 'Ready' until cordite telegraph has been put to 'Ready'
12 Cannot open shell door until No 5's lever is put to 'Lower'
13 Cannot open shell door until main cage is down

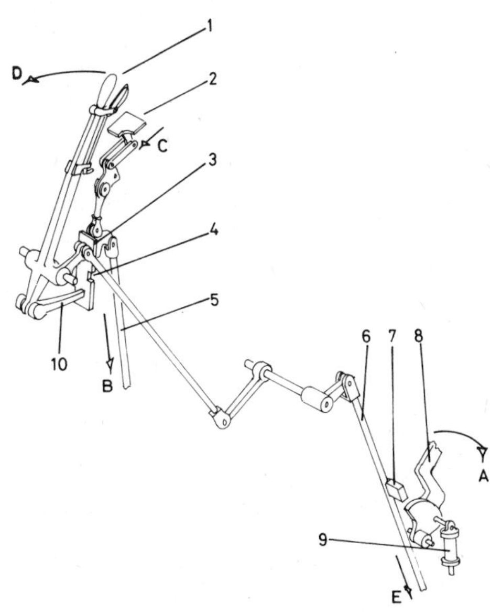

BRITISH 15in Mk I – TYPICAL INTERLOCKS

1 Gunloading cage control lever in gunhouse
2 'Cage Ready' telegraph plate
3 Interlock plate
4 Interlock slot
5 Link-rod from cage unlocking gear in working chamber
6 Link-rod to cage hydraulic control valve
7 Interlock block
8 Breech workers' 'Breech Open' foot-pedal
9 Spring box
10 Interlock bar

Sequence
A Breech worker opens breech, operates foot pedal and clears 8 from 7
B 'No 6' unlocks cage in working chamber
C Telegraph plate shows 'Cage Ready', slot 4 aligns with bar 10
D 'No 1' operates lever to raise cage
E Link-rod opens cage control valve to 'Raise'

14 Cannot traverse shell trolley until bogie is in line with trunk opening
15 Cannot traverse shell trolley if bogie is clutched to ship
16 Cannot unclutch bogie from trunk when trolley is in trunk
17 Cannot train bogie when trolley is traversed to trunk

Cordite handing room

18 Cannot open cordite hopper until No 5's lever is put to 'Lower'
19 Cannot open cordite hopper until main cage is down

Gunhouse

20 Cannot open breech (in power) until gun has run out far enough for breech to swing clear of loading arm
21 Cannot open breech (in power) if gun is at more than 20° elevation (Mk I/N only)
22 Cannot close breech (in power) until 'spoon tray' is clear
23 Cannot raise gunloading cage until No 2's pedal has been depressed, ie until breech is open (Note: pedal operation is drill, not auto)
24 Cannot raise gunloading cage until gunloading cage has been freed
25 Cannot raise gunloading cage until flash doors around cage are open
26 Cannot raise gunloading cage if the gun is elevated to 20° or above (Mk I/N only)
27 Cannot lower gunloading cage until chain rammer is fully withdrawn
28 Cannot lower gunloading cage until cordite dropping lever is in forward position
29 Cannot put hand lever for chain rammer to ram until gunloading cage is up
30 Cannot work cordite dropping lever until chain rammer is fully withdrawn
31 Cannot elevate gun above 20° with breech open (in power) (Mk I/N only)
32 Cannot elevate gun above 20° with gunloading cage at loading arm (Mk I/N only)

Auxiliary cordite hoist

33 Cannot open handing room doors until cage is down
34 Cannot 'free' the cage until handing room doors are closed

Working chamber

35 Cannot open access door unless hoist lever is to 'Lower'

Gunhouse

36 Cannot raise cage until access doors in working chamber are closed
37 Cannot raise cage until cage has been 'freed' in handing room

'Gun Loaded' position

1 Gunloading cage loaded and down
2 Main shell cage loaded
3 Cordite hoppers in handing room loaded with one full charge
4 One full charge each side, out of cases in magazine

When gun fires

1 Gunloading cage is raised
2 Main cordite cage loaded, cage raised
3 Shell and cordite transferred to waiting position in working chamber
4 Main cage sent down and reloaded with shell only
5 One full charge passed from magazine to handing room (through flashtight scuttle) and placed in hopper
6 One full charge removed from cases in magazine
7 When gunloading cage returns to working chamber, shell and cordite are rammed into it from waiting position, thus returning to 'Gun Loaded' position (Note: when gunloading cage leaves working chamber floor, it moves a telltale in handing room to 'Load')

15in Mk I – TELEGRAPH PLATES (for each gun)

Shell room

1 Shell
Down↔Not down
Cage

2 Central
Ready↔Not ready
Cage

3 Cordite
Ready↔Not ready
Cage

1 is operated by shell cage; cannot open shell door unless cage is down
2 is operated by shell telegraph handle, cannot be moved until cordite cage is ready
3 is operated by cordite telegraph handle in cordite handing room

Cordite handing room

4 Load
(Blank)

5 Cordite
Down↔Not down
Cage

3 Cordite
Ready↔Not ready
Cage

4 moves to 'Load' when gunloading cage leaves working chamber
5 is operated by cordite cage

Working chamber

6 Central
Up↔Not up
Cage

7 Central
Ready↔Not ready
Cage

6 and **7** were repeaters operated by the shell telegraph handle
When cordite cage arrives at working chamber level, **6** goes to 'up'; **2**, **3** (in shell room), **3** (in cordite handing room) **7** and **8** all go to 'Not ready'

Gunhouse

8 Cage
(Blank)↔Not
Ready

15in TURRET CREW (*VANGUARD*)

83 men with officer in charge

Captain of turret	1 CT
Second captain of turret	1 2nd CT
Gunlayers	2 GL
Turret trainer	1 TT
Sight setters	3 SS
Phoneman	1 Phone
Two guns crews of 6 men each	12 men
FCB operators	2 men
Cordite handing room crew	11 men (10 in 'X' and 'Y')
Shell handing room crew	13 men
Shell room crew	16 men
Magazine crew	20 men (17 in 'X' and 'Y')
	83

(Note: 'X' and 'Y' had 3 instead of 4 fixed structure hoists)

APPENDIX 4: THE BRITISH 16in MkI MOUNTING

LOADING ARRANGEMENTS

From the schematic sketches, one can see the passage of shell from source to gunhouse. The huge projectiles were stowed horizontally, in bins, in shell rooms set around a compartment called the shell handing room. They were lifted from their stowage by powerful grabs and carried by overhead conveyors to a power-operated traversing tray, capable of holding two shells. Either shell position could be aligned between a fixed feed tray and a hydraulic rammer. When operated, the rammer thrust the projectile through an aperture, in the shell room bulkhead, on to a pivoted tray in the adjacent shell handing room. A watertight door opened to allow the shell to pass and closed as soon as the shell room rammer had withdrawn. By having a traversing tray, it was possible to load one of its two troughs while the other was in the ramming position.

The shell handing room surrounded the revolving turret trunk, to which a pair of contrarotating, power-driven, geared rings were attached. These could be clutched to drive four shell bogies, set at 90° apart. When three projectiles, from three separate shell rooms, had arrived on the pivoting trays the bogies were traversed around the trunk to a lined-up position and locked 'to ship'. Each pivoting tray was then revolved until it lined up with a shell bogie and an integral tray rammer transferred the shell. The rotating power-driven gear-rings were next connected to the bogie bodies through a complex arrangement of power drives and clutches. The bogie, now connected to the rotating rings, was of cradle style with a geared quadrant and, in being turned through 90°, it caused the shell to take up an upright attitude. When the three bogies had thus tipped, they were unlocked from the ship, reclutched to 'traverse' and driven around the trunk until each was in line with a shell hoist. The three independent shell hoists – one for each gun – were themselves displaced 90° apart, so that one of the four bogies was unused. This, referred to as the master bogie, was normally kept upright and was used solely as a position from which all four bogies were traversed. It was, of course, used as a spare when one of the others became defective as the bogie traverse could be controlled from any of the four positions, their operating levers being mechanically linked together.

When the mounting was first conceived each bogie was to have been completely independent, but all were linked together when the basic ship design was altered. This lack of independence was something of a drawback because it meant, in effect, that all three guns had to be loaded at the same time. Ideally, one would have wished to be able to engage a target with a proportion of the guns in a mounting while the other – or others – were being loaded, as was the case with the 15in.

Having located the bogies opposite the shell hoists, the complete bogie ring was locked to the trunking and would then revolve with it should the turret train. Each shell, now resting on its base, was next moved towards the hoist by the bogie rammer (again powered by the common power drive), all bogie movements being mechanically interlocked to prevent accidental malfunction. For example, it was impossible to unlock 'from ship' until all three working bogies had been tilted upright, nor would the bogie rammer function until the bogie had been locked to the trunk.

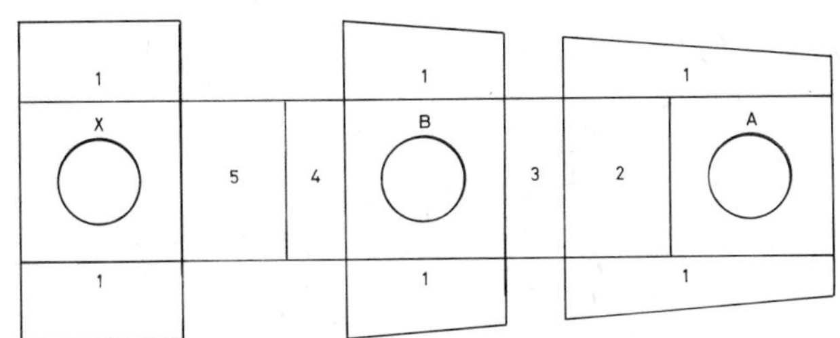

BRITISH 16in Mk I – SHELL ROOM DISPOSITION

A 'A' shell handing room
B 'B' shell handing room
C 'X' shell handing room
1 Wing shell rooms
2 'A' midship shell room
3 'B' forward midship shell room
4 'B' after midship shell room
5 'X' midship shell room
(Note: Cordite handing rooms and magazines vertically below, in each case.)

BRITISH 16in Mk I – SHELL ROOM TO SHELL HANDING ROOM ARRANGEMENTS

1 Shell grab traverse wire
2 Shell grab truck
3 Shell grab lifting and lowering wire
4 Rammer casing
5 Shell traverser
6 Shell feed tray
7 Watertight door
8 Pivoted tray
9 Pivoted tray rammer

Sequence

A Lower shell into vacant trough on twin-trough traverser (5)
B Open watertight door
C Ram shell on to pivoted tray (8)
D Withdraw rammer
E Close watertight door
F Traverse tray to bring second shell to rammer, reload vacant trough
G Revolve pivoted tray when shell bogie is locked 'to ship'

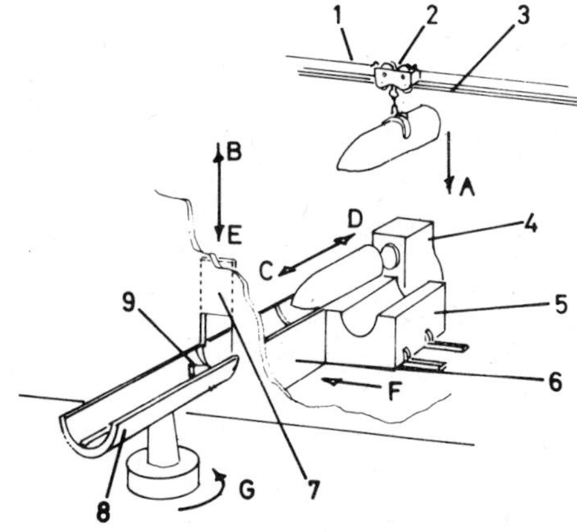

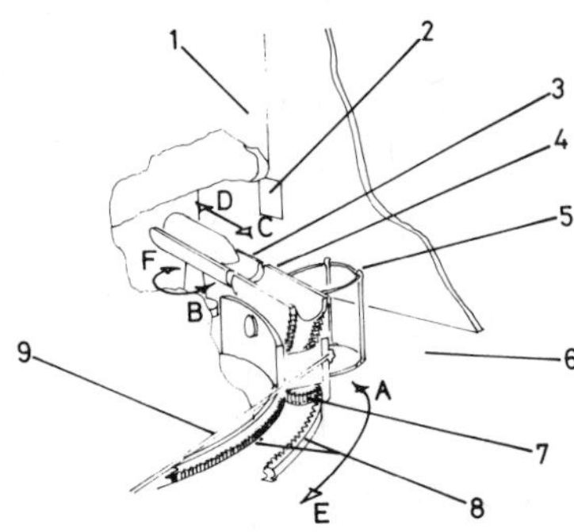

BRITISH 16in Mk I – PIVOTED TRAY TO SHELL BOGIE ARRANGEMENTS

1 Revolving trunk
2 Watertight door to shell room
3 Pivoted tray
4 Shell bogie
5 Bogie operator's position
6 Shell handing room
7 Gear-wheel drive to bogie
8 Contra-rotating gears to bogie drive
9 Link rod to adjacent bogie

Sequence
A Slew bogie 'to ship' and lock 'to ship'
B Revolve pivoted tray
C Ram shell from pivoted tray to bogie with pivoted tray rammer
D Withdraw rammer
E Unlock bogie 'from ship', slew 'to trunk'
F Revolve pivoted tray back to watertight door

BRITISH 16in Mk I – SHELL BOGIE TO SHELL SCUTTLE ARRANGEMENTS

1 Shell hoist trunk
2 Shell scuttle
3 Shell bogie (tilted to vertical)
4 Bogie control console (Inset: console lever gates)
5 Inner drive-ring
6 Outer drive-ring
7 Drive pinion, meshed to both rings
8 Power drive from hydraulic motor
9 Drive pinion to 'Tilt' and 'Ram' shafts, meshed to both rings
10 Pinion meshed only with inner drive-ring for 'traverse left' motion
11 Band-brake clutch
12 Clutch disc: when band brake 11 is engaged, pinion 10 cannot revolve, and bogie traversed right
13 Duplicate traverse gear, meshed to outer drive-ring for 'traverse right'
14 'Tilt' clutch
15 Drive to tilt gearing
16 'Ram' clutch
17 Drive to ram gearing
18 Shell bogie envelope

Sequence
A Bogie traversed from pivoted tray
B Lock bogie 'to trunk', bogie revolves with mounting structure
C Ram shell from bogie to shell scuttle
D Withdraw rammer
E Unlock bogie 'from trunk'; traverse bogie left or right to adjacent pivoted tray

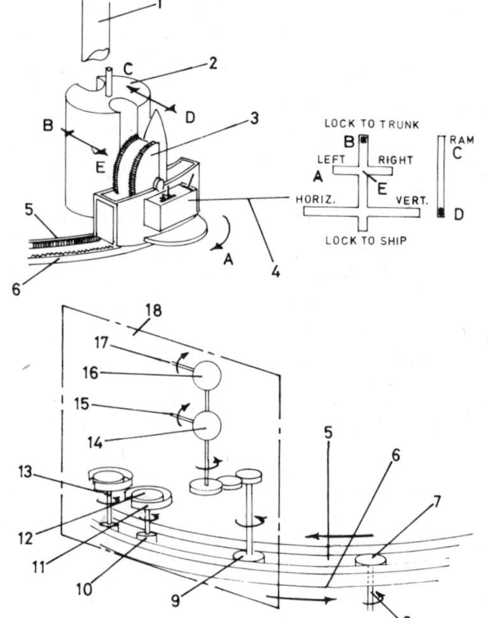

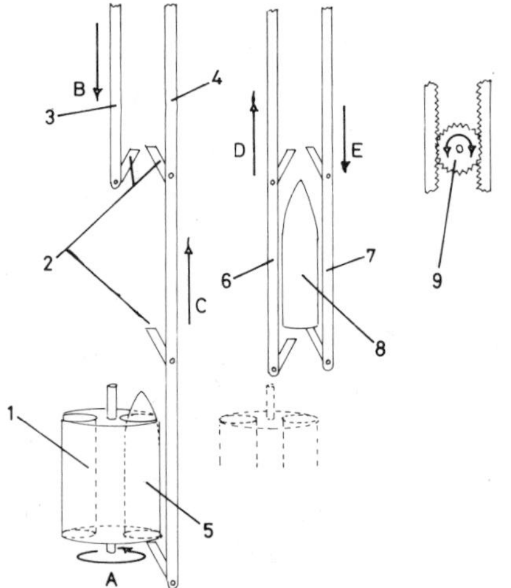

BRITISH 16in Mk I – SHELL SCUTTLE TO SHELL HOIST ARRANGEMENTS

1 Vacant shell compartment awaiting reload from shell bogie
2 Spring-loaded shell lifting pawls
3 Left-hand pawl bar in upper position
4 Right-hand pawl bar in lower position
5 Shell at foot of hoist
6 Left-hand pawl bar in lower position
7 Right-hand pawl bar in upper position
8 Shell lifted to first step
9 Pawl bar drive pinion

Sequence
A Shell scuttle revolved 180° from bogie (Note: for modifications to scuttle drive in service, see text)
B Pawl bar about to descend
C Pawl bar about to ascend
D Pawl bar about to ascend
E Pawl bar about to descend

BRITISH 16in Mk I – CORDITE HANDING ROOM ARRANGEMENTS

1. Cordite hoist trunk
2 Combined flash door and rammer control lever
3 Twin 3-charge cordite hoppers
4 Twin rammer casing
5 Hopper door, manually operated
6 Hopper door grip-bar

Sequence
A Open hopper door, place charges in hopper, close hopper door
B Open flash door
C Ram cordite
D Withdraw rammer
E Close flash door

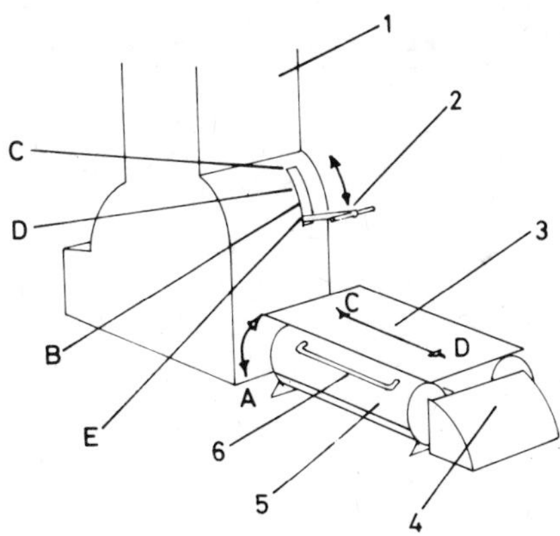

Between the shell bogie and the hoist base there was a cylindrical drum called a scuttle which accepted the shell when it was rammed inwards. The scuttle was rather like an enormous pistol cylinder, with two shell positions diametrically opposite each other, and it, too, had to be locked before the bogie rammer could operate. Once the shell had been transferred and the scuttle unlocked, the latter was engaged with the shell hoist mechanism. Its downstroke operation spun the scuttle around half a turn, placing the shell at the foot of the hoist tube, at the same time exposing its empty shell position. The scuttle drives gave persistent trouble and were prone to shear completely. In 1936 the automatic feature was removed, the scuttles being modified for hand-rotation, and an extra crew member added for each.

The shell was now moved upwards towards the gunhouse by a pusher hoist that worked on the ratchet principle, shown schematically in the sketches. As soon as all shells had been transferred to their respective hoists, the bogies were unlocked and traversed back to the nearest convenient pivoting tray; and so the process went on until the three hoists were full. By this time, they held a vertical column of four shells each (the highest projectiles having reached the gunhouse) and there were thus 12 tons of shell in the hoist trunks.

In the cordite handing room the six cordite charges were laid in trios into the hopper trays, swung into the hopper trunking and then power-rammed horizontally into a double-cylinder canister. A wire rope skip tipped it vertically upwards and hauled it to the gunhouse in one movement, where it appeared alongside the waiting shell ready for loading.

GUNHOUSE LOADING ARRANGEMENTS

Remembering that there were three identical guns in each mounting, we need only consider the loading process for one. However, it is worth mentioning that the left gun breech hinged open on the left-hand side, whereas both the centre and the right guns had right-handed breeches. This was not particularly significant since, clearly, the centre gun had to be 'handed' on one side or the other, but it did, of course, make the hoists asymmetrical. British interrupted screw breech mechanisms opened, door-wise, either to left or right but the Americans favoured a mechanism hinged at six o'clock so that, even in a multi-gun turret, the breeches were identical, gun to gun.

A gun's crew consisted of three men. The captain of the gun (CoG) operated the loading control levers and the chamber wash-out squirt; No 2 looked after the electric firing circuits and the air-blast gear (to discharge the cordite fumes from the chamber when the breech was reopened); and No 3 worked the shell and cordite hoists by two operating levers. He could see immediately when a shell was available by its presence at the top of the shell hoist, but waited until a mechanical telegraph plate moved to reveal 'Cage Loaded' before raising the cordite.

BRITISH 16in Mk I – CORDITE HOIST ARRANGEMENTS

1 Cordite hopper in magazine
2 Twin 3-charge cordite canister
3 Canister lifting head
4 Cordite tilting tray
5 Tilting tray hydraulic cylinder
6 Lifting wire
7 Hoist trunk
8 Lifting wire lead to hydraulic press sheaves
9 Tilting tray buffer
10 Gunhouse floor level
11 Guide lugs for traverse motion
12 Flash door

Sequence
A Ram cordite to canisters
B Tilt tray up in alignment with hoist
C Raise cordite canister to cordite tray in gunhouse

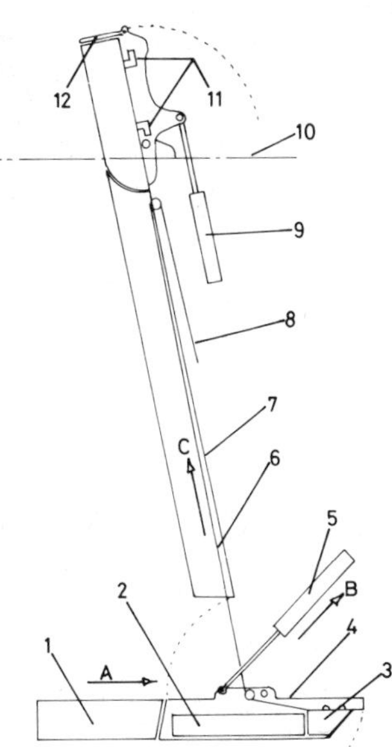

The CoG now took over, operating his two hand-levers. These were known colloquially as 'churn levers' because of their motion around three sides of slotted square box – shown on the schematics. Complex mechanical interlocking rods (very similar to those found beneath a railway signal box) were fitted to prevent malfunction. The first movement was towards 'Lock Slide', whereupon the gun was divorced from the layer's control and automatically moved, as required, in either elevation or depression, until it reached the fixed loading angle of 3°. There, heavy pawls engaged it, holding it rigidly. Shifting the same lever sideways aligned it with the 'Tilt Tray' slot and, at the same time, opened the power-operated breech. The shell hoist terminated in a hinged section which held the shell and moving the lever to 'Tilt Tray' tipped the shell downwards to the 3° loading angle. The cordite canister, linked to the tilting gear, tipped automatically to the same angle so that both shell and cordite were now aligned alongside each other. At this stage, however, they were to one side of the breech, clear of the gun's recoil, so, as soon as the tipping motion of the shell tray was complete, it tripped a traverse gear which carried it sideways on a carriage, pulling the cordite canister after it. At this point, the situation was:

1 Gun locked at loading angle
2 Breech open
3 Shell tray tilted and traversed to position in line with chamber

The CoG now operated his second lever towards 'Ram Shell', whereupon a seven-section telescopic rammer extended, from a rammer casing anchored to the turret deck-plate, and thrust the shell through the chamber until its copper driving band bit into the commencement of the rifling. When he returned it to the 'Withdraw' position, it became aligned with the lateral 'Traverse' slot. Moving it in this new direction caused the whole assembly to traverse a step inwards, so bringing the first three charges into line between the rammer and the chamber. The same lever, pulled backwards into the 'Ram Cordite' slot, again extended the rammer, but its stroke was automatically reduced as the cordite did not have so far to travel as the shell. The rammer was withdrawn by returning the lever to the 'Withdraw' position again, the assembly traversing another step inwards automatically, to bring the second trio of charges into the ramming position. The rammer was then extended for the third time, pushing the second three charges into the chamber and shunting the first three before them.

The first movement of the reverse sequence traversed the shell tray and cordite canister back towards their hoists, where the empty cordite container re-entered the hoist skip-cage and the shell tray reconnected with the hoist tilt gear. Thereafter, the shell tray was tilted upright, the breech closed, a firing tube inserted into the lock, the slide unlocked, and the layer resumed elevation control of the gun. The gun-drill order 'Free the slide' was adopted in the messes as a request to 'Pass the butter' and is still sometimes used today, although its significance is rarely appreciated.

Once the cordite canister had returned to the top of its hoist trunk, and the shell tray had been tilted upright by the CoG, No 3 sent the cordite cage back down to the lower quarters for reloading and brought another shell up into the shell tray by operating his 'Raise Cordite' and 'Raise Shell' control levers. The three drill conditions were:

1 Gun loaded Gun on pawls and loaded, no tube in vent; firing circuit interceptor open; shell tilting tray loaded; shell hoist full; cordite cage up, and full
2 Half-cock Gun loaded; tube in vent; interceptor open; gun free from pawls
3 Gun ready Gun loaded; tube in vent; gun layer 'on', by matching receiver pointers; interceptor closed

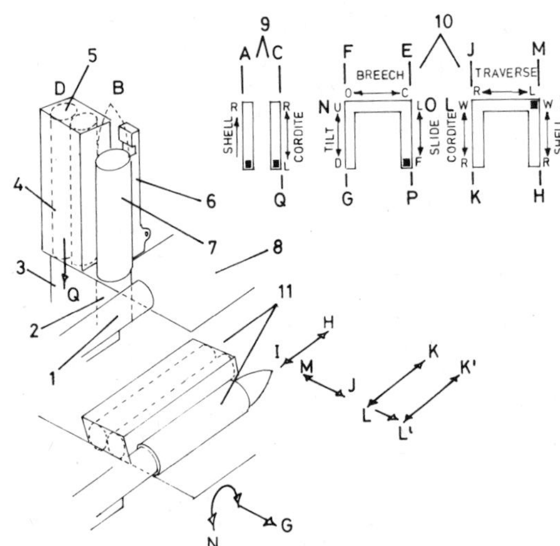

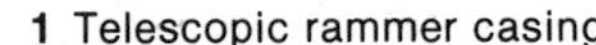

BRITISH 16in Mk I – GUNHOUSE LOADING ARRANGEMENTS

1 Telescopic rammer casing
2 Shell hoist trunk
3 Cordite hoist trunk
4 Cordite tray
5 Cordite canister
6 Tilting tray
7 Shell 'bucket'
8 Gunwell
9 Hoist control levers
10 'Churn' levers' position at 'Gun ready'
11 Shell and cordite tilted to loading position

Sequence
A Raise shell
B Shell arrives in shell 'bucket'
C When cage indicator shows 'Ready', raise cordite
D Cordite canisters arrive in cordite tray
E After gun has fired, lock slide, gun moves to loading angle and locks
F Open breech
G Tilt down: shell and cordite tilt to loading angle, then both traverse automatically to bring shell into line with rammer
H Ram shell
I Withdraw rammer
J Traverse: first canister tube moves into line with rammer
K Ram first three cordite charges
L Withdraw rammer: automatic traverse brings second cordite canister tube into line
K1 Ram second three cordite charges
L1 Withdraw rammer
M Traverse left: empty units move back into line with hoists
N Tilt up: cordite canisters and shell buckets tilt upright
O Close breech
P Free slide
Q Send down cordite cage to magazine

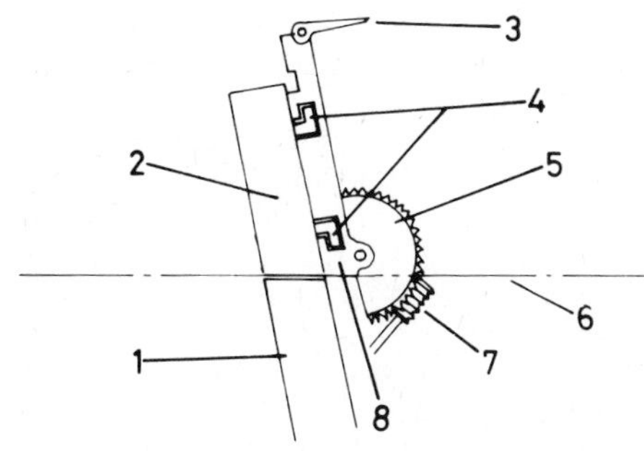

BRITISH 16in Mk I – SHELL BUCKET ARRANGEMENTS

1 Shell hoist trunk
2 Shell bucket
3 Hinged breech-thread protection tray
4 Guide lugs, for traverse motion
5 Geared tilting quadrant
6 Gunhouse floor
7 Tilting power-drive from hydraulic motor
8 Tilting tray

In the rear corners of the gunhouse there were two auxiliary stowage positions for shells, each with an associate radial crane capable of plumbing a striking-down hatch, through which shells could be returned directly to the shell room. The normal shell supply arrangements, described above, were not reversible and there had to be a means of emptying the hoist and stowing the shells therefrom, should the type of projectile be changed during an action – from armour-piercing to high explosive, for example. The hydraulic radial cranes could plumb the adjacent outer hoist, the shell bin and the striking-down hatch, making the process for the outer guns fairly straightforward, but the centre shell hoist was beyond the span of either crane and special slinging arrangements had to be arranged to unload it.

SUMMARY OF MODIFICATIONS IN HAND OR UNDER CONSIDERATION IN 1938

	Detail	Remarks
1	Improved air blast	Fitted in *Nelson*
2	Reintroduction of No 1A interlock	Fitted in *Nelson*
3	Solid forgings for traversing tray cross-heads	Fitted in *Nelson*
4	Modification to run-out control arrangements	Under consideration
5	Redesign of breech obturator pads	New pads pressed to 8 tons/sq in, supplied to both ships
6	Modification to depression control gear	Fitted in *Rodney*
7	Modification to elevating cylinder	Gear manufactured
8	Redesign of bogie training arrangements	Under consideration
9	Conversion of shell scuttles to hand operation and interlocking gear modified	Complete
10	Modification to control valves of shell room overhead gantries	Fitted in *Nelson*
11	Fitting of interlock to prevent double-loading of cordite cage	Under consideration
12	Fitting of oil coolers	Complete
13	Modification to pump governors	Two fitted in *Nelson* for trial
14	Cross-connection to run turret pumps in parallel	Under consideration
15	Fitting of access doors to cordite hoists above flash doors	To be fitted

THE 16in GUN MOUNTING CREW

The full turret crew comprised one officer and 98 men[1] who closed up as follows:

Gunhouse, 'silent cabinet' and training engine space
1 captain of turret (quarters rating, 1st class)
3 gun's crews of 3 men each
1 rangetaker, plus one, for rangefinder
1 LDS layer
1 LDS trainer
1 sight-setter
1 OOQ
1 telephone operator
Plus, for quarters firing:
1 range officer
1 rate officer
1 Dumaresq calculator operator
3 gunlayers[2] (quarters ratings, 3rd class)
1 turret trainer

Shell handing room
1 second captain of turret (QR1)
4 shell bogie operators
4 pivot tray operators
3 shell scuttle operators (after modifications – see above)

Shell room
1 petty officer in charge plus 24 men ('B' turret only – 6 men per loading tray; 'A' and 'X', with only 3 trays, had 18 men)

Cordite handing room
1 petty officer, plus 15 men (5 men per gun)

Magazine
1 petty officer, plus 24 men ('B') or 18 ('A' and 'X') – 6 men per supply scuttle manned)

GUNCREW DUTIES

1 Gunhouses etc: (see earlier descriptions)
2 Shell handing room:
(i) Pivot tray number – loads shell bogie and operates serving port
(ii) Shell bogie number – controls the bogie and loads the revolving scuttle at the shell hoist
(iii) Shell scuttle number – revolves scuttle by manual operation

Loading procedure
(i) opens serving port
(i) of shell room advances shell room rammer; withdraws rammer trains pivot tray into line with shell bogie
(ii) puts bogie tilt lever to 'Tilt Left'; when bucket is horizontal, replaces tilt lever to 'Locked to Ship'
(i) advances pivot tray rammer; withdraws pivot tray rammer
(ii) puts bogie tilt lever to 'Tilt Right'; when bucket is vertical, replaces lever to 'Locked to Ship'

[1]Varied slightly between individual turrets
[2]Senior gunlayer in charge

(i) trains pivot tray back to serving port
(ii) of master bogie puts churn lever to 'Train Right' or 'Train Left'
(ii) of other bogies put their churn levers to 'Locked to Trunk' (Note: all bogies lock to trunk automatically when in line with hoist). In the case of 'B' only, its fourth tray was initially loaded but then remained in line with its serving port
(ii) of loaded bogies ram projectiles into scuttles, withdraw rammers and clutch scuttle 'to hoist' as soon as rammers have withdrawn (Note: drill changed when scuttles were modified)
(ii) of master bogie trains bogies back to pivot trays
(ii) of working bogies lock bogies 'to ship' and tilt buckets to horizontal (Note: master bogie is kept free with bucket vertical)
The cycle was repeated until the shell hoists were full and the tilting trays in the gunhouse were loaded

State on completion of 'Load Hoists'
1 Shell hoists full
2 Shell scuttle loaded and clutched to hoist
3 Shell bogies loaded and locked to ship
4 Pivot trays loaded and in line with serving ports
5 Serving ports closed

At the order 'Load'
When scuttle has rotated, (ii) of working bogies lock to trunk, reload scuttles, clutch scuttles 'to hoist' and free bogies from trunk

Duties of shell room crew
PO takes general charge in the main shell room
No 1 (in charge of the crew) works rammer of traversing tray
No 2 traverses tray
No 3 removes grab at traversing tray
No 4 works lifting and traversing levers of the overhead shell gantry
Nos 5 and 6 work in shell bins, placing grabs

Duties of cordite handing room crew
PO takes general charge of all cordite supply
No 1 operates cordite rammer and is in charge of hoppers
Nos 2, 3 and 4 – cartridge supply numbers
No 5 operates flashtight scuttle between handing room and magazine

Duties of magazine crew
PO takes general charge; supply numbers provide cartridges to scuttles as required

Loaded state
1 Cordite cage up and loaded
2 Cage telegraph showing 'Cage not down'
3 Both hoppers loaded and closed
4 Flashtight scuttle open to cordite handing room, closed to magazine, and empty
5 No other cordite in handing room

Procedure to test cordite loading gear
1 'Open right hopper' – No 3 opens right hopper
2 'Advance rammers' – should not be possible
3 'Close right hopper, open left hopper' – No 3 closes right, No 2 opens left
4 'Advance rammers' – should not be possible
5 'Close all hoppers' – No 2 closes left
6 'Out cordite rammers' – No 1 advances rammers
7 'All cordite rammers out' – report passed to captain of turret
8 'Open both hoppers' – should not be possible
9 'Withdraw rammers' – No 1 withdraws rammers
10 Cordite cages can now be raised

SAFETY INTERLOCKING GEAR[1]
1 Cannot put lever to 'Open Breech' until slide locking pawls are out
2 Cannot put lever to 'Close Breech' until shell tray is tilted up
3 Cannot put lever to 'Tilt Down' while hoist is on up stroke
4 Cannot put lever to 'Tilt Down' until breech is open
5 Cannot put lever to 'Tilt Up' while ramming or traversing
6 Cannot put lever to 'Ram' until shell tray is tilted down, or while trays are traversing
6A Cannot put lever to 'Ram Shell' after trays have traversed to cordite loading position
7 Cannot put lever to 'Traverse' with trays tilted up
8 Cannot put lever to 'Traverse' unless rammer is right back
9 Cannot put cordite hoist lever to 'Lower' unless cordite tray is tilted up
9A Cordite tray cannot be tilted up unless cordite tray is at top of hoist ready to receive canister
10 Cannot put cordite hoist lever to 'Raise' when bottom flash door is open, or until it has been opened and closed since hoist was last lowered
11 Cannot put shell hoist lever to 'Lower' until hoist has completed an upstroke
11A Cannot put shell hoist lever to 'Raise' until shell hoist has completed a down stroke
12 Cannot put shell hoist to 'Raise' (in 'B' turret, to 'Lower') until scuttle locking bolt is free and scuttle is clutched to hoist
13 Cannot put shell hoist to 'Raise' unless shell tray is tilted up and is empty
13A Cannot put lever to 'Tilt Down' while shell hoist lever is being put to 'Raise', and vice versa
A Cannot put ramming lever to 'Withdraw' until shell ramming stroke is complete
B As **A** above, for cordite ramming stroke

Additional notes on gunhouse controls
1 Slide could also be locked by a hand-operated locking bolt
2 No 1A interlock ('Slide cannot be unlocked unless breech is closed') removed during development; replaced by No 1 (later reinstituted – see modifications)
3 The cordite cage could not be raised unless the cordite handing room rammers had been withdrawn.

Shell handing room
15 Cannot put pivot tray levers to 'Slew' or 'Ram' unless shell room rammer head is back
20 Rammer lever on pivot tray is locked until shell bucket is horizontal
21 Bogie is locked to ship until telescopic portion of pivot tray is home
21A Shell bogies cannot be unlocked from ship unless pivot tray is trained to a serving port
22 Shell bucket of bogie cannot be tilted to vertical until pivot tray is clear
23 Bogie cannot be unlocked from ship unless shell bucket is vertical
24 Cannot put pivot tray lever to 'Slew' unless bogie is locked to the ship
28 Cannot put bogie rammer lever to 'Ram' unless bogie is locked to the trunk and shell scuttle is locked in the receiving position
29 Cannot unlock bogie from trunk unless bogie rammer is right back
31 Cannot unlock bogie from trunk until shell scuttle has been clutched to shell hoist

[1]Numbers refer to gunhouse interlocks

38 Cannot put pivot tray lever to 'Slew' unless rammer lever is to 'withdraw'
39 Cannot put lever to 'Slew' while pivot tray lever is out
40 Cannot put lever to 'Ram' unless slewing lever is hard over to 'Train to Bogie'
41 Cannot put lever to 'Ram' unless pivot tray is in line with bogie

Shell room
14 Cannot put rammer lever to 'Ram' until the watertight door is open
14A Cannot put rammer lever to 'Ram' until pivot tray is in line with serving port
16 Cannot put watertight door operating lever to 'Close' until shell room rammer is fully back

Cordite handing room
33 Cannot move loading lever to 'Open Bottom Flash Door' unless both hopper doors are closed
34 Cannot put loading lever to 'Ram' until bottom flash door is fully open
35 Cannot put loading lever to 'Withdraw' until rammer has completed its stroke
36 Cannot put loading lever to 'Close Flash Door' until rammer is right back
37 Cannot open hopper doors until bottom flash door is closed

APPENDIX 5: THE BRITISH 14in Mk II AND Mk III MOUNTINGS

MOUNTING DIMENSIONS

The trunnion axis was only 7ft from the turret front, with the rear of the breech describing an arc of 14ft 6in radius behind it, but the gun sat back a further 4ft 3in on recoil, at 40° elevation, when it was accommodated in a gunwell extending 12ft below the gunhouse floor. The guns were spaced equidistantly about the centreline with approximately 7ft 6in between the axis of adjacent bores, the outer guns being 22ft 6in apart.

The training base diameter was 35ft and the maximum width of the gunhouse slightly larger at 38ft 6in. The vertical height above the main deck was 20ft but the lower 10ft 6in was the non-rotating armoured barbette. Taking into account the thickness of its roof armour, this gave a clearance of nearly 8ft in the gunhouse proper. There was 40ft between the outer surface of the vertical front-face armour and the curved gunhouse rear – a dimension repeated in the twin. The latter's barbette was 22ft high to super-fire over 'A' mounting, but was reduced in width to a training base diameter of 29ft 6in. The overall distance between the armoured roof and the bottom of the turret trunk was 53ft in the case of the quadruple and 72ft in the twin.

CORDITE HANDING ROOM MACHINERY

At its lowest level, in the cordite handing room, the trunk was of rectangular cross-section and simply contained the four two-layer cordite cages, side by side. There were, of course, only two such cages in the case of the twin. A circular platform, recessed to lie flush with the surrounding deck plate, was attached to the trunk and so revolved with it. On one side, two cordite hoppers, side by side, served the centre cages, and on the opposite face of the trunk, a further pair served the outer cages. The hoppers were double-layered and aligned with the cages in their lowest position. Ports, cut into the trunking, were sealed by power-operated, sliding, flashtight doors.

The cordite was passed from the magazines into the square-shaped handing room through watertight doors and placed in the open hopper trays. Each hopper had its own double-headed power rammer, whose control level opened the flashtight door with its first movement and extended the rammers with its second. In the reverse action, the rammers were withdrawn and the flash-doors closed. Following the usual 'safety-first' British practice, all the movements were mechanically interlocked to prevent malfunction.

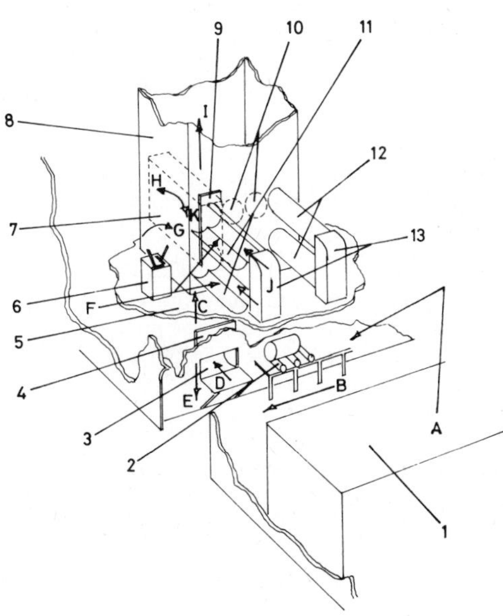

BRITISH 14in Mk III MOUNTING – MAGAZINE TO CORDITE CAGE ARRANGEMENTS

1 Cordite bay
2 Roller conveyor
3 Serving port
4 Watertight door
5 Loading platform on revolving trunk
6 Control console
7 Left outer gun cordite cage
8 Revolving trunk
9 Flash door
10 Inner gun cordite cages
11 Cordite hopper trays
12 Right outer gun cordite hoppers
13 Cordite rammer casings

Sequence
A Cordite manhandled from cordite bay
B Pushed along roller conveyor
C Open watertight door
D Cordite to receiving tray in handing room
E Close watertight door
F Cordite placed on hopper trays
G Close hoppers
H Open flash door
I Flash door opens, triggers rammers
J Rammers advance
K Retract rammers, close flash doors

BRITISH 14in Mk III MOUNTING – SHELL ROOM AND SHELL HANDING ROOM ARRANGEMENTS

1 Shell bin
2 Combined rammer, flash door control console and shell waiting trays
3 Hinged trays
4 Watertight door
5 Shell-ring locked 'to ship' in one of four positions 90° apart
6 One of four groups of quadruple shell troughs, 90° apart
7 Turret trunk, revolving with gunhouse
8 Shell-ring gearbox
9 Shell-ring traversing engine, 'traverse' and 'to ship' locking-bolt control console
10 Shell room bulkhead
11 Traveller
12 Overhead rail, spanning shell bins
13 Shell grab raise/lower cable
14 Traveller traverse cable
15 Quick-release shell grab

Sequence
A Traveller returning for shell from shell bin
B Open watertight door
C Watertight door opens
D Rammer advances
E Retract rammer
F Rammer retracts
G Watertight door closes
H Unlock shell-ring 'from ship'
I Shell-ring traverse lever inoperative
J Shell-ring 'called' to trunk by on-mounting shell-ring traverse lever

BRITISH 14in Mk III MOUNTING – SHELL-RING TO SHELL CAGE ARRANGEMENTS

1 Shell-ring
2 Watertight door
3 Ammunition cage trunk
4 Rammer machinery compartment
5 Control compartment
6 Control console
7 Rammer head

Sequence
A 'Call' shell-ring to trunk
B Shell-ring traverses
C Centralise shell-ring control lever
D Lock shell-ring to trunk
E Rammer lever to 'Ram'
F Watertight door opens, rammer advances
G Rammer lever to 'Withdraw'
H Rammer withdraws, watertight door closes
I Unlock shell-ring from trunk
J 'Call' shell-ring to trunk with second group of four shells or to reload emptied shell positions
K 'Call' shell-ring 'to ship'

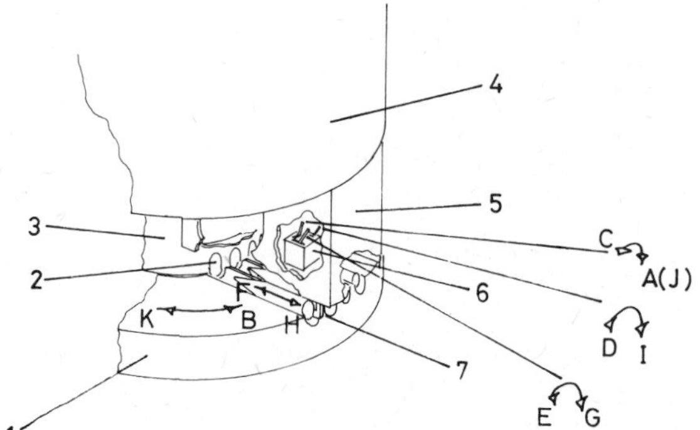

SHELL HANDING ROOM MACHINERY

The shell cages reached their lowest point aligned with ports cut in the trunk in the compartment above the magazine, called the shell handing room. It was square shaped and each side was served by a shell room wherein the shells were stowed horizontally in bins. From these, they were carried by overhead travellers and placed on to four parallel troughs, called waiting trays, facing the exit ports, each trough having its own rammer, interlocked with a vertically sliding watertight door.

Surrounding the turret trunk, there was a massive shell-ring having four groups of four parallel troughs set 90° apart, such that when the ring was locked 'to ship' the four groups lined up with the exit ports of the four shell rooms. Operation of the shell room rammers now thrust the shells across hinged bridging trays, until all sixteen troughs on the shell-ring were loaded. Once the turntable was loaded, it was independently power-rotated around the trunk by a hydraulic engine until one group of four waiting shells was aligned with the ports leading through the trunk to the shell cages. It was then locked 'to trunk' thereafter moving with the mounting as it trained.

Above the shell-ring, an overhead compartment – rather like a signal box – was constructed outwards from the turret trunk. Four rammer heads projecting downwards beneath this cab thrust the four shells into the shell cages. When the rammers had been withdrawn – depending upon the demands for ammunition from above – either the empty troughs on the ring could be recharged from the nearest shell room, or the ring simply unlocked from the trunk, power-rotated to bring a second quartet of shell into line, and re-aligned with the shell-cage ports.

The shell-ring itself had gear teeth cut on its outer and inner rims. The outer gear teeth meshed with a gearbox driven by a hydraulic engine mounted on the shell handing room deck and the inner gear teeth with a pinion driven by a second engine in the trunk.

A control console in the shell handing room contained a shell-ring traversing lever which controlled the ring when it left the trunk and was to be slewed into line with a shell room. This console also contained a lever controlling the 'to ship' locking bolts. A second console, in the trunk rammer compartment, contained levers controlling the rammers together with the 'to trunk' locking bolts and the shell-ring traversing engine in the trunk itself. From this position, the ring was 'called' to the trunk and locked thereto, while the shell handing room arrangements 'called' the ring back to the shell room loading positions.

Both engines were hydraulically linked (via the central pivot swivel) and ran in parallel irrespective of their controlling position. However, hydraulic-mechanical interlocking prevented conflicting lever movements. The twin controls for the shell-ring were incorporated because the shell handing room operator would never be unsighted from the 'to ship' locking positions, while the trunk rammer operator would never be unsighted from the trunk shell-ports.

Effectively, a fully loaded shell-ring provided projectiles for four successive broadsides, but if it became defective – perhaps jammed in a position where it could be locked neither to the trunk nor to the shell rooms – the supply of shells dried up. It is understood that a defect in this area occurred in *Prince of Wales* during action against *Bismarck*.

From the schematic sketches, it will be noted that the projectiles entered the trunk nose-first and that they were, therefore, already correctly positioned in the direction of their eventual loading into the guns.

WORKING CHAMBER MACHINERY

On their arrival at working chamber level, the four composite cages came to rest in alignment with triple chain rammers arranged vertically to suit the three layers of ammunition. It was at this point that the transfer from the ammunition hoist to the gunloading cages took place. However, it could not be done directly because the spacing between the guns was, necessarily, much greater than the width of the lower trunking.

The first set of working chamber rammers ('ammunition hoist to traverser'), bearing against the base of the shell and the two double charges of cordite, thrust them into a trolley called a traverser which ran on rails at right angles to the axis of the guns – in other words, across the mounting. Likening the arrangement to a railway, it was a single track with four trucks on it – one for each of the four main cages. The traverser was next moved sideways, by a hydraulic ram, until it came to rest before the second set of working chamber rammers ('traverser to gunloading cage'). These thrust the ammunition in the reverse direction, across bridge trays spanning the central ammunition hoist trunk and into the gunloading cage.

The working chamber was like a railway terminus with four main lines entering and four branch lines leaving. But in the same way that bombs on a junction can seriously disrupt rail traffic so action damage to this compartment could starve the gunhouse of ammunition. It was all very well to put four guns in one gunhouse but if it were knocked out – or even became defective in a key position like the shell-ring or traverser trackway – the ship lost nearly half its main armament.

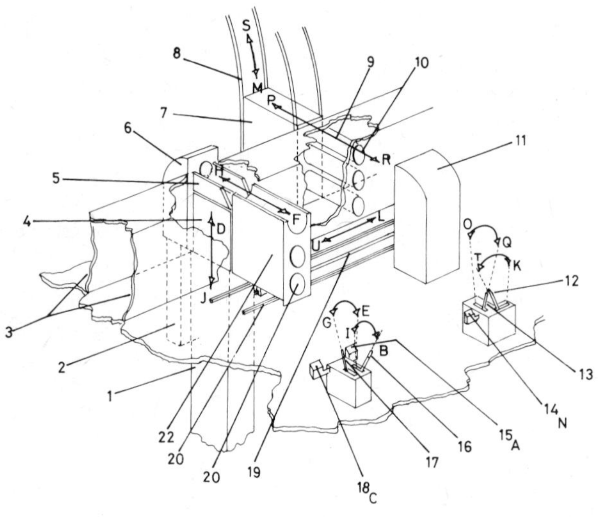

BRITISH 14in Mk III MOUNTING – WORKING CHAMBER ARRANGEMENTS FOR ONE GUN

1 Ammunition hoist trunk
2 Chain rammer trunk
3 Flashtight bulkheads (common for all ammunition hoists)
4 Cordite cage
5 Shell cage
6 Triple rammer, 'ammunition hoist to traverser'
7 Gunloading cage
8 Cage rails
9 Bridge trays
10 Flash doors
11 Triple rammer, 'traverser to gunloading cage'
12 Traverser control lever
13 'Traverser to gunloading cage' rammer control lever
14 'Gunloading Cage Down' indicator
15 'Ammunition Hoist Ready' indicator
16 Ammunition hoist control lever
17 'Ammunition hoist to traverser' rammer control lever
18 'Ammunition Hoist Up' indicator
19 Traverser piston
20 Flash doors
21 Traverser rails (common for all traversers)
22 Traverser, cordite sealed, shell in upper trough

Sequence
A Ammunition hoist indicator registers 'Ready'
B 'Raise' ammunition cages
C Ammunition hoist indicator registers 'Up'
D Shell and cordite cages arrive at working chamber lever
E Rammer lever to 'Ram', flash doors on cages open
F Triple rammer advances
G Rammer lever to 'Withdraw', flash doors close
H Triple rammer withdraws
I 'Lower' ammunition cages
J Shell and cordite cages descend to shell room/magazine levels
K Traverser control lever to 'Gunloading Hoist'
L Traversers move into line with bridge trays
M Gunloading cage arrives from gunhouse
N Gunloading cage indicator registers 'Down'
O Rammer lever to 'Ram'
P Triple rammer advances
Q Rammer lever to 'Withdraw'
R Triple rammer retracts
S Gunloading cage free to be called to gunhouse
T Traverser control lever to 'Ammunition Hoist'
U Traverser moves back in line with ammunition hoist

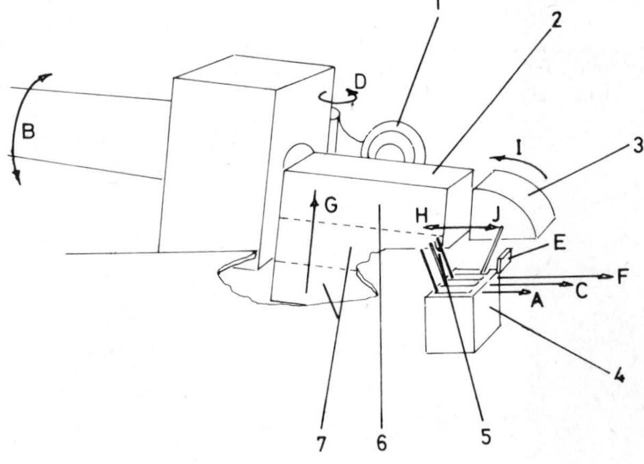

BRITISH 14in Mk III MOUNTING – GUNHOUSE ARRANGEMENTS

1 Breech-screw
2 Gunloading cage
3 Chain rammer casing
4 Control console
5 Locking panel clutch lever on gunloading cage control lever
6 Shell compartment
7 Cordite compartments

Sequence

A Slide locking lever to 'Lock'
B Gun moves to 5° elevation and locks, breech lever unlocked
C Breech lever to 'Open', interlocks slide locking lever
D Breech opens
E Gunloading cage indicator shows 'Ready', gunloading cage lever unlocked
F Cage lever to 'Raise', interlocks breech lever. Panel locks cage lever at 'Raise'.
G Gunloading cage rises to bring shell into line with rammer
H Rammer lever to 'Ram'
I Rammer advances
J Rammer lever to 'Retract', gunloading cage 'zones' up automatically for first pair of cordite charges and rammer stroke is automatically reduced. Second retraction of rammer causes the gunloading cage to 'zone' up automatically, bringing lower cordite compartments into line with rammer. Control levers then operate in reverse sequence and last operation – 'unlock slide' – returns elevation control to gunlayer

The ammunition hoist and traverser controls were positioned in the working chamber in two separate lever standards. The first had a 'raise – lower' lever, for the shell and cordite cages, and a rammer control lever – 'hoist to traverser'; the second had a lever to operate the traverser and another to control the rammer – 'traverser to gunloading cage' – movement.

GUNHOUSE MACHINERY

Gunloading cage operation was carried out from a control standard, having four levers, in the gunhouse in rear of each gunwell. It looked very like the 'ground frame' often seen on important railway sidings to control turnouts. The left hand lever, called the slide lock control lever, brought the gun to the loading angle of 5° elevation. A complex arrangement of valves and levers divorced the elevation control from the layer and moved the gun in the appropriate direction; in other words, it either depressed or elevated to 5°, depending on what its position had been when the lever was initially moved to 'Lock'. The next lever opened and closed the breech in power; the third raised or lowered the gunloading cage; and the fourth advanced or withdrew the gunloading rammer.

The four levers were sequentially interlocked. The rammer lever could not be moved until the hoist lever was to 'Raise'; this lever could not be moved unless the breech was to 'Open', which in turn could not occur until the slide lock control was to 'Lock'. The hoist control lever, alone, also had a hand-grip clutch to ensure that it was positively positioned during the ramming cycle.

When all was ready, moving the rammer lever to 'Ram' admitted pressure to a cylinder whose piston was attached to a horizontal toothed rack. As it moved, a gear wheel revolved, driving a shaft with a sprocket wheel on its opposite end. A chain rammer contained in a vertical trunk below the gunhouse floor then moved outwards and, supported by the shell trough of the gunloading cage, pushed the shell forwards into the gun. When the rammer was withdrawn, the cage automatically 'zoned' up one step to bring the first pair of cordite charges in line with the chamber and these, too, were rammed. The throw of the rammer was automatically restricted (because the cordite did not have to travel so far into the chamber as the shell) and left the first two charges in the rear end of the chamber. The second withdrawal of the rammer again 'zoned' the cage upwards ready for the second pair of charges, and when these were rammed they pushed the first pair fully into the chamber ahead of them. There were, therefore, three separate ramming strokes, after which the hoist control lever was unlocked and put to 'Lower', sending down the empty cage to the working chamber. At the same time the breech was closed and the slide unlocked.

In certain conditions of mechanical defect, it became possible to advance the rammer while the cage was still down, when its chain plunged unsupported down the gunwell, like a massive mechanical tongue!

The loading sequence, as described above for the quadruple mounting, was applicable in broadside fire, when all guns fired together. In salvo fire, left outer and right inner guns alternated with the other pair, with a similar alternation in the twin, and the individuality of each gun meant that any permutation of barrels could keep firing – as long, of course, as no disaster occurred on the shell-ring or traversers. The shell-ring idea had some merit in that it allowed for a measure of flexibility in type of ammunition. Two sets of shell troughs, for example, might be loaded with HE and the other two with AP, either type being then immediately available for dispatch to the working chamber.